Theatre and War

WHAT IS THEATRE?
Edited by Ann C. Hall

Given the changing nature of audiences, entertainment, and media, the role of theatre in twenty-first century culture is changing. The **WHAT IS THEATRE?** series brings new and innovative work in literary, cultural, and dramatic criticism into conversation with established theatre texts and trends, in order to offer fresh interpretations and highlight new or undervalued artists, works, and trends.

ANN C. HALL has published widely in the area of theatre and film studies, is president of the Harold Pinter Society, and is an active member in the Modern Language Association. In addition to her book *A Kind of Alaska: Women in the Plays of O'Neill, Pinter, and Shepard*, she has edited a collection of essays, *Making the Stage: Essays on Theatre, Drama, and Performance*. Hall is also the author of a book on the various stage, film, print, and television versions of Gaston Leroux's *Phantom of the Opera*, *Phantom Variations: The Adaptations of Gaston Leroux's Phantom of the Opera, 1925 to the Present*.

Published by Palgrave Macmillan:

Theatre, Communication, Critical Realism
  By Tobin Nellhaus

Staging Modern American Life: Popular Culture in the Experimental Theatre of Millay, Cummings, and Dos Passos
  By Thomas Fahy

Authoring Performance: The Director in Contemporary Theatre
  By Avra Sidiropoulou

Readings in Performance and Ecology
  Edited by Wendy Arons and Theresa J. May

Theatre and War: Theatrical Responses since 1991
  By Jeanne Colleran

Theatre and War

Theatrical Responses since 1991

Jeanne Colleran

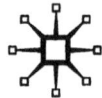

THEATRE AND WAR
Copyright © Jeanne Colleran, 2012.

Softcover reprint of the hardcover 1st edition 2012 978-1-137-00629-5

All rights reserved.

First published in 2012 by
PALGRAVE MACMILLAN®
in the United States—a division of St. Martin's Press LLC,
175 Fifth Avenue, New York, NY 10010.

Where this book is distributed in the UK, Europe and the rest of the world, this is by Palgrave Macmillan, a division of Macmillan Publishers Limited, registered in England, company number 785998, of Houndmills, Basingstoke, Hampshire RG21 6XS.

Palgrave Macmillan is the global academic imprint of the above companies and has companies and representatives throughout the world.

Palgrave® and Macmillan® are registered trademarks in the United States, the United Kingdom, Europe and other countries.

ISBN 978-1-349-43499-2   ISBN 978-1-137-00630-1 (eBook)
DOI 10.1057/9781137006301

Library of Congress Cataloging-in-Publication Data

Colleran, Jeanne M. (Jeanne Marie), 1954–
  Theatre and war : theatrical responses since 1991 / Jeanne Colleran.
    p. cm.—(What is theatre?)
  Includes bibliographical references.

  1. War and theater. 2. War in literature. 3. Press and journalism in literature. 4. Political plays, American—History and criticism. 5. Political plays, English—History and criticism. 6. Theater—Political aspects—United States. 7. Theater—Political aspects—Great Britain. 8. War in mass media. 9. War—Press coverage. I. Title. II. Title: Theater and war.

PN2041.W37C65 2012
809.2′93581—dc23   2012010460

A catalogue record of the book is available from the British Library.

Design by Newgen Imaging Systems (P) Ltd., Chennai, India.

First edition: September 2012

10 9 8 7 6 5 4 3 2 1

Transferred to Digital Printing 2014

To Richard
Tá grá agam duit

To James and Julia
Ná bíodh amhras ort choíche faoi sin, is tusa mo chroí agus mo shaol.

Contents

Acknowledgments ix

Introduction: Spectator of Calamities 1
1 Five Political Crises: The New Semiotic Environment 13
2 Turning History into Happening: The First Iraq War 29
3 The Persians 57
4 From the Ruins of 9/11: Grief and Terror 87
5 Facing Terror 105
6 War Documents 131
7 Bodies Count: In/Visible Scandal at Guantanamo and Abu Ghraib 169
8 Afghanistan and "the Spectacle of Our Suffering" 199

Notes 215
Works Cited 223
Index 237

Acknowledgments

> What else is love but recognition?
>
> —Tony Kushner, *Homebody/Kabul*

MY MOTHER, REGINA COLLERAN, GAVE ME THE GREAT GIFT of reading, and my father, William Colleran, gave me a deep love of music. These gifts and their love have immeasurably enriched my life. My dear brothers, James, William, Daniel, and Robert, have given me affection and affectionate deflation in equal measure. I am also very lucky to have many kind relatives—Collerans and Weavers—who are too numerous to mention but on whose support I have relied.

I am also thankful for good friends, especially Sheila Haney, Brenda Wirkus, Maryclaire Moroney, Ellen Grace, Marcia Blumberg, Jenny Spencer, Katherine Burkman, Peggy Finucane, Tom Hayes, Graciela Lacueva, Pam Mason, Nick Santilli, Rose Nicholson, Peter Kvidera, Deb Straneiro, Jill Fulton, Karen Clifford, Mark Storz, James Krukones, and Mary Rycyna. Special thanks to Ann Hall for her support throughout this project, and to Nicole Garner for her assistance. Sincere thanks to my many generous colleagues at John Carroll University, but especially in the dean's office and the AVP's office. I want to recognize Bernadette Sferry and Tina Guzik and to thank John Day, provost, and Robert Niehoff, S. J., president, for their support of my work.

My children, James Weaver and Julia Weaver, make me glad and proud and hopeful. I carry you in my heart.

And to Richard Weaver: my deepest love and deepest thanks.

Introduction

Spectator of Calamities

> Being a spectator of calamities taking place in another country is a quintessentially modern experience.
> —Susan Sontag[1]

WHEN COMPOSER KARLHEINZ STOCKHAUSEN WAS ASKED FOR HIS REACTIONS to the September 11, 2001, attacks on the World Trade Towers, he infamously observed that the event was "the biggest work of art there has ever been." The attacks were the ultimate achievement of the sublime since

> people practice ten years madly, fanatically for a concert. And then die. [Hesitantly.] And that is the greatest work of art that exists for the whole Cosmos. Just imagine what happened there. There are people who are so concentrated on this single performance, and then five thousand people are driven to Resurrection. In one moment. I couldn't do that. Compared to that, we are nothing, as composers... It is a crime, you know of course, because the people did not agree to it. They did not come to the "concert". That is obvious. And nobody had told them: "You could be killed in the process."[2]

As performances of the highest order, Stockhausen implied, the difference between sublime art and terrorist crime is only contractual: did one agree to "come to the concert"?

Although Stockhausen had warned his listeners to "adjust [their] brains" to what he was about to say, his words incited deep, if misplaced, anger. He was correct in comparing the terrorist attack to an experience of sublimity: like sublime art that astonishes its spectators, the terrorist attacks overwhelmed us with their immensity. They also produced a discourse of enormous transformation: American history was divided on "9/11" into "before" and "after."

George Packer, writing for *The New Yorker* on the ten-year anniversary of the attacks, argued that the 9/11 attacks "transfixed" America. He used another word associated with the experience of sublimity: astonishment so immense that one is halted, frozen in spectatorship. Packer went on to discuss the elements that kept America transfixed:

> A crime that felt like a war, waged by a group of stateless men occupying the fringe of a widespread ideology, who called themselves holy warriors and wanted to provoke the superpower into responding with more war: this was something entirely new. It raised vexing questions about the nature of the conflict, the enemy, and the best response, questions made all the more difficult by America's habitual isolation, and its profound indifference to world events that had set in after the Cold War (2011, 67).

Like Stockhausen, Susan Sontag also touched a public nerve when she disagreed with the prevailing view that the terrorist bombers were "cowards." Sontag wrote less than two weeks after the attacks,

> Where is the acknowledgment that this was not a "cowardly" attack on "civilization" or "liberty" or "humanity" or "the free world" but an attack on the world's self-proclaimed superpower, undertaken as a consequence of specific American alliances and actions?... And if the word "cowardly" is to be used, it might be more aptly applied to those who kill from beyond the range of retaliation, high in the sky, than to those willing to die themselves in order to kill others. In the matter of courage (a morally neutral virtue): whatever may be said of the perpetrators of Tuesday's slaughter, they were not cowards (2001, 29).

In the immediate aftermath of the attacks, Sontag's words stung: nothing could assuage the raw grief and fear felt in the United States, and nothing but outright condemnation could be countenanced. As President Bush ordered retaliation, first bombing Afghanistan and then Iraq, the quality of American public sentiment changed quickly from grief to atavism, from vulnerability to violence. An increasingly Manichean rhetoric dividing the world into the civilized and the barbaric muted the critical, especially self-critical, assessments voiced by thinkers like Sontag and others.

The reactions that Sontag's and Stockhausen's comments provoked raise two issues that are explored in this book: how have changes in media and information technology affected the public sphere where judgments can be made, expressed, and acted upon; and, given this profound shift in public dialogue, what role can art and culture, especially theatre, assume? Postmodern theorists have traced the rise of a symbolic economy and the enormous cultural shift that it has brought about, but in this discussion I am most interested in one particular aspect of this change: the simultaneous emergence of rapid mediazation (first termed "total television") and the "virtuous war," which began in 1991 with the first Persian Gulf War.[3] "History progresses at the speed of its weapons systems," observed Paul Virilio, but when military technologies overlap with those of media, information, and entertainment, a qualitatively different kind of history is being written (1977, 68). The 1991 Gulf War inaugurated real-time war spectatorship, making visible the tactical and symbiotic role of the media in military planning and governmental action. The freeze frame of this new relationship was the televised sight in 1991 of George W. H. Bush in the White House watching CNN broadcast live the bombing of Bagdad that he had just ordered. A perverse but telling bookend to this early scene was the stage-managed "Mission Accomplished" speech that George W. Bush gave on board a Navy destroyer in May 2003. His deep desire to achieve the victory that had eluded his father prompted Bush to go forward with his specious announcement, but what is most pertinent here is the conscious displacement of political fact by a public staging of a military/morality script proclaiming that might had vanquished evil. The fact that victory had not been achieved was not a mere exaggeration or an inconsequential lie. Changing the language about the Iraq War meant changing military strategy, with the tragically ludicrous result that the "war" lasted six weeks and the "postwar" lasted close to a decade longer. In the meantime, terrorist cells migrated into Iraq, and attacks continued around the world—Madrid, Bali, London—while the ever escalating war of images fed a pervasive and highly manipulated sense of insecurity and vulnerability. Until this cycle can be interrupted and until, as Judith Butler has written, the cry of grief can find some outlet other than a cry for war, terrorism and the struggle against it becomes the new reality, one with incalculable costs, limitless expansion, and no political objective except to exterminate the other (2004, xii).

The men, whose evil imaginations envisioned planes as bombs, humans as deadly cargo, civilian workplaces as military targets, and their own deaths as holy, are called terrorists, but it is useful to call them by the more neutral term that defined their actions: they were hijackers. It is difficult not to make the immediate metaphorical leap: they hijacked planes, of course, and American security about its own inviolability, but they also hijacked every human imagination. Certainly every American—if not every human in reach of a television—has an indelible imprint of now iconic images: the plane about to strike a tower, the imploding buildings, the descending bodies, the rubble of Ground Zero, the damaged Pentagon walls, the empty field in Pennsylvania. Such an imaginative hijacking, such a huge act of terrorist fear accomplished in less time than a Shakespeare play or the first performance of Beethoven's Fifth Symphony, could not have occurred even ten years earlier: it required the ubiquity of mass media, the instantaneous dissemination of the wired world, and the new capacities of quick reproduction and exchange. It required the extremist imagination of the hijackers, who have been called primitive and barbaric, but it relied on the highly developed technologies of Western media, entertainment, travel, information exchange, and digital reproduction.

In particular, these new habits of perception involve understanding the relationship of aesthetics to perception and hence to ethical judgment. Terrorism obviously depends on aesthetic strategies, whether they be the Grand Guignol of 9/11, the minimalism of Osama bin Laden's prophecies from within a hidden cave, or the neorealist videos of captured soldiers costumed in shalwar kameez. Triumphalism—the toppling of the statue of Saddam Hussein, the inked thumbs of Iraqi voters, or Bush's victory speech—does as well. In *Art and Fear*, Virilio insisted that art and politics inhabit different but connected points on the trajectory of representation and are thus mutually influential. He took artists and critics to task for their failure to produce or to describe how representation enables atrocity, arguing that contemporary artists are "spellbound by human violence" and "have abandoned their function of continually reassessing the creative practices and sensibilities, imagination and cultural meaning of the advanced societies." (2003, 4). While artists have specific abilities and commitments, every human living in the contemporary world of spectacle, sonority, and speed must, of necessity, become a semiotician. Virilio admonishes his reader to see connections between artistic crises of meaning, the decline of participatory governance, and ongoing violence:

> At the end of the millennium, what abstraction once tried to pull off is in fact being accomplished before our very eyes: the end of REPRESENTATIVE art and the substitution of a counter-culture, of a PRESENTATIVE art. A situation that reinforces the dreadful decline of representative democracy in favor of a democracy based on the rule of opinion, in anticipation of the imminent arrival of *virtual democracy*, some kind of 'direct democracy' or more precisely a *presentative* multimedia democracy based on automatic polling. In the end 'modern art' was able to glean what communications and telecommunications tools now accomplish on a daily basis: the *mise en abyme* of the body, of the figure, with the major attendant risk of *systematic* hyperviolence (2003, 35).

In less-frenzied language, art historian W.J.T. Mitchell agrees:

> My sense is that 9/11 has been so fetishized as an apocalyptic moment, and has been so resistant to a proper process of mourning and commemoration, that there is still no comprehensive verbal or visual image to put it in

perspective. The failure to provide an adequate memorial to the World Trade Center is symptomatic in this regard. (2011a)

Nevertheless, Mitchell sees analytic value in works of art still being created about global terrorism, especially through "the efforts of artists to regenerate a sense of democratic public space, and to engender a corresponding sense of critical, oppositional consciousness".

The desire for art to assume a larger burden of ethical and political oversight and to provide an alternative public space for exchange and reflection as a response to terrorism may seem naïve to some. Yet, developing a critical disposition toward image and narrative is an indisputably necessary skill in the mediated, networked world. While visible evidence and witness were once touchstones for truth and fact, the proliferation of signs and images, disseminated more widely than ever before because of television, cell phones, and computers, has changed the status of proof and altered conceptions of authenticity. Similarly, the "sonorization," as Virilio terms it, of the world, the constant commentary, infinite parsing by talking heads, and incremental revaluation by ever-ready experts has produced a surfeit of opinion but little final insight. This combination of visibility and sonority has so defined information delivery that it is impossible to step outside the "cyberblitz." We seem to be simultaneously technophobic and technophilic: absorbed by immediate images and instant narratives, but also aware of their malleability.

Jacques Ranciere has identified two seemingly opposite conceptualizations of the relationship between image and reality that may account for our present wariness. One point of view is that reality has been displaced by simulation and virtuality—therefore nothing is real, and images are without substance. The other point of view discards images themselves: lacking critical separation from reality, there can be no place of representation and hence no image (Mitchell and Ranciere, 2008). As subjects of contemporary culture, we find ourselves in a state of permanently agitated desire: the desire to see the "real" thought to be anterior to the represented persists, but it is wrapped in doubt about whether this desire can ever be satisfied and whether the desire itself is illusory. Our response to public events displays this discomfort, and hence we argue about the "authenticity" of the Abu Ghraib photos and whether Americans commit torture. This skepticism about what we are seeing (and not seeing) and whether anything can be done to gain access to truth results at times in a kind of private emotional and cognitive shut down. Such inertia fails us as citizens and humans; it is "the raw form of despair" (De Saint-Exupery, 1982, 9).

In short, while it is impossible to avoid mediatization, to live outside the cyberblitz, or to be immune to manipulation, it is very possible to be critical of the production of images and stories. We need, as Douglas Kellner has argued extensively, the ability to employ a "diagnostic critique" that is commensurable to the complexity of our wired environment. Such a critique would "analyze the circuits of production, textuality, and reception, deploying a dialectic of text and context to provide critical readings of media texts and that use the texts to illuminate the contemporary era" (Kellner 2005, 15).

While all art forms make claims to particular skill sets, it seems especially true that a deeper knowledge of performative strategies is useful, even essential, to understanding political conflict as it is currently waged and staged. One supposition of this book, then, is that seeing theatre, reading drama, and understanding performance does not merely enhance aesthetic appreciation or provide content knowledge, but rather, that such exposure enables a fuller inquiry into the overlap of politics and aesthetics characteristic of contemporary events. Additionally, this book argues for the particular power of theatre as a live, embodied, communal art form to raise awareness of complex issues flattened out through hype and spin, to offer a public space of exchange, and to invigorate political analyses and action. The rise of the blogosphere manifests the appetite for alternate means of information, connection, and expression, but it does little to satisfy the desire for face-to-face interaction and shared live experience. Socially conscious art, particularly theatre, provides a common experience and a critical apparatus with which to engage our most urgent ethical and political problems.

The primary aim of this book is to investigate how the media, beginning with the Persian Gulf War, has altered political analysis and how this alteration has in turn affected socially critical art. To this end, I discuss some 40 plays, most of which were written in direct response to the emergent New World Order and the subsequent 1991 war in Iraq and, a decade later, the 9/11 attacks and the retaliatory actions in Iraq and Afghanistan. These works are drawn primarily from the British and American stage since these two nations were the principal partners in these conflicts. Works included are from various sources: some were written by prominent figures (Harold Pinter, Caryl Churchill, Sam Shepard, Peter Sellars, Tony Kushner, David Hare, Trevor Griffiths, Naomi Wallace, Neil LaBute), others are by theatre groups and artistic directors (San Francisco Mime Troupe, Nicolas Kent and the Tricycle Theatre, Alan Buchman and Culture Project), and still others are by emerging playwrights and by writers who work primarily as journalists or in other media (Anne Nelson, Lawrence Wright, George Packer, Alan Havis, Richard Norton-Taylor, Robin Soans, and others). The plays I discuss take up issues of political policy, executive decision, military practice, and international law. They examine the mechanisms and consequences of adopting torture techniques and of holding prisoners in indefinite detention. They raise questions about how domestic injustices persist and are exacerbated during time of war. They acknowledge and respond to aspects of public discourse, whether it be the exploitation of feelings of shock and vulnerability, the manipulation of security threats, the demonization of Arab and Muslim identities, or the rhetoric of American exceptionality and moral superiority. They work, both explicitly and implicitly, within the mediated sphere, knowing that the audience has entered the theatre with visual and information overload. They depict real events and real figures to counter the superficial flattening of media coverage. They offer political commentary and ethical critique. They are outraged, and they are mournful. There are surely plays that I have inadvertently missed or make only brief reference to as I attempt to demonstrate the breadth of theatrical response to over two decades of conflict. And there are subjects that might well have been broached but space would not allow: the performative aspects of mass demonstrations, for example, the therapeutic use of drama for wounded soldiers, or the work of individual performance artists. Instead, I have tried to capture the response of writers primarily offering their work through "mainstream" theatrical venues—by which I mean theatres with some presence and history and longevity—and I do so chronologically (the 1991 war; 9/11; the 2003 war), through issues (indefinite detention, collateral damage, women's roles, torture), with an awareness of media blitz, with attention to political discourse, and with an interest in theatrical form, especially the revaluation of political theatre and documentary theatre.

One of the threads woven throughout these discussions is how theatre enacts a political/ethical critique during a time when dissent has been termed unpatriotic and when media technologies manage public opinion. Theatre director Peter Sellars has commented, "One of the reasons, possibly, for theater to continue to exist in our technological age is as kind of alternative information system that is able partially to humanize the denatured results of our vaunted and costly objectivity" (1993, 8). I begin the book with a brief discussion of the rise of media spectacle and, drawing on the categories that globalization theorist Arjun Appadurai has devised, I attempt to chart the new semiotic environment in which information is shared and in which all politically engaged art must take place. In response to this environment, I make the case for two essential critical capabilities that arise from theatrical practice: its ability to discern different discursive formations at work and identify their rhetorical stance and implicit arguments, and its capacity to read and make sense of the proliferation of images, without reducing their visceral effect, their reliance on context, or even their ambiguity. In writing this book, I was as interested in the pedagogical and critical value of theatre studies as a means of developing the capability of identifying ideology, whether in language or in image, as I was in the particular political criticisms the plays enunciated. The first chapter, then, outlines how the complexity of the global and virtual contemporary world may be approached through the resources of theatre. It goes further to enumerate the particular value of political theatre in enabling critique and in offering alternative forms of embodied knowledge and live community. These are not new claims, but they are linked to the crisis in democratic consent that marked the American entry into the Iraq War.

This thread appears elsewhere in the book. It is apparent in my discussion of the proliferation of verbatim or documentary theatre as one form that highlights a dissatisfaction with the media's management of information and fact. Documentary theatre, which has deep roots in the work of writers such as Erwin Piscator, Peter Weiss, Heiner Kipphardt, and Rolf Hochhuth, is most associated with the "tribunal plays" that originated at London's Tricycle Theatre. These plays took testimony around controversial public events and re-presented it in a shortened but otherwise unaltered format.[4] The testimony has subsequently assumed various forms, from oral histories taken from returning Iraq soldiers, such as *In Conflict*, to the mixture of interview and spectacle in the National Theatre of Scotland's "Blackwatch." Another expression of journalism's limitations are the plays produced by newsmen, such as Lawrence Wright and George Packer, to supplement their journalistic accounts (*My Trip to Al-Qaeda*, *Betrayal*"). Implicit in documentary theatre is the view that since theatrical techniques have "leeched into politics, religion,...news, commerce, warfare, and crime," offering consumers a steady diet of "reality" shows, "docudramas," and "factions," it make sense that theatre reverse the dynamic but in such a way that demystifies the "pseudo-real" media event from either the real or the theatrical (Hedges, 2009, 16).

Another way in which recent political theatre deconstructs mediatization is by making media coverage the subject of the drama. The San Francisco Mime Troupe makes it critique through broad and obvious satire of news reporters, while Judith Thompson's *My Pyramids* is built around three recognizable stories that had garnered high media attention but that made stick figures of those involved. David Hare's *Stuff Happens* juxtaposes imagined behind-the-scenes interactions between world figures with bits instantly recognizable from televised reports, and while the latter seems familiar but broadly satiric, the former is all the more disquieting for the way in which the depictions of pettiness, religiosity, and hubris at work in the Bush administration has since been confirmed by alienated former cabinet members. One of the characters in Sellars's version of *The Persians* excoriates the West for producing technology that can see the hair on the enemies head but does nothing to produce empathy.

While much political theatre draws on well-publicized events, political theatre about the Iraq Wars and the War on Terror has also dedicated itself to depicting events that have been less-covered. Gillian Slovo and Victoria Britain's spoken evidence play, *Guantanamo: Honour Bound to Defend Freedom*, for example, appeared in advance of a widespread public understanding that Guantanamo was both an illegal detention camp and that it permitted the use of torture. Heather Raffo's *Nine Parts of Desire*, rebuts stereotypical views of Muslim women; Eve Ensler's "The Treatment" focuses on the psychological distress born by soldiers complicit in prisoner abuse; and Naomi Wallace connects domestic racism and homophobia to the Persian Gulf War—all topics that exceed the interest and the ability of media to explore them adequately. Robin Soan's *Talking to Terrorists* unpacks distinctions between terrorists and freedom fighters, finding that common threads of political exclusion and poverty connect radical groups. Allan Havis, Frank Lentricchia, and Jody McAuliffe attempt to enter the mind of Mohammad Atta, one of the 9/11 suicide pilots. Anne Nelson writes of the deep grief experienced by firefighters in New York, focusing as much as possible on the trauma more than the politics. Neil LaBute, on the other hand, depicts selfishness and opportunism at work even in the midst of such outsized tragedy.

Other plays examined here are more directly interventionary: Sam Shepard staged *States of Shock*, a "vaudevillian nightmare," three months after the 1991 war, to protest American complacency. Trevor Griffiths wrote *The Gulf Between Us* to register the rage and pity he felt as he watched the 1991 bombing of Baghdad. Tony Kushner offered his satire which features Laura Bush reading bedtime stories to dead Iraqi children (*Only We Who Guard the Mystery Shall be Unhappy*) to be performed free across the country. These plays attempted a more immediate interruption in the political discourse justifying war and openly hoped to provoke dissent and action.

If all of the plays mentioned above are, in the manner of what is usually thought of as political theatre, issue-oriented, another group of plays written against the war is committed to examining the mechanisms of power and control. These works, especially those by Caryl Churchill and Harold Pinter, may make no reference at all to any specific conflict; instead they depict rationalizations of torture, the workings of traumatic memories, connections between late capitalism and oppression, violence and sexism, authoritarianism and cultural genocide. In comparison to the documentary or issue plays, these investigations into structural violence are indirect, even purposefully obscure; however, they too want to expose operative discourses of power. In addition to asking spectators to understand the veiled power dynamics underlying specific kinds of brutality, they also invite us to consider connections between representational violence and political violence.

As the distance between discursive and material forms of violence narrows or disappears, the possibilities of ethical and political action seem also to diminish; these plays work against such disappearance.

As Jochen and Linda Schulte-Sasse have pointed out, the "reality of politics is being shaped, from the outset, by the imaginary of media images and language" (1991, 71). Stubbornly, idealistically, perhaps naively, theatre artists continue to use theatre to enact and encourage critiques of crises that may seem, like the Gulf Wars or the War on Terror, to be beyond effective protest. My reading of these plays suggests that theatre can, against media hegemony, offer itself as a critical alternative, addressing issues and enacting perspectives that are otherwise unavailable. Specifically, political theatre can eschew the false objectivity and speculations of minutia-driven reportage in favor of a presentation that acknowledges its own biases. Political theatre about these ongoing conflicts can make connections between the conflict "over there" and the domestic pressures at work in its prosecution. And it can enact a politics of recognition, honoring a responsibility to the presentation of otherness, to the actual suffering behind each theatrical representation. Further, theatre can expose the constructedness of media images, and in Brechtian fashion, lay bare the devices that underlie the illusory realism of the hyper-visible. Finally, it can attempt to enunciate a coherent ethical position, one that is supranational, beyond tribal alliances, blind patriotism, or economic advantage.

I conclude my examination of theatre written within and against the conflict that is now entering its third decade with a discussion of the war in Afghanistan. Here I examine the play cycle "The Great Game," which attempts to stage the historical past and present of Afghanistan, and I discuss Tony Kushner's great work *Homebody/Kabul*. The opening monologue of *Homebody/Kabul* offers a clear ethical imperative: "What else is love but recognition?" (2002, 28). The difficulty, however, is that the Afghanistan that the Homebody has read about and imaginatively entered is nothing like the Afghanistan where she visits and meets her death. The deep disjuncture between the two halves of the play—the imaginative and lyrical monologue and the grim events of the realistic second act—opens up a variety of issues, the chief one being the same question raised in Raffo's *Nine Parts of Desire* and Thompson's *Palace at the End*: is there any sense in which political intervention can ever not be motivated by self-interest? It is appropriate, I believe, to end the book with a discussion of a war that lasted a decade, even as it was sidelined by the overreaching of regime change. It is also important that I end with some discussion of the ethics, challenges, and possibilities of representational, live art. The search for the missing mother in the second half of *Homebody/Kabul* can be read as a family's entrance into a world larger than their own, an entry made possible only by the risky effort of bearing witness to the mother's violent death and the reasons for it. But leaving home to recover the mother's body, and failing this, bringing another body back, is a challenging political gesture. Judith Butler, reflecting on whether an encounter can ever avoid appropriation, concludes, hopefully, "If I am confounded by you, then you are already of me," and thus, "You are what I gain through this disorientation and loss" (2004, 49). Kushner stages these disorienting encounters to suggest that truth-telling is always about loss, but this loss lies at the enigmatic heart of art's restorative powers. It is this vision and these acts of human restoration that this book ardently seeks.

CHAPTER 1

FIVE POLITICAL CRISES: THE NEW SEMIOTIC ENVIRONMENT

IN 1989, AN EAST EUROPEAN DICTATOR AND HIS WIFE were arrested and executed, brief scenes of which were broadcast on the evening news over several days. In 2005, another East European dictator was indicted for war crimes, and for five years until his unexpected death in March 2006, his deluded self-defense was broadcast in lengthy excerpts to a world audience. The time between the arrest and trial of Romanian president Nicolae Ceausescu in 1989 and that of Serbian and Yugoslavian president Slobodan Milosevec in 2005 is chronologically brief but technologically vast. The changes in information technology and media coverage since the 1990s have been so profound that they have completely reconfigured the sphere of public knowledge, social analysis, and political response. What we know, how we analyze it, and what conclusions we can draw—the entire realm of debate and discussion that characterizes democracy—has changed, and with that, skepticism and wariness have deepened while partisanship has grown.

During this time, the media not only conveyed information about war but also became an instrument of it. By 2001, the constructive power of the media had become increasingly evident, and nowhere more so than on 9/11. The attacks in New York, Washington, and Pennsylvania were a double hijacking: first the planes, then the airwaves. Few of us could look away from the horrific sight of our countrymen dying before our eyes, but watching was part of terrorism's arsenal. The images became part of the strategies of counterterrorism, and America entered a new psychological and political era. We were terrorized, traumatized, vulnerable, provoked, angry, defensive, and retaliatory. For a decade, the War on Terror was successful in ways that mattered little—as the initial bombing of Afghanistan proved—and unsuccessful in ways that mattered most, wreaking lasting damage on America's families, soldiers, economy, and international reputation. Instead of a historical timeline drawn from major events, the decade between 2001 and 2011 can be summoned by iconic images. We can visually chart it: the planes into the towers, Bush reading to children, the falling man, Ground Zero, anthrax in envelopes, bombing Baghdad, toppling Hussein's statue, pulling him from a hole, blue thumbs of Iraqi voters, the aircraft carrier speech, the cave speech, the Abu Ghraib man, Lynndie England, Hussein's hanging, the Al-Qaeda deck of cards, the Green Zone, Cindy Sheehan, Osama bin Laden in a cave, the raid on bin Laden's compound, Osama bin Laden dead. The important point here is that not only do these images convey what has happened, but they also provoke public response and *policy* response. Media coverage may appear to be reporting what has been discovered, but it is also delivering what it has constructed.

The impossibility of being untouched by media images constitutes the common social life of advanced nations. One consequence is that we pay less attention to what is not shown: seeing so much, we think we have seen it all, and we forget the fundamental truth that for everything screened, something is left unscreened. In terms of war's use of instantaneous visibility, we know that capturing an audience to witness acts of violence is the very definition of terrorism. Yet, invisibility also plays its part. Arguably, the tactics of invisibility—keeping detainees out of sight, censoring journalists, refusing to make public documents such as the infamous Bybee-Yoo torture memo, hiding the body count, never showing wounded soldiers or dead civilians or returning coffins—seem to be operationalized best by military planners such as the Pentagon or Department of Defense. But the capacity for terrorist cells to hide, move stealthily, and replicate themselves has generated viral levels of anxiety that are costly in every way imaginable.

The seen/unseen dynamic that is the very definition of the theatrical experience—the *fort/da*, the show, the stage and offstage, the *entr'acte*—is also what characterizes contemporary warfare that is waged via media. War as theatre is no longer a metaphor. With this in mind, this book examines war as performances, but it also contends that performance (the insights of performance theory and the theatre works themselves) can examine war. As various playwrights and directors have observed, contemporary theatre offers itself as a form of political discussion, engagement, and critique. This kind of theatre may at times function as agitation propaganda, but more often, it reclaims theatre's pedagogical function. Theatre's intimate knowledge of the decisive impact of framing, of deploying cultural symbols, and of narrating a scene or performing a role offers an array of critical skills that can enable spectators to make the kind of informed judgments that have become harder to reach because of the cultural shifts brought about by mediatization.

A brief review of how the media treated six political crises that occurred between 1989 and 2011 illustrates how a "politics of spectacle" has become the provenance of both those who are orchestrating political events and those who are covering them, and that these "spectacular politics" have, as terrorist acts have so compelling shown us, as much power to inflict harm as rocket launcher. The first political event, already mentioned, is the 1989 Romanian Revolution, which culminated in the firing-squad death of the vicious dictator Nicolae Ceausescu and his wife, Elena. Next are the identical beginnings of the Persian Gulf Wars: twice in a dozen years, American aircraft bombed the Iraqi capital of Baghdad. The fourth public event is President George W. Bush's May 1, 2003, declaration aboard the aircraft carrier the USS *Abraham Lincoln* that the United States had accomplished its military mission in Iraq. The fifth is bin Laden's January 2006 taped message, warning of further attacks against the United States and proclaiming the resilience of Al-Qaeda against the American War on Terror. The sixth is the death of bin Laden.

The Ceausescu arrest is memorable both because it appeared on television and because it became the subject of a widely produced play, Caryl Churchill's *Mad Forest: A Play from Romania*. (1993). The arrest demonstrates both the state of media coverage just a brief time ago and how a theatre piece such as Churchill's was created to fill in an informational void. Like early plays by Athol Fugard, it communicated both externally, to a world largely ignorant of Romanian politics, and internally, to a society where strong barriers prevented public expression and political debate. In one of the scenes of Churchill's play, Lucia Vladu has just returned from America to visit her hospitalized brother, Gabriel, who was wounded during the revolutionary melee. She tells him about watching the uprising on television and how she videotaped it:

> All the way over on the plane I was terrified of what I was going to see. But you look beautiful. In America, everyone's thrilled. I told my friends, "My brother was there, he was wounded, he's a hero." I watched TV but they never showed enough. I kept playing it and stopping when there was a crowd, I thought I must know somebody, I was crying all the time, I was so ashamed not to be here (51).

Like Lucia, many American television viewers can also recall watching the taped revolution and the subsequent trial and conviction of the Ceausescus. The footage was brief, and it was the quickness of the overthrow and execution of a head of state that made the coverage so riveting. Unlike Lucia, few of us bothered to tape the televised snippets of roughly ten days of demonstration, revolution, and execution, and no subsequent videos were produced for a mass audience.

Churchill wrote *Mad Forest* after traveling to Romania (with collaborator Mark Wing Davey and theatre students) to gather oral testimonies that she then shaped into a series of scenes depicting the steel grip the Ceausescus held on all aspects of Romanian life and the immediate, postrevolutionary period of confusion. Churchill's play rightly assumed that audiences knew little about the history behind the events or much about the events themselves. Audiences might recognize the grim portraits of Nicolae and Elena from photos in the news, but little else. Through Churchill's play spectators learned, possibly for the first time, about the degradations experienced during the Ceausescu reign: the scarcity of food, the cult of personality, the constant surveillance and the suspicions it produced. The play's ominous ending hinted that the newly installed Iliescu regime might replicate Ceausescu's reign.

In contrast to the Romanian Revolution, the opening moments of both the 1991 and 2003 wars against Iraq were telecast by means of live, instantaneously transmitted reports and continuous television coverage.[1] On January 16, 1991, the start of the first Gulf War was planned to coincide with the evening news. The first air strikes were broadcast live at 6:34 p.m., interspersed with shots of President George Bush and Prime Minister John Major shown watching on television the war they had just declared. In a perverse kind of mirroring, we watched the war, and we watched world leaders watching the war. In 2003, Americans, now knowing they had a living room seat for the beginning bombing raid, viewed the first wave of live nighttime battles, heard accounts from "embedded" reporters, and listened to endless commentaries from military strategists, experts on the Middle East, and the anchors themselves. Having grown accustomed to the coverage of the first Gulf War, Americans watched the second raid in real time as if it were a nonstop miniseries. As a result of the media coverage of the 1991 Gulf War, the new phenomena of "total television" had emerged whereby the events of major trials, natural disasters, or political events erupted on to the screen and remained there for hours or days at a time. With the 1991 war, the age of the "media spectacles" and "megaspectacles," Douglas Kellner's terms for media events that distract the public from substantive understandings of public issues (2003, 2005), had begun.

On May 1, 2003, George W. Bush donned a flight suit and helped steer a jet onto the USS *Abraham Lincoln*, an aircraft carrier docked off the California coast. In a live broadcast, the president declared the "mission accomplished" in Iraq. Three years later, in January 2006, Americans viewed a prerecorded tape of bin Laden. In grainy footage, bin Laden not only showed himself alive and functioning, but he also cited opinion polls that Americans opposed the war to which they saw no end. If we pair these two scenes, we see first how the megaspectacle has grown its parasitic economy: the event and its coverage are thoroughly merged and simultaneous. It amasses the world's attention on the basis of a faux-announcement that makes a show of the president's belief in the lie he is about to utter. The staged farce eventually became its own mockery. In the meantime, bin Laden cannily understood that the weapons of invisibility, the inverse of the megaspectacle, possess their own potency. His pronouncements in low-tech videos filmed at unknown sites tauntingly suggest that if he is outside the reach of Western technology, he is also outside of capture. Of course, this is a specious claim: the footage may be technologically primitive but the means of circulating it require the same wired resources as Bush's sophisticated production. Nevertheless bin Laden's tapes felt more like a haunting than a broadcast.

These events illustrate how mediatization, in changing from covering an event recently past to constituting it in the present, has affected public events in every way possible from creation to reception. During the Romanian Revolution, there was no causal connection between event and reportage: the arrests and executions could have been publicized in the print media or by word of mouth in Romania, and the presence of television cameras did not precipitate these events or shape their outcome. Just two years later, the overlap between the start of the bombing and the media transmission of it began the phenomenon of the "technowar," whereby the control of information and imagery became a vital part of military and political strategy. This phenomenon grew in the shadow of the larger emergence of "infotainment" and "technocapitalism," so-named for the interpenetration of information, entertainment, technology, and commerce. The 2003 case of Bush aboard the naval vessel depended on this hybrid media form: the display of military might and presidential confidence required the already blurred boundaries of news and entertainment, fact and fiction.

The "Mission Accomplished" speech was the most significant megaspectacle since the 9/11 attacks. Although it came back to haunt Bush's reputation as the war continued, the speech was not an empty lie or inconsequential act. Like all illocutionary acts, the pronouncement had consequences even though it failed to do what it intended: to replace the spectacle of 9/11 loss with the spectacle of American triumph. Bush's staged message illustrates how the exchange of images can be regarded as part of what Francois Lyotard called the "gaming" quality of postmodern language (1985). Bush's ploy is a "figure," a specific event of narration that asserts its power and claims its owns disruptive space over any competing discursive act. That this figure would be challenged by other figures—bin Laden's tape can be seen also as part of the Lyotard language game—moves political pronouncements away from definitive or determinative utterances of fact or truth to a field of play.

The tape made by bin Laden was an announcement of a different kind. There was no occasion for his speech—not even the invented occasion of the "Mission Accomplished" event. Bin Laden produced the contents and engineered its distribution, sending the tape to Al-Jazeera, an Arab network that would broadcast it to both Muslim and Western audiences. In effect, the bin Laden tape was a scripted reaction, a counter performance. In contrast to the set and props of Bush's live, spectacular announcement, bin Laden's low-tech, prerecorded tape produced an eerily effective rebuttal: its unspecified locale and the unknown date of recording served as an unspoken reminder of bin Laden's status as the most elusive and potent of terrorist masterminds. Yet, despite the differences in choosing live over taped presentation and immediate transmission against indirect circulation, both events were literally made for television. Each performed acts of aggression through the media. Bin Laden's tape was not ancillary to the War on Terror; it was itself an act of terrorism. Bush's declaration was not just an announcement; it was a battlefield maneuver played out on a landscape more important than the Iraq desert or Afghan mountains: the television screen.

The Bush event and the bin Laden tape are performative in several senses. First, both were illocutionary acts. If a terrorist promises that terrorist acts are coming, he has, by definition and illocutionary force, committed a terrorist act. If the commander-in-chief declares that the mission is accomplished, he enacts at least some kind of ending even within the liminoid space of the pronouncement. In fact, the Bush administration changed its rhetoric to one of "reconstruction" and "postwar," a shift that required changes in military strategy. That Bush's remarks appeared to finalize what was not final suggests one of the complications of performance: Bush's words wield authority—they have material costs and consequences and appear to have illocutionary force at the time of utterance—but they are a *play of finality* that places his desire (for victory and vindication) above fact or probability (that the conflict may be the new status quo).

Secondly, both events are performative in the sense that Alice Rayner describes: they gesture toward the immediate moment, the "total thisness of here and now," but they are also "relational, mediated through signs, norms and symbols" (1994, 34). In Baz Kershaw's discussion of radical theatre, he describes the capacity of performance to act as cultural intervention because of its "relationship with the wider social order, in all of its discursive and institutional complexity" (1992, 2). Rayner's and Kerhsaw's definitions of performative power apply to the Bush and bin Laden events: each is a cultural act that reveals through sign and symbol its historical moment; each is a political intervention that wants to shape the wider social order. The live performance and the taped performance are deeply "relational": they are in dialogue with spectators, with the status of the war, and with each other. The performances are also intertextual: they refer to something that the spectator recognizes. Bush's aircraft carrier speech implicitly cited the most durable of imperial images, the triumphant naval battleship; it also referenced the popular film *Top Gun*. Bin Laden's message also had familiar echoes, framing bin Laden as the solitary but inviolable holy man. The Bush and bin Laden "announcements" were not really about anything "accomplished"; rather, each man sought to stage the social reality he wanted to shape. For Bush, Americans would go back to shopping and stimulating the economy; for bin Laden, Americans would cower in fear.

Finally, there is the discovery of bin Laden's compound in Pakistan and his death in May 2011. For years, bin Laden's elusiveness nettled Americans, most of whom assumed he was living primitively in a remote cave in Afghanistan. When his extensive compound was discovered in Pakistan, and we learned that he was hiding in plain sight even as Americans were still stationed in the wrong battleground—Iraq—American pride took another blow. Before President Barack Obama announced the raid and killing, he ordered bin Laden's body to be dumped at sea. In the age of images, the most wanted terrorist was killed in secret and buried anonymously. While the official explanation was that bin Laden was buried quickly, in accordance with Muslim tradition, it is difficult not to imagine that the Obama administration wanted to control the firestorm of responses that images of the dead leader would provoke.

In sum, the six incidents I have described illustrate a change in the media from what might be called an authenticating role (such as the reportage that confirmed the Ceausescu overthrow) to that of coproducing an environment that partially constructs knowledge about the events (such as the narration that accompanied the real-time coverage of the 1991 Persian Gulf War) to becoming the events themselves (such as the performative utterances of both Bush and bin Laden). While this "progression" points to changes in technology and media practices that developed over two decades, it does not imply the elimination of one model by another, but instead indicates a mixed environment of communication practices. The media thus has become, in Douglas Kellner's opinion, the "dominant form and site of culture in contemporary societies," and the place where "the battles are fought for the control of society" (1995, 35).

One of the "paradoxes" of so much information, as William Leiss has noted, is that "on the great issues of society and politics, the role of knowledge in the composition of informed judgment very well may decline in proportion to the increase of available information" (1989, 207). As a case study, the Gulf Wars and the War on Terror bear out both Kellner's and Leiss's conclusions: as Americans and others watched the instantaneously transmitted images from the battlefield, they experienced a greater sense of immediacy but not a corresponding depth of insight.[2] To understand this disjunction, I begin this book by discussing the advent of "total television," a phenomenon initiated during the 1991 Gulf War, developed further in the 2003 Gulf War, and now the model for the media's treatment of all significant social crises. The profound effect of constant media coverage can be summarized simply by pointing out that few spectators enter a playhouse without bringing some media-produced image of the drama's subject along with them. Whatever political effect a drama may hope to create, it must first dislodge the images or assumptions the media has already manufactured.

Today, arguably, there is no "empty space," to use Peter Brooks's famous phrase, where public dialogue can take place. Mass media has so turned political crises into "informational events" that art of any kind, political or not, can hardly act independently of the mass-produced images that fill first our televisions and then our cultural imaginations (Patton 1995, 12). Moreover, not only does the media occupy most public space, but it can also incapacitate public action: the act of spectatorship displaces deliberation and, some would argue, "substitutes for the social action needed to address real life concerns" (Angus and Jhally 1988, 1). For Pierre Bourdieu, the "media are overall a factor of depoliticalization" (1998, 73). Technology, some darkly predict, leads only to virtual engagements with virtual realities; glued to television screen or computer monitor, we watch alone while narratives of history are spun before facts are gathered or communities are assembled. Citizens have become, in Baudrillard's stark analysis, "terminals of multiple networks," seduced by simulations (1983, 16).

THE NEW SEMIOTIC ENVIRONMENT: MEDIASCAPES AND IDEASCAPES

Arjun Appadurai, one of the most prominent theorists of globalization, has tantalizingly described "electronic propinquity" as one of the key features of current cultural processes (2004, 101). On the one hand, the media has produced an unprecedented experience of closeness: Americans watched the sufferings of the tsunami victims in Southeast Asia; Southeast Asians saw the despair and displacement of hurricane victims in the southern United States. On the other hand, the "media create communities with no sense of place," and the world appears "rhizomic," or even "schizophrenic" (101). "Electronic propinquity," producing competing feelings of intimacy and distance, connection and isolation, information and incredulity, is characterized by its unevenness. In some parts of the world, an abundance of information, images, and news is available; other parts of the world are premodern, passed-over pockets that remain invisible, unconnected, inaudible.

In order to better understand this complex and disjunctive global cultural economy, Appadurai proposes a framework of five elements—people, technology, money, media, ideas—coined around the suffix "scape" to indicate that the terms are not "objectively given relations that look the same from every angle of vision," but rather "deeply perspectival constructs, inflected by the historical, linguistic, and political situatedness of different sorts of actors" (102). Two of Appadurai's terms, mediascape and ideascape, are especially useful for understanding the new, albeit deeply uneven, public sphere of information exchange. They complement and expand an understanding of the increasingly performative nature of the public sphere.

Mediascape is Appadurai's coinage for both the "distribution of the electronic capabilities to produce and disseminate images" and "the images of the world created by these media" (104). "What is most important about these mediascapes," writes Appadurai, is that

> they provide (especially in their television, film, and cassette forms): large and complex repertoires of images, narratives, and ethnoscapes to viewers around the world, in which the world of commodities and the world of news and politics are profoundly mixed. What this means in that many audiences around the world experience the media themselves as a complicated and interconnected repertoire of print, celluloid, electronic screens, and billboards. The lines between the realistic and the fictional landscapes they see are blurred, so that the farther away these audiences are from the direct experiences of metropolitan life, the more likely they are to construct imagined worlds that are chimerical (104).

Appadurai is surely right that global interaction and security are affected by the imagined worlds constructed by those who live some distance from metropolitan centers, but it is also true that those situated in the heart of the metropolis—saturated by images generated through the mediascape—also must process an endless array of images and information. From either vantage point, the challenges of living in the new information order are enormous, especially when it comes to regarding images of Otherness, whether on a one-dimensional billboard or some form of advanced digital technology.

This challenge is made more complicated when a second of Appadurai's notions is taken into account; this is his concept of an ideascape, defined as a "concatenation of ideas," that are "often directly political and frequently have to do with ideologies of states and the counter-ideologies of movements explicitly oriented to capturing state power or a piece of it" (104). These ideascapes "are composed of elements of the Enlightenment worldview, which consists of a chain of ideas, terms, and images, including *freedom, welfare, rights, sovereignty, representation,* and the master term, *democracy*" (104, emphasis in the original). Appadurai argues that these terms have become more fluid as they have detached from an internal coherence they previously had when bound to a Euro-American master-narrative; they are parts of new "terminological kaleidoscopes," functioning as keywords around which different nation-states or groups organize their political cultures (104). These keywords, whose reference points and meanings are often strategically ambiguous, become rallying points. Nevertheless they lie at the heart of often violent assertions of essential differences. One can imagine a different chain of ideas, terms, and images, rooted not in Western Enlightenment ideals, but in other founding premises, particularly those of religious fundamentalism. These terms—*clericalism, piety, brotherhood, scriptural*—also work strategically and affectively to produce nonnegotiable identity claims.

Mediascapes and ideascapes are mutually dependent: my introductory descriptions of Bush aboard the military vessel and bin Laden's tape point to how these media events, both in their content and mode of distribution, are connected to certain animating ideas—the right to security; the right to self-determination—that are articulated as irrevocable, timeless principles. These events also possess an illocutionary force, dependent upon their invocation of such touchstone truths as "democracy" or "divine will," terms that circulate within an ideascape and that justify or legitimate a course of action by attaching it to a time-honored principle or sacred belief. In sum, a complex semiotic environment of images and of looser semantic signification characterizes our time and complicates everyday understandings of global events or political crises. To a defensible extent, the argument can be made that a greater critical understanding of performative strategies and of visual and verbal semiotics is a necessary component of civic, global engagement. This principle underlies every chapter in this book.

Problems of the Real

In the age of high visibility and rapid, real-time dissemination, spectators must deal with a problem Rosalind Krauss identified in 1977: the problem of the index (68). The index, as Hal Foster notes, is a "mark like a footprint that makes its meaning through a direct relationship to its referent" (1996, 80). In the political theatre that will be discussed in this book, most works claim a relationship to a factual, historical referent. Implicitly, principles associated with realism are assumed, specifically that language, scene, and performance can *signify directly*. This principle—the one that underlies naturalism as a kind of scientific method, and underlies realism—which drew upon both the material and symbolic valences attached to concrete objects but nevertheless insisted on the writerly control of such signification, persists in the privilege accorded to presence, of the body as the irreducible site of meaning. The documentary urge, which manifests itself in the appearance of the verbatim theatre discussed in Chapter 6, can be traced back to the desire to connect the indexical to the photographic, a desire that Susan Sontag famously interrogated (1973, 2004). Other works discussed later, particularly Heather Raffo's *Nine Parts of Desire* (2006), a one-woman show based on ethnographic research in which the actress embodies a range of Iraqi female Muslim identities, also draws its power by foregrounding indexical, bodily presence. The performance explicitly draws upon particular and identifiable referents and thus offers itself as more real and authentic for its use of gathered testimony; it does not, however, connect truth only to word but also to how the body on stage substitutes for the body elsewhere. Like Anna Deavere Smith, Raffo has developed a performative and epistemological strategy that sympathetically inhabits the Others she brings to the stage rather than impersonates or mimics them, thus further increasing a sense of a verifiable, even trustworthy, depiction of these women's lives.

Nevertheless, in recent political theatre a tension persists between the view that the spoken word or the photographic image is indexical and referential and the view that the word or image contains an ideological function whose power must be interrogated. Some theatre artists have adopted a journalistic perspective since they believe that journalism has been co-opted by the infotainment phenomena—an issue discussed more fully in the next chapter. Other theatre artists want the public to recognize how word and image have been manipulated, so they call attention to how it is very difficult to have direct, impartial access to historical events. That these two views constantly vie with each other was unwittingly and ludicrously illustrated by George W. Bush's secretary of defense, Donald Rumsfeld. In his April 11, 2003, Department of Defense news briefing, Rumsfeld asserted indexical accuracy and denied it in the next breath. Sometimes, for Rumsfeld, the index is proof—the rioting and looting in Baghdad in 2003, though untidy, is the mark of freedom. "The images of thousands of cheering Iraqis, celebrating and embracing coalition forces, are being broadcast throughout the world, including the Arab world," Rumsfeld observed. "And possibly for the first time, Arab people are seeing the people of Iraq waving American flags and thanking the men and women in uniform for risking their lives to free them from tyranny. I think it's important that that message be seen, for America is a friend of Arab people. And now, finally, Arab people are hearing the same message, not from U.S. officials, but from their fellow Arabs, the liberated people of Iraq." Yet, when pressed about the scenes of lawlessness and looting, Rumsfeld argued that the photographic index lies:

> Does that mean you couldn't go in there and take a television camera or get a still photographer and take a picture of something that was imperfect, untidy? I could do that in any city in America. Think what's happened in our cities when we've had riots, and problems, and looting. Stuff happens! But in terms of what's going on in that country, it is a fundamental misunderstanding to see those images over, and over, and over again of some boy walking out with a vase and say, 'Oh, my goodness, you didn't have a plan.' That's nonsense (Rumsfeld 2003).

As Rumsfeld breathtakingly demonstrated in his glib answers, while postmodern theory may struggle with how to determine the truth and validity of whether the image, the word, and even the body can be a site of direct signification, much popular and political discourse is happy to play either side of the equation. It veers between asserting that the body or scene, as photographed or televised, is a verifiable historical and material referent and suggesting that the body or scene has been staged or mediated. This specific question of the witness capacity of the body is especially crucial in a war that has been not only dehumanized but also *unhumanized*. Weaponry has become more detached from its human operators in the form of unmanned drones and smart bombs, and its deadliness has been made the stuff of video games. Bodies are hidden through direct policies of censorship or through media decisions driven by consumer ratings. The practice of embedded reportage or restricted journalist pools has effectively "weaponized" the press. But it is foremost the suffering body—whether injured or abused—and the hidden body—whether dead, captured, or detained—upon which ethical judgments about the conduct and cost of war are made. The Pentagon's decision to hide the coffins of the American dead or the wounds of the injured soldier is directly tied to a concern that such bodies would mutely convey the excessive costs of a controversial war.

There is the corollary issue of the enemy body and the heroic body. The Muslim body and the American body must also be managed by marking them: the first as zealous and murderous and the second as brave and unyielding. Here we again find elements of Appadurai's ideascape and mediascape. When there is a fissure in the representation of the latter, that body must be re-marked. The mother of a soldier killed in Iraq, Cindy Sheehan, who became an antiwar activist, was re-marked as a strident leftist; John Walker Lindh, the young man whose ideals led him to explore Islam, is the "American Taliban." The difficult interpretive task lies in evaluating how presence is marked or unmarked: whether bodies can convey anything that is not already appropriated by the gaze of those looking upon it. Very quickly, the indexical becomes the mythical.

Two examples present themselves. The first is the management of the body and story of the female American soldier. It is curious that two women soldiers from West Virginia were emblematized at different points in the war. During the triumphant stage of the war in 2003, Jessica Lynch, a West Virginia soldier who was captured and rescued, became a national heroine, though she later testified before Congress that she disliked such fabrication. Lynndie England, another West Virginia soldier, became the scapegoat for the prisoner abuse at Abu Ghraib, and though her culpability was clearly linked to widespread practices of torture, she bore the brunt of public scandal more than any officer who knowingly sanctioned torture. Both women became more mythic than indexical: America's sweetheart; America's trailer trash.

Another example of the turn to the mythic through the real is the case of bin Laden's video message. With his access to great wealth and his habitation in Afghani camps and caves, bin Laden lived in an uncanny place of the postmodern and the premodern, and as he spoke from within ruinous spaces, his taped images seemed simultaneously indexical and mythic. He was the richest bogey man on the planet. His seeming asceticism, in contrast to Saddam Hussein's hedonism, was more frightening: how do you fight a wraith, a specter with spectacular power?

IMAGES AND INVISIBILITY: FALLING TOWERS, BAGHDAD BURNING, CUBAN CAGES, ABUSIVE CELLS, KABUL FATIGUE

Five places, I believe, can convey the problem of evaluating and intervening in the extended War on Terror, a war that can be traced backward several decades, but at least to the 1991 Gulf War. These five sites each speak to the complicated questions of image and referent, visibility and invisibility.

For American citizens, the implosion of the falling towers on September 11, their ruins, and the mass grave of the three thousand dead is remembered as the nation's greatest trauma. That day and that site have coalesced in the national memory as the time and place when the unimaginable produced the dust of the dead. No event has wreaked so much pain, so quickly, as we watched it happen, paralyzed by the fear that there may be countless suicide hijackers manning many planes, each bearing down on us. W.J.T. Mitchell reminds us that alongside the high visibility of terrorism and its carnage, the anxiety of the invisible was also at work. He notes, "All terrorism is bioterrosm in the sense that, although the *end* may be a spectacle and an iconized event, the *means* are generally invisible... The chief characteristic of terrorism *tout court* is in the invisibility of its instruments and its agents, whose aim is to pass through all systems of surveillance without detection" (2011, 84). If we are to take 9/11 as the date when American vulnerability exploded into American consciousness, we must also acknowledge it as the originary date that introduced the anxiety over the capacity of an enemy whose goal is our eradication to live unnoticed among us, attack us when we travel, poison our mail, and keep us in a debilitating state of "orange alert."

Imperial power, conversely, must be visible power. The real-time transmissions of the 1991 and 2003 bombings of Baghdad were meant to put the world on another kind of alert—one about American invincibility. Significantly, the bombings were coded through the metaphors of visibility—"shock and awe"—as retaliation against the invisible agents who injured us. Both the spectacle of the 9/11 attack and the spectacle of the 2003 military retaliation were motivated by a display of power. In different ways, the spectacular excess of the 9/11 attack and the 1991 and 2001 bombings effectively, albeit temporarily, derealized its consequences. Only when the injured or dead body was admitted back into the scene did the traumatic real displace the spectacular real.

This alternation between what is visible and what is not has been essential to the exercise of power during the War on Terror. As I discuss in Chapter 4, Guantanamo and Abu Ghraib relied on policies of invisibility and unaccountability that were ultimately exposed through uncontrollable low-level technology. Digital cameras and cell phones brought down Rumsfeld and Dick Cheney's legally manipulated practices of detention and torture. Internet delivery of the Abu Ghraib photos exposed American moral hypocrisy and ratcheted up the tide of anti-Americanism. Before this eruption into the public sphere, the abuse used at Guantanamo, Abu Ghraib, Bagram Air Base, and other unnamed prisons was so secretive that the slang term "black site" captures their stealth and illegality. To keep our moral sensibilities intact, we outsourced torture (Mayer 2005). Invisibility connects with inaudibility. Judith Butler discusses how the detainees at Guantanamo inscribed poems on Styrofoam cups with shards of rock (2010, 52). Lines such as those composed by Abdullah Maijid al-Noaimi sound like an ancient psalm of suffering:

My rib is broken, and I can find no one to heal me
My body is frail, and I can see no relief ahead (Falkoff 2007, 59).

This invisibility and inaudibility were ruptured by the photos of the Abu Ghraib torture that exposed the fact that "acts of brutality and purposeless sadism" lay at the heart of Abu Ghraib (Danner 2004a, 51). Theatre artists, notably Gillian Slovo and Victoria Brittain, who helped to expose the illegality of Guantanamo, and others, such as Frances Cowhig and Judith Thompson, who have constructed works that interrogate American policies of abuse, have contributed directly to a larger public protest against such "democratic" illegality. These plays, and others, take on the project Butler describes in these terms:

> If certain lives are not perceivable as lives...then the moral prohibition against violence will be only selectively applied...The critique of violence must begin with the question of the representability of life itself: what allows a life to become visible in its precariousness and its need for shelter, and what is it that keeps us from seeing or understanding certain lives in this way? The problem concerns the media, at the most general level, since a life can be accorded a value only on the condition that it is perceivable as a life, but it is only on the condition of certain embedded evaluative structures that a life becomes perceivable at all (2010, 51).

Butler's contention about the "certain evaluative structures" that make a life perceivable pertains, devastatingly, to the Afghani people. As the first and the longest of the Wars on Terror, Afghanistan has remained largely offscreen. Perceived as an uninhabitable terrain populated by warring tribes and cursed by the Taliban, whom the United States has alternately aided and hunted, Afghanistan remains as unknown in 2012 as it was a decade ago. During those ten years, public discussion about Afghanistan has diminished, even as the Obama administration continues its military policy of pursuing Al-Qaeda there. Nevertheless, as Clyde Haberman observed in a *New York Times* commentary, "The near-invisibility of Afghanistan and Iraq reflected the remoteness of the wars for most people" (2010). For Butler, "Part of the very problem of contemporary political life is that not everyone counts as a subject" (2010, 31). If Afghanis "count" and are counted, they surely number among those with the most precarious existences on the planet. It is on this subject of erasure and invisibility that the book ends.

CHAPTER 2

TURNING HISTORY INTO HAPPENING: THE FIRST IRAQ WAR

> Skin has become inadequate in interfacing with reality. Technology has become the body's new membrane of existence.
> —Nam June Paik[1]

"IF THERE WAS ONE UNDISPUTED VICTOR IN THE GULF War I it was CNN." So claimed Danny Schechter, a former producer at two large television news shows (NBC and ABC), and he had the numbers to prove his case: CNN increased its audience from a few million in the early eighties to 184 million in the 1990s (1998, 10). The announcement of the war on January 16, 1991, was broadcast to over sixty million households, the largest audience at that point for a single event in television history. George H. W. Bush and his advisors, convinced they would be the undisputed victors of the Gulf War, celebrated that they had, in Bush's own words, "kicked the Vietnam syndrome" once and for all.[2] They jeered at the "opportunity" that Saddam Hussein had given the Western world when he invaded Kuwait; James Baker, Bush's secretary of state went so far as to say that the "entire planet is in this madman's debt" because Hussein's "brutal invasion of Kuwait provided the unexpected opportunity to write an end to fifty years of Cold War conflict with resounding finality" (Engle 2010, 26).

More than two decades later, any gains from extricating the nation from Vietnam-era malaise or Cold War superpower tensions have receded, replaced by worse fears about self-replicating terror cells that aim to destroy the West. This chapter and the next examines the 1991 war as a historical juncture in which new information technology and media practices converged with military planning and politics to reshape the public sphere. This new symbiosis is both collusive and competitive. In its emerging moments, it seeded the dynamic that would define the age of terrorism: the management of the imaginary.

In addition to looking at how what came to be known as a "megaspectacle" helped to produce the very political crisis it was also "covering," I want to raise three other issues that materialized in the 1991 war, all with lasting effects. One is George H. W. Bush's political doctrine of a New World Order, a forerunner of the "Bush Doctrine," which his son would develop. The second is how domestic problems, particularly of economic justice and civil rights, played out in military conflict. Here, we can see a more straightforward continuum between the first and second Gulf wars: soldiers in the 2003 conflict experienced the racism, homophobia, misogyny, and classism that their 1991 counterparts did. Finally, the model of the technowar surfaced in 1991 and became the model of a quick, low-casualty war that Americans would support.

The 1991 Persian Gulf War can be viewed as a "historic juncture" because covering the war was controlled in unprecedented ways by the Pentagon and describing it was shaped in equally unprecedented ways by media corporatism (Anderson 2006, 172). The 1991 war set the stage for the ways that visibility, reproduction, and speed would affect military planning and media coverage, for how public debate would occur, and for how oppositional practices, including socially engaged art, would need to rethink their strategies.

The theatre produced in response to the 1991 war clearly grapples with this new "constructive" aspect of media: the subject is central to the San Francisco Mime Troupe's *Back to Normal* and to Sam Shepard's *States of Shock*. These plays also foreground American bellicosity and American greed: they connect the Gulf War to the Vietnam war and they link American nationalism to American consumerism. They offer depictions of the economic suffering of those most affected by the war's costs and those most excluded from the American dream the war putatively protects. Naomi Wallace, who has written the most aesthetically complex and emotionally powerful of the plays considered here, also engages the Vietnam syndrome by ghosting the Gulf War with Lt. William Calley and one of his My Lai massacre victims. She also depicts profound social exclusion, based not only on class, but also on ethnicity, religion, gender, and sexual orientation. None of these three plays are single-issue plays, and I look at each of them in relation to four issues: the New World Order; media spectacles and technowars; the domestic costs of militarism; the Vietnam syndrome and American imperialism.

With hindsight, it is possible to see that some of the rhetorical rationalizations used in 1991 were repeated in 2003. Both Bushs, father and son, appointed themselves the protector of freedom and rationality. George H. W. Bush praised the American rule of law, implicitly suggesting that its opposite, the rule of the jungle, operated everywhere else. George W. Bush's verbal touchstones were "freedom" and "democracy": he was the liberator who extended American values to the oppressed while protecting us from those, maddened with envy, who hated our fundamental decency and individual rights. The early expression of these ideas can be found in the concept of the New World Order. Nor surprisingly to any who know his fierce political intelligence, Harold Pinter was among the first to call out the weasel lurking beneath the rhetorical cabinet.

THE NEW WORLD ORDER

In his Nobel Prize acceptance speech, Harold Pinter filleted the American government whose leaders, he contended, were empowered not only by extensive arsenals but by a "vast tapestry of lies" that has hypnotized citizens (2005). Experts at manipulation, they had hit on a "scintillating strategy," which Pinter went on to describe:

> Language is actually employed to keep thought at bay. The words "the American people" provide a truly voluptuous cushion of reassurance. You don't need to think. Just lie back on the cushion. The cushion may be suffocating your intelligence and your critical faculties but it's very comfortable (2005).

The corrective, Pinter concluded, was an "unflinching, unswerving, fierce intellectual determination, as citizens, to define the *real* truth of our lives and our societies" (2005).

The New World Order, Pinter's 1991 play, is an unflinching, intellectually determined assessment of George H. W. Bush's platform for re-drawing the post–Cold War map. Though only ten minutes long, it is as brutal as a knife across a throat.

The derisive title of Pinter's brief play has a fairly long history, stretching back to Woodrow Wilson. The phrase apparently seized George H. W. Bush's imagination during a fishing trip he took with his national security advisor, Brent Scowcroft, in August 1990. Initially formulated to describe American global presence at the end of the Cold War, it accrued meaning when used to justify a military response to Iraq's invasion of Kuwait. Bush regarded Iraq's action as an opportunity for the United States to "lead the world community to an unprecedented degree," even as the United States pursued its "national interests, wherever possible, within a framework of concert with our friends and the international community" (Bush and Scowcroft 1998, 399–400). The date of Bush's policy speech "Toward a New World Order," to a joint session of Congress is retrospectively ironic: September 11, 1990.

"Out of these troubled times," Bush argued, "our fifth objective—a new world order—can emerge: A new era—freer from the threat of terror, stronger in the pursuit of justice and more secure in the quest for peace. An era in which the nations of the world, east and west, north and south, can prosper and live in harmony." This world, Bush went on, would be "a world quite different from the one we've known" since it would be

> a world where the rule of law supplants the rule of the jungle. A world in which nations recognize the shared responsibility for freedom and justice. A world where the strong respect the rights of the weak (Bush 2001).

What, then, did the term "new world order" signify, in 1991 and subsequently? A brief list of politicians who have used it since Bush's congressional address makes the point that the phrase has become (or may always have been) an empty signifier: Dick Cheney, Henry Kissinger, Tony Blair, Gordon Brown, Iranian President Mahmoud Ahmadinejad, and Turkish President Abdullah Gul. Initially Mikhail Gorbachev used the term to discuss the goals of nuclear disarmament and greater global co-operation and power sharing. It increasingly acquired different resonances after Bush began speaking about a new world order in connection with the war in the Persian Gulf. Eric Miller and Steve Yetic suggest that initially Bush imagined the new world order as one where the United States took the global lead but did so with respect for the rule of law and with broad consultation and co-operation in order to enhance security (2001, 57). But in fact, the "new" in the new world order began to look suspiciously like unipolarity, just as the "world order" was vertiginously changing. In the 1990s, "previously stable territorial formations—nation-states, ideological blocs, global markets, or ethnonational communities" became chaotic even as "typically unstable exterritorial flows—communication networks, trade arrangements, cultural codes, or capital reserves" began to evolve into new coherent cohesions (O Tuathail and Luke 1994, 381). This opportunity to rechart the world may have begun (or been publically announced) as a co-operative vision, but President Bush repeatedly emphasized the "unique" role of the United States to bring freedom to the rest of the world. In O Tuathail and Luke's analysis, the

> old Cold War military-industrial complex seemed as necessary as ever as "instability" became the new discourse of danger. Although the New World Order suggested a recognition of one deterritorialization of world politics in the wake of the disappearanceof the Soviet threat, as the blocs formed by East/West or capitalist/communist struggle collapsed, it attempted to re-territorialize world politics by keeping familiar Western geopolitical structures intact albeit with the United States as the "sole remaining superpower" (383).

In order for the United States to fulfill this manifest destiny, "a permanent state of alert was seen as imperative for the U.S. as leader of the free world" (383). It is difficult not to hear post-9/11 language, especially about security, terrorism, and alertness, in these earlier formations, just as it is impossible not to mourn the lost opportunity that post–Cold War cooperation might have brought about. In hindsight, the discourse of danger has defined American international and domestic politics for over two decades.

Pinter immediately grasped the real effect of such discursive reformulations, and he just as quickly lampooned America's role as guardian of the rule of law. In his Nobel speech, he brings together the fact of Soviet dissolution and the rise of an American belief that it "had carte blanche to what it liked" (2005). His theatrical response, *The New World Order*, visualizes the corporatization of political policy and anticipates the American use of torture.

The New World Order, which premiered at the Royal Court Theatre in 1991 as part of the London International Festival of Theatre, depicts the dynamics of brutal oppression as part of common business dealings rather than as political machinations. Des and Lionel, thuggish businessmen, chat in front of the blindfolded man they are about to assault. Though quite different in setting, the play recalls Samuel Beckett's *What Where* in which an authoritarian figure repeatedly asks his subordinate if he gave the prisoner "the works" in order to make him confess. In Beckett's play, when there is no confession, the underling disappears, only to be replaced by an exact double, until in the final round, he takes the place of the tortured prisoner. The parallel between Beckett and Pinter occurs not only in the euphemistic language, with all its potent menace, but also in the sense that exercising power is an end in itself, while extracting information is secondary. Since the abusers don't even know what information they are seeking, they cannot obtain it, and Beckett's play suggests that the desire for absolute domination must ultimately feed upon itself.

In Pinter's new world, the corporate hirelings are similarly ignorant about the crime the prisoner has committed: their victim was once a "big shot," a "lecturer in fucking peasant theology" who "never stopped shooting his mouth off" (28). The captive "never stopped questioning received ideas," but the thugs intend him to silence him by torturing his wife first. Pleased that he has been brought down a peg, Des and Lionel observe that now he is "just a prick. Or a cunt" (30). At this point, the torturers become a comedy duo: the Abbot and Costello of persecutors. Lionel upbraids Des, the stupider, more servile of the two, for changing insults. He tells him, You've "got to learn to define your terms and stick to them" (29). If you don't, Lionel says, with the pomposity of one who is just a few points higher on the intelligence scale, all credibility will be lost. The advice confuses Des, who does his best thereafter to let Lionel take the lead. The pair are similarly muddled a few minutes later when they can't decide what would be the most menacing construction: to assert that they are "finished with" the victim or that "they've just begun" (29).

Torture has been Pinter's subject before; arguably it has always been his subject. But unlike even *One for the Road*, *The New World Order* invokes a specific political doctrine and visualizes how its self-interestedness is masked as a defense against extremism—the radical thought of a liberation theology. In this, the play foretells the "discourse of danger" that radicalism, frequently linked to religious fanaticism or ethnic extremism, poses to American rationality, democracy, and corporate interests. The play's demonization of dissent, especially by linking it with non-Western irrationality expressed via tribal alliances or religious zealotry, and its operative misogyny appear in the political rhetoric of the second Bush administration.

MEDIA EVENTS, MEGASPECTACLES, TOTAL TELEVISION IN THE 1991 GULF WAR

On January 17, 1991, the day after George H. W. Bush ordered the bombing of Baghdad, CNN signed on more than a million subscribers in Europe alone, and because it allowed its signal to be re-transmitted, some analysts estimated that a billion people watched the cable news' coverage (Hall 1997). For CNN, the Gulf War was "a windfall of profit and prestige" (Schecter 1998, 10). Its round-the-clock coverage of the forty-three-day war introduced audiences to a phenomena that George Gerbner has called the first "global media crisis orchestration" (1992, 244). His description echoed journalist Tom Englehardt's claim that the Persian Gulf War was the "ur-production" of a "new media conglomerate" of the sometimes competitive and sometimes collusive spheres of government and television (1992, 630). In the war, Englehardt asserted, "boundaries between military action and media event broke down in such a way that military planning could become a new form of media reality" (630). Terming this new media reality "total television," Englehardt noted that it represented a shift "toward a world in which, increasingly, everything gets done for the media; in which the more fully meshed media systems of the twenty-first century will need to discover new, more powerful, more all-purpose sponsoring relationships" (632). A year later, as Iraqis suffered intensely from the imposed sanctions, the first war that television viewers watched in real time was largely forgotten, though the model it employed—a technowar of short duration fought by as few ground troops as possible—installed itself as the American public's new expectation for military engagements.

Though the 2003 Iraq War has disproven this model, the expectation after 1991 was that wars needed to be short and bloodless, without domestic sacrifices, and broadcast live.

In describing this new media reality, it is useful to contrast the differences between "media events," "megaspectacles," and "total television." The first term refers to the coverage of an incident by the media in such a way that the coverage itself weights the event with significance. In June 1994, millions watched the real-time televised sight of a two-and-a-half-hour slow-speed car chase of O. J. Simpson fleeing after his wife was murdered. Neither Simpson nor the police sought coverage: it became an event only because the media decided to air it on the basis of Simpson's fame and the suspense of its outcome. A megaspectacle, alternatively, is constructed for the media and by the media; the event's power is directly related to its visibility. The megaspectacles of the twin towers attacks and the "Mission Accomplished" speech are alike in their desire to amass as large an audience as possible to disseminate a political message. Attached to a compelling visible image, the megaspectacle remains alive in the collective memory because of the image's power which is in turn enhanced by constant reproduction and dissemination through computer networks. "Total television" adds the third dimension of constant coverage. An event—hurricanes, tsunamis, celebrity trials, the first Gulf War—is televised in both live and in taped formats for long periods of time, supplemented with commentary and analysis to protract the event even further until it finally disappears—sometimes because the event has ended, but more often because something else has displaced it, or the audience has lost interest.

In current practice, the semiotic field is even more complex and fluid since the procession of media events, megaspectacles, and total television overlap, and the circuit of information is further amplified and disseminated by other information technologies. The portability and connectivity of hand-held, wireless computer/camera/phones, the proliferation of blogs, the popularity of social media networks, and the emergence of more real-time technologies have deeply affected the accessibility of information, the form it takes, and the speed at which it is shared. Henry Jenkins offers the term "media convergence" to describe the entire gamut of new technologies that allow information to be annotated, forwarded, archived, or otherwise used.[3] Technologies of simulation further complicate interpretation, blurring the real and the virtual. It is also inaccurate to speak of an event and coverage as if there is time and critical distance between them in which to produce analysis and judgment. The instantaneous reproduction of the event results in an image that is itself already coded and part of a signifying chain, even if that signification later gets reversed or debated. To indicate the entire range of this complexity, James Der Derian has devised the term the "military-industrial-media-entertainment-network" (2009) to describe the enmeshed network of actors who may be operating somewhat independently but are always cognizant of each other's presence. As spectators encounter the flux, speed, and recombinant possibilities of these boundary-blurring networks, they paradoxically find themselves in a labyrinth of infinite choices and a desert of judgment.

THE 1991 PERSIAN GULF WAR: THE NEW MODEL OF TECHNOWAR

We have no opinion on Arab-Arab conflicts.
—April Glaspie, US ambassador to Iraq[4]

The beginning of the Persian Gulf War is attached to two dates: August 2, 1990, when Iraq invaded Kuwait, and January 16, 1991, when the United States and its coalition allies bombed Baghdad at 6:38 p.m. EST, just 24 hours past the deadline that the United Nations had set for withdrawal. These two dates demarcate the pre-invasion, diplomatic phase, known as Desert Shield, and the war itself, Desert Storm.

The United States had supported Iraq in the 1988 Iran-Iraq War, continued to provide aid despite the abuses committed against the Kurds, and appears to have sent signals that it would not intervene should Saddam Hussein decide to invade Kuwait. But when Iraq invaded its oil-exporting rival, the United States led the deployment of a coalition of troops from some thirty countries (Kellner 1992, 12). In November 1990, the UN Security Council set January 16, 1991 as the deadline for an Iraqi withdrawal from Kuwait, and on January 17, the air bombardment began. President George H. W. Bush addressed the nation to justify the intervention. In retrospect, his speech enunciated the rationale and strategies that his son would use in 2003, although it also set forth principles that would be discarded. The first portion of the speech laid out the operation's necessity, legitimacy, and righteousness, establishing the operation as a "virtuous" war:

> This conflict started August 2nd when the dictator of Iraq invaded a small and helpless neighbor. Kuwait—a member of the Arab League and a member of the United Nations—was crushed; its people, brutalized...Tonight, the battle has been joined. This military action, taken in accord with United Nations resolutions and with the consent of the United States Congress, follows months of constant and virtually endless diplomatic activity on the part of the United Nations, the United States, and many, many other countries...Now the 28 countries with forces in the Gulf area have exhausted all reasonable efforts to reach a peaceful resolution—have no choice but to drive Saddam from Kuwait by force. We will not fail (Bush 1991).

Bush went to great lengths to emphasize extensive, multilateral diplomatic efforts—an effort at which his son would fail in the 2003 Iraq invasion and would attempt to gloss over with his euphemism of the "coalition of the willing." But he then goes on to press the same hot buttons that his son would push twelve years later: Saddam must be prevented from developing his "nuclear bomb potential," and his "chemical weapons factories." He is a rogue who must be stopped from the "rape, pillage, and plundering" of a tiny nation and from further maiming and murdering "innocent children." Promising that the war would not be another Vietnam, that soldiers would not "fight with one hand tied behind their backs," Bush set forth the military model that would underlay the planning for the 2003 war: short with minimal American casualties. Finally, Bush offered his global vision, that the 1991 war would help establish a "new world order" that would be governed by the "rule of law," and where a "credible United Nations can use its peacekeeping role to fulfill the promise and vision of the U.N.'s founders" (Bush 1991). His son ultimately discarded this collaborative vision by announcing the right to make a pre-emptive strike, a policy known as the Bush Doctrine.

As a case study, then, the 1991 Persian Gulf War is a pre-eminent example of the implications of how megaspectacles shape events and enervate political critique. For Paul Patton, the Gulf War "witnessed the birth of a new kind of military apparatus which incorporates the power to control the production and circulation of images as well as the power to direct the actions of bodies and machines. It involved a new kind of event and a new kind of power which is at once both real and simulacral" (Patton 1995, 5–6). The desert conflict also exemplified how media coverage can abound but also be heavily censored, hijacked by nationalist fervor, and indebted to its advertisers. While the Pentagon adeptly managed access, forcing journalists to participate in a pool system operated by the military or have no access at all to the battlefront, the hastily-formed "Citizens for a Free Kuwait" group managed congressional approval by hiring a public relations firm, Hill and Knowlton, to concoct a story about Iraqi troops throwing Kuwaiti infants out of incubators. The media also played its part in rubber-stamping the war as it acceded to sponsors who objected to having their products associated with grisly war photos. News anchors who declared themselves incapable of impartiality abetted the nationalist fervor, inflaming listeners by comparing Hussein to Hitler. Instances of dissent received very little air time: one study states that in the five months before the bombing, ABC offered 0.7 percent of its coverage to opposition, CBS gave 0.8 percent and NBC delivered 1.5 percent, roughly 13 minutes worth of air time (Anderson 2006, 158).

In addition to how the media abandoned objectivity, the unveiling of astonishingly sophisticated military technology with claims to surgical accuracy bred a sense of indomitability. The war—or at least the war planning—was to be as bloodless as the video games that mimicked it. But the facts are that between 125,000 and 150,000 Iraqis, both military and civilian, died in the short war, against 148 American combat deaths (Dunnigan 1992). In addition, the sanctions imposed against Iraq for the next decade caused extensive malnutrition, resulting in estimates ranging from 170,000 to 500,000 children's deaths.[5]

Baudrillard's Critique: From Outrageous to Obvious

For Jean Baudrillard, the fallout from the relentless visibility of media coverage is an "obscenity of the visible, of the all-too-visible...of what no longer has any secret, of what dissolves completely in information and communication" (1983, 131). The crucial notion in Baudrillard's analysis is surely that of "dissolution," for it is this idea that underlies the three provocative essays, collectively titled *The Gulf War Did Not Take Place*, he published immediately before, during, and after the 1991 Gulf War (1995). The thesis of the first and third essays—one announcing the Gulf War will not take place and one concluding that it did not take place—is actually the same: that is, the Gulf War is not a war if war is understood as an "antagonistic and destructive confrontation between adversaries" (Patton 1995, 17). Rather, Baudrillard deems the conflict an "ultra-modern process of electrocution" and concludes that no amount of "direct transmission by CNN of real time information is sufficient to authenticate a war" (1995, 61). Certainly, death and carnage have occurred; "the flesh suffers just the same," Baudrillard writes, "and the dead combatants count as much" but alongside combat, virtual engagements must be examined foremost for the "murderous capacity of images" (1995, 70, 10). His intentionally outrageous claims counter what he sees as equally outrageous lies: that this war is, for example, a "clean war" or a "surgical war" (62). Calling the war "promotional, speculative, and virtual," Baudrillard concluded that the "media promote the war, the war promotes the media, and advertising competes with the war" (30, 31). War is not meant to vanquish enemies but to incorporate them into regimes more compatible with the new world order of commerce.

At the time of its pronouncement, Baudrillard's rhetoric seemed extreme. The subsequent rise in hybridized viewing experiences—the popularity of reality shows, for example, the common practice of product placement, the open political affiliations of news outlets—now makes Baudrillard sound as though he were simply describing the obvious. Indeed, the analysis of Baudrillard's second essay, "The Gulf War: Is It Really Taking Place," seems prescient in light of the September 11 attack on the World Trade Center and the Pentagon:

> Thanks to this *war*, the extraordinary confusion in the Arab world is in the process of infecting the West—just revenge. In return, we try desperately to unify and stabilize them in order to exercise better control. It is an historic arm-wrestle: who will stabilize the other before being destabilized themselves? Confronted by the virulent and ungraspable instability of the Arabs and of Islam...the West is the process of demonstrating that its values can no longer lay claim to any universality than that (extremely fragile) of the U.N. (1995, 36).

The conclusions drawn by researchers at the University of Massachusetts Center for the Study of Communication are offered in far less polarizing language but point as well to a critical breakdown in how knowledge is constructed, disseminated, and received in the public sphere. They constructed a survey instrument to measure whether an increased amount of time viewing television coverage of the 1991 Persian Gulf War resulted in deepened knowledge of that conflict. Motivated by a belief that democratic decisions depend upon the quality of the information available, the Massachusetts researchers concluded that despite months of television coverage, few respondents could answer questions about the US foreign policy toward the region or even provide rudimentary facts. That 81 percent of the respondents could name a kind of American weaponry but could not articulate inconsistencies in American foreign policy led the researchers to conclude that media viewers have been "selectively misinformed" (Jhally 1991).

FIRST RESPONSE: SHEPARD AND THE SAN FRANCISCO MIME TROUPE RESTAGE THE WAR

Two long-established dramatic voices made the earliest theatrical responses to the 1991 Persian Gulf War: those of Sam Shepard and the San Francisco Mime Troupe. Shepard's *States of Shock* opened at the American Place Theatre in New York on April 30, 1991, a little more than two months after the declaration of victory.[6] In part because it was the first work by the rockstar/actor/playwright to appear in six years, and in part because it featured noted actor John Malkovich, the run sold out. *Back to Normal*, gestating since the war's beginning, followed the Mime Troupe's usual calendar and played in outdoor venues in the Bay Area from July 4 to Labor Day, 1991. There's no surprise in how quickly the Mime Troupe put together *Back to Normal*. As the oldest antiestablishment theatre in the United States, the Mime Troupe is widely known for its topicality and leftist political satires.

Read or re-viewed in tandem, these plays reveal the first wave of American criticism voiced against the 1991 war, and while the plays are differently satiric, they enact similar critiques on similar grounds. Both set scenes in a quintessential American locale, the diner, and each performance addresses the effects of the Persian Gulf War domestically. Each also voices concern about whether activism or dissent can occur any longer in the United States, tracing its demise to the unacknowledged ties among the spectacularized conflict, consumption patterns, and contagious nationalism. Thirdly, both plays engage a very specific discursive formulation enunciated during the 1991 Gulf War when Bush asserted, "By God, we've kicked the Vietnam syndrome once and for all." In this, Bush was wrong: references to Vietnam reappeared after the 2003 war disintegrated into military and political chaos.

At the time of the performance, the political judgments offered in each play reflected a minority viewpoint; as Ed Holmes, the director of *Back to Normal* observed, the cast and writers of the Mime Troupe were among the mere "9 percent" who opposed the war (Mason 2005, 239). Yet, while both plays condemned the war for its brutality and for its effect on America, they depart in their performance of political empowerment. The Mime Troupe, in the play's thematics and by virtue of its own performativity, reaffirms the possibility of critical dissent by tying it to a citizen's fundamental need to know how much the war is costing, partially in jobs and the de-funding of essential services, but even more basically in terms of lives.[7] Through the addled but ultimately vindicated protagonist Hetty Counts, the play asserts the right to know the ultimate bottom line of a war: a head count of lives lost. *States of Shock* does not offer such a sanguine message about political activism: it ends with a suicidal lament and an image of a father poised to kill his son. If there is a message about empowerment at all, it is an angry warning about American violence, self-sabotage, and obliviousness. Shepard's play offers a stunning example of Guy Debord's notion of a "diffuse spectacle," that is, the "commodity abundance associated with the undisturbed development of modern capitalism" (1987, 65).

Both plays, however, depict how, early on, political theatre recognized the shaping powers of media-driven images and commentary. From the moment the United States began military action against Iraq, the war became a nightly (or in the case of CNN, constant) miniseries. However obvious the markers of this fictionalization appeared throughout the miniseries, they were, nonetheless, subsumed in the onslaught of minute-by-minute coverage, which exerted the nearly unassailable pull of live experience. Hence, the "instantaneity of sight" that characterized coverage of the Gulf War tacitly suggested that spectacularity in and of itself provides sufficient and comprehensive insight that needs no further critical analysis (Polan 1986,

56). Indeed, distanced critical analysis is displaced in this model of communication transmission in favor of a "pure performing present" (Connor 1989, 170). When CNN televised President Bush watching the opening bombardment, it affirmed the connection between instanteity and fact. And if the commander-in-chief needed to watch, surely every other American did, too.

The San Francisco Mime Troupe's *Back to Normal* directly confronts the new dynamic of total television by starting the action with the recognizable music from the news show *Nightline*. Reporter "Muffy Chung" appears, expressing her exasperation with the tedium of the war. Her viewers have "had it with sand," she says, "They've waited six months—they want to see action" (Mason 2005, 242). Fortunately for Muffy—a thinly disguised version of television reporter Connie Chung, in the Mime Troupe's tradition of recognizable spoofs on public figures—she gets a story when two American sappers, Jimmy and Virgil, meet a surrendering Iraqi. When the Iraqi soldier inadvertently steps on a live mine, the American soldiers must choose whether to risk their lives to save him or let the "raghead" blow. Muffy is delighted.

States of Shock opens with a re-enactment of the televised bombings, the "shock and awe" of new weaponry. In a disorienting assault on the senses, a backdrop cyclorama shows lit tracer fire, rockets, and exploding bombs. A driving percussionist rhythm builds in intensity until the war panorama and drumming cease, and, in the silent aftermath, a spot illuminates a sepulchral white couple, two cadavers outfitted in West Palm Beach attire. They are seated at a diner, ignoring the noise. If the soldiers in *Back to Normal* are ready to serve, the couple in *States of Shock* are ready to be served.

The two plays begin by drawing upon what every audience member has already seen and heard. This is perhaps the most fundamental change that has occurred in political theatre: because of media saturation and instant connectivity, no one enters the theatre without some previously formed image or narrative in mind, and the performance necessarily works within/against established visual and verbal discourses. While political theatre artists have always sought aesthetic forms and performance strategies to counter political propaganda, they must now engage the complex epistemological challenges that arise in the new media environment: that reality is and is not virtual; that pseudo-events and constructed spectacles have material effects; that we select information and are summoned by it. In the 1991 Gulf War plays, the beginnings of the paradigm shift are evident. While the two plays still engage in old "us"/"them" political dichotomies—such as the classic antagonism between government secrecy and citizen activism—they also demonstrate an awareness that it is more difficult to tell what is fact and what is hype.

The San Francisco Mime Troupe's *Back to Normal* is one of the earliest examples of a theatre company exposing the constructive role of media coverage. The plot of *Back to Normal* takes place in three locations: the desert; the small town of Normal, California; and the Oval Office. While her son, Jimmy, is serving in Iraq, Hetty, a 1960s burn-out, obsessively pursues government conspiracies stories that she airs on her radio program, *Reality Sandwich*. Her current project involves tracking Bush's movements in order to shatter the myth of unsupported, unilateral Iraqi aggression. To her dismay, the working-class, multicultural community she lives in has been infected by the nationalist fervor, and she feels herself a double outcast as mother and citizen. When a genie magically grants her three wishes, she squanders the first two in the usual fairy-tale manner, but inadvertently makes good use of the third.

Part of the comic bluntness in *Back to Normal* stems from reporter Muffy's bald admission that the media is the real hero of the story being told. When she gravely informs the television audience that she is standing "witness to an act of individual heroism" as a young American soldier has "risked his own life to save an Iraqi soldier just as I, Muffy Chung, risk my life to bring you this story," she mocks the hyperbole of the Gulf War journalists who became their own best news stories (Mason 2005, 243). In her essay "Military Censorship and the Body Count in Persian Gulf War," Margot Norris writes about how the "majority of articles about the press...inevitably produced more self-dramatizations" (1991, 227). Arthur Kent, an NBC journalist known as the "Scud Stud" got more air time for adding sex appeal to the reports—a formula repeated in the handsome Anderson Cooper and the beautiful Lara Logan—and he appears briefly in *Back to Normal* as "Arthur Pent."

This cult of celebrity increased with the number of media events and megaspectacles that would dominate the news: obtaining the story became the story. Muffy's drive to *find* a story or *be* the story underscores how the news is part of the larger entertainment industry, but it also points to a problem in total television: how to deal with empty air time, tedium, and the need for constant commentary. While the air raid on Baghdad showcased the power of advanced weaponry, the images of it could not be aired in silence. The challenge of total television is to eliminate any lag-time between what can be seen and what can be told; hence, news anchors became proficient at providing on-the-spot coverage. With little new to report, commentators relied on narrative devices to fill out the time and give a sense of coherence to what was piecemeal. These conspicuous narrative ploys included frequent chronological markers ("Day One"; "Day Thirteen"), the use of captions or other titles ("The War from the Gulf: Operation Desert Storm"), and the presence of reliable narrators (Peter Arnett of CNN; Dan Rather of CBS).[8]

The need for instantaneous comment led to casting every event in terms of a mythic struggle or, as Baudrillard would have it, turning it into a scenario from an already written disaster script. In his study of the development of mass audiences, David Chaney compares the narrative performance of mythical tales and the narrative performance of news, finding that both promote "structural amnesia." This amnesia, caused by a "focus upon simultaneity and novelty" induces "a radical indifference to the past," in which the past is reduced or simplifies to exist as a "series of spectacular tableaux and allegorical figures" (1993, 237). In *Back to Normal*, Muffy's language, part empurpled hyperbole, part homely cliché, raises ordinary events to mythic status: she describes Jimmy and Virgil "cutting a swath of safe road through the heavily mined desert" and with coded language concludes that the mixed-race Jimmy is a "special breed" who will return home to a "proud black mother" (Mason 2005, 243). This latter focus on the human interest side to the news will be raised to such a level during the 2003 war that heroes and villains—Jessica Lynch, Lynndie England—will serve as distractions from more important issues—such as why the United States countenanced torture.

To counter the faux-transparency of television coverage, *Back to Normal* puts the tedium, Chung's impatience, and the construction of boiler-plate news on view. By drawing the media coverage into a theatrical frame, the play exposes the great homogenizing effects of network presentations that tell the same story however much they highlight the exclusivity of their "first" reports. The theatrical frame works as any framed narrative does, drawing implicit contrasts that can expose ideology. The Mime Troupe's audiences see how instantaneously reported stories are inscribed into larger narratives—depoliticized mythic tales of generosity, courage, or ingenuity—that do far more to reify national identity than to provide factual coverage. When Muffy is whisked off stage by a military police officer, the audience immediately grasps that ubiquitous coverage does not mean the end of censorship.

Back to Normal also connects media coverage to a hystericized public sphere, the "yellow-ribboning" of America, where dissent is unpatriotic. The performance of a faux-inclusiveness and its manufacturing of consent is played out in the next scene, which shifts to a diner in Normal, California, where Frank, formerly known as Farid, has thought it best to delete "eggs and falafel" from his menu. All the gathered customers support the war (they sing, "You can tell King Tut, America's gonna kick butt"), however little it is in their interest to do so. Neither economic considerations nor past prejudicial treatment affect the judgments of the Vietnam vet turned failing farmer, the mayor who loves "smart bombs" but must lay off teachers, or the Japanese American who remembers internment. The war spectacle prompts an uncritical desire for national affiliation, in part because of sheer emotionalism and in part because it is better to join the cause than to lose access to economic and cultural capital. The incipient racism of the Gulf War is put on display primarily through the Arab American character of Frank/Farid who fears reprisal, but also via the cultural amnesia of the Japanese American.

All of this denial frustrates Hetty. Her predicament deepens when she is invited to the White House to watch her son receive a presidential commendation, an event that will be aired live. The scene points to the administration's willingness to pile on to the media's mythology. But now Hetty must choose: son or cause. The intertext between Hetty and Brecht's Mother Courage derives from their parasitic dependence on war at the expense of their children even though Hetty is driven by her conscience rather than profit. Her deep psychic investments have damaged her relationship with her son who feels neglected by his endlessly distracted and embarrassing throw-back mother. As in Brechtian drama, the Mime Troupe exposes the false choices; here Hetty must elect the historical amnesia of her neighbors to have a relationship with her child or continue to expose the truth but lose her son.

Though motherhood compels Hetty to accept the invitation to the White House, she cannot bear to hear the president speak. She inadvertently uses up her third wish when she mutters to herself that Bush should stop lying, and Bush instantly spews out his real feelings, all caught on-air. Once revved up, Bush can't stop: the United Nations is a pawn of American business, he couldn't care less about giving "Sambo a badge," and no one worries if Saddam Hussein's "sadass country" is bombed "back to the Stone Age." While Secret Service men try to pull him out from in front of the television cameras, Bush unzips his pants—a nod to the public characterization of Bush as a "wimp"—to prove he is a president with "brains, bucks, and balls" (Mason 2005, 263).

Hetty goes back to Normal, but this time her son is with her. While Hetty's penchant for Sixties activism is ambivalently treated, it is not wholly dismissed even as *Back to Normal* acknowledges the increased difficulty of finding the truth amid both government war-management and media saturation. *Back to Normal* therefore offers a mixed message of political empowerment, one symptomatic of its timing. While it advises its spectators to be aware of how the media is constructing events, it fails to suggest ways to respond except with vigilance. Though Hetty is vindicated, she is an outmoded model of political activism. Few would take her as a role model.

More darkly comic, *States of Shock* stages an Artaudian performance of political shock. Its brevity and savage images, even its lack of depth, are the marks of a work written in a passionate hurry in order to make a passionate point. In *States of Shock*, the juxtaposition of war's victims and voyeurs implicates the audience as well as the on-stage diners and makes explicit connections between consumerism, nationalism, and political isolationism. One character, a waitress named Glory Bee, gives voice to this profound obliviousness, in terms prescient of the September 11 attacks:

> The thing I can't get over is, it never occurred to me that Danny's could be invaded. I thought we were invulnerable to attack. The landscape. The lighting. The parking lot. All the pretty bushes. Who could touch us?
> Who would dare? When the first wave of missiles hit, I kept studying the menu. I thought the menu would save me somehow... the catfish dinner. The chicken-fried steak. I worshipped the menu... To me it held a life. An unthreatened life. Better than the Bible (40–41).

States of Shock enacts its critique by placing the war spectacle within the framework of consumption. Unlike the Normal diner, this family restaurant is not fervidly patriotic nor hysterically nationalistic: as a "White Couple" waits impatiently for their food, they seem hermetically sealed from any outside events. At the sound of a whistle, a colonel enters, dressed in a motley of past military uniforms and war paraphernalia, from Civil War sabers to various pins and medals. In the German production, he wears a Gulf War T-shirt. He pushes a young soldier in a wheelchair festooned with American flags and good-luck charms. The juxtaposition of the diner's iconic realism with the disturbing expressionism of the cyclorama produces a setting that links American consumption to violence, underscoring America's desire to wage wars abroad without troubling domestic peace. The European production at the Staddtheatre Konstanz further emphasized these connections by incorporating both Edward Keinholz's sculpture *The Portable War Memorial* and Bruce Naumann's neon sculpture *EAT/DEATH* into the background (Shewey 1997, 219). The white couple shows no curiosity even when a bomb hits the restaurant, the cook is killed, the manager dies, and the soldiers wrestle each other to the floor.

Instead, *States of Shock* offers what Guy Debord called a "defuse spectacle," that is, the kind of spectacle that "accompanies the abundance of commodities, the undisturbed development of modern capitalism" (1987, 64). Associated with advanced capitalism, diffuse spectacles operate via seduction, on desires. The white couple wants what they want. Their impatience with the waitress—inflected with racism when she is played by a black actress, as was the case in the premiere production—is in part because she is delaying them from further consumption. More than once, they rebuke her: "We could be buying things as we speak" (Shepard 1993, 11). In the manner Debord describes, the white couple exemplify the "banalization" that dominates modern society when commodities are so overabundant that what produces satisfaction is not their use but their existence per se. The white couple doesn't necessarily want to eat the clam chowder they ordered, but they want it delivered immediately. The chowder is, in Debord's terms a "pseudogood" that produces "pseudo-gratification." Shepard places this mini-parable of commodity fetishism on top of an older, still operative, story of race and gender oppression (the white woman declares the waitress "ought to be shot" for her inadequacies) and associates both with the didactic moralism of right-wing rhetoric about "family values." Another of Debord's observation applies here: that "vestiges of religion and the family" are often "blended with ostentatious pretensions of worldly gratifications" (1987, 59). When Stubbs tells the white couple directly, "The middle of me is all dead. The core. I'm eighty percent mutilated," they ignore him. When he begins to shout, "My thing hangs like dead meat," they complain about the unseemly disruption in a "family restaurant"(Shepard 1993, 12). The soldier disturbs the peacefulness of "blissful social unification through consumption" and so the white couple are happy to sing him a suicide lament ("Goodnight Irene") at the play's end (Debord 1987, 69).

As the first two theatrical responses to the Persian Gulf War, *Back to Normal* and *States of Shock* both drew attention to the media's role in producing the story, an insightful achievement given that media criticism was still an emergent discourse. *States of Shock* reproduced Shepard's signature dark satire; however, its depiction of the alliance of consumption patterns with war and national isolation held American self-righteousness up to ridicule. Shepard also underlines the long history of American militarism. In their rush to the stage, the two pieces may have recirculated old dramatic messages and styles, but each work signaled that new approaches to war, to war coverage—and to theatre—were in the making.

GHOSTING IRAQ: VIETNAM REINCARNATED

Both *States of Shock* and *In the Heart of America* strip away the Persian Gulf War narrative of principled objection to the violation of national sovereignty and replace it with the longer narrative of American neo-imperialism. Both plays similarly insist that the militarized American culture has deepened the fractures in America society. In this, the plays anticipate the cultural split that showed itself in the 2003 war: on the one hand, George W. Bush advised Americans to "go shopping" as part of the war effort; on the other, the sensational news stories depicted women soldiers from the economic underclass, such as Jessica Lynch and Lynndie England. Naomi Wallace explicitly compares Vietnam and Iraq in her play *In the Heart of America* by reincarnating the ghost of Lt. William Calley, famous for the My Lai massacre, in the person of an American soldier and by having a murdered Vietnamese woman appear as a wandering spirit in search of her killer. In an interview in 2001, Wallace spoke about the American desire to "think that what is happening to Iraq is not part of our story." But, Wallace insisted, "what has happened and is happening with Iraq is part of the context of our story now." [9]

Unlike the prevalent rhetoric of "regime change" in the 2003 war, the earlier Bush administration tried to avoid such unilateral language, cultivating international approval for the operation. Yet, in Bush's public pronouncements, comments about America's strategic interests in the region crept in among the alternatively inflammatory accounts of Hussein's brutality and idealistic defense of political principles. However much Bush defended the rationality of the New World Order, emphasizing its co-operative aims, it clearly served Western economic and political interests. In *A World Transformed*, he stated that the "premise [was] that the United States henceforth would be obligated to lead the world community to an unprecedented degree, as demonstrated by the Iraqi crisis, and that we should attempt to *pursue our national interests*, wherever possible, within a framework of concert with our friends and the international community" (Bush and Scowcroft 1998, 399–400).

As strategically important to the United States as Vietnam had been, Iraq also posed the same problem of becoming a no-exit failure. Even in the 1990s, vestiges of the dreaded "Vietnam syndrome" remained, despite Ronald Reagan's effort to put it to rest by contending that the defeatism was part of the North Vietnamese propaganda machine. Bush's willingness to use overwhelming force suggests that he followed Reagan's script very closely. General Norman Schwarzkopf also promised the American public "this is not going to be another Vietnam." After declaring the six-week war a victory, Bush declared in his radio address that "the specter of Vietnam has been buried forever in the desert sands of the Arabian Peninsula" (1991).

Both *States of Shock* and *In the Heart of America* enact performative dialogues with the public pronouncements that linked the Persian Gulf War to the Vietnam War (1998).[10] Acknowledging the deep trauma of Vietnam-era MIA's as well as that of veterans and injured soldiers, the plays form themselves around the metaphor of the mutilated or missing soldier's body. In Shepard's drama, the colonel actually prefers his son to be missing rather than to be the injured wreck that has been shipped home; in Wallace's work, the action begins with a sister looking for information about her missing brother's whereabouts. Both plays reject the idea that the short Iraq war has exorcized the ghost of Vietnam's failure, and they do so quite explicitly. Shepard's soldier and colonel wear a motley collection of past-war paraphernalia that includes Vietnam and Iraq war references. Wallace's play pairs

Vietnam war figures (Calley and Lue Ming) with figures from the Iraq war (Remzi, Fairouz, Craver), connecting them through a character (Boxler) who incarnates American aggression. Both Shepard and Wallace imply that the Vietnam syndrome has not disappeared; it has mutated to become a deeply militarized/corporate culture that will betrays its own citizens in pursuit of the goods, markets, and prominence it requires.

In Wallace's America, unlike Shepard's, the focus is not on blind consumption habits: her characters are too far down the social ladder to exert much influence over anything. Rather, Wallace examines how the competition that sustains this militarized/corporate culture requires an enemy, a loser, or an outcast, and she shows how constantly demonizing someone else, even a fellow-soldier, is required to keep the race going. The goal for a successful American in the new order is to be in the position of setting the terms of the game and naming the players—and the enemies. Hence, Remzi, who wants to be a fully assimilated American, joins the US Army, ignoring the fact that his Palestinian father had been killed by Americans and that he himself is killing Arabs—even as he is called a "sandnigger" by his commanding officer. Willing to kill and die for one's country does not guarantee full entitlement, a fact Wallace underscores by allowing the audience to see the self-deluding optimism of characters who by ethnicity, class, and sexual orientation will remain outcasts, however deep their patriotism. The painful unraveling of Remzi's hope suggests that the ideals of a fully inclusive, equitable, multicultural democracy are themselves chimerical.

Shepard's one-act, 80-minute play is extraordinarily fast-paced, and like other plays he has written, it depends upon a searing image. In *States of Shock*, the image of two military men, a colonel and an injured young veteran in a wheelchair, opens and closes the drama, though by the end, their posture is reversed. Ostensibly taking the young soldier out on a break from the military hospital, the colonel's desires are quickly unmasked. He needs—indeed his professional, familial and sexual identity requires it—to hear how his son, possibly the injured soldier, Stubbs, "died" in the war. He cajoles the maimed and traumatized Stubbs into reliving the moment he was attacked by friendly fire, asking him to use toy soldiers to re-enact the exact moment when his "son" saved Stubbs's life and died in the process. If Stubbs offers the quintessential story of American heroic selflessness, the colonel can install his "son" in the mythic line of American frontiersman whose common purpose has been to save the nation from wallowing in "various states of insanity and self-abuse" (25). But Stubbs cannot tell the tale the colonel wants. In one of the exchanges that conflates paternity with militarism, Stubbs tells the colonel that he "remembers the moment you forsook me. The moment you invented my death" (23). The painted face on one of the "smart" missiles that hit Stubbs looked like the colonel's, "smiling and lying, peering down from a distance...bombing me" (43). In his equation of the failures of fatherhood and fatherland, Stubbs realizes that for him, "America had disappeared" (21).

Such a parting would be, in Shepard's world, a perversely optimistic ending. But in something akin to the fertility rites of *Buried Child*, the ritualistic restoration of Stubbs must take place: he must be revived in order, though currently impotent, to replace the colonel and to father more sons to send to war. Alfred Nordman and Hartmut Wickert, in their discussion of the 1993 European premiere, which Wickert directed, make the incisive observation that just as the United States sought to heal itself from the bad war of Vietnam through the good war of the Gulf, the colonel attempts to heal himself by replacing the story of his son's actual war experiences with a folktale that allows him to preserve his own militaristic instincts. As the action accelerates, the relationship between Stubbs and the colonel grows increasingly more violent while the waitress and couple remain preternaturally unfazed. Even as the colonel savagely whips Stubbs with his belt, exhorting him to "become a man," the white woman laps her soup with bovine lassitude, and the white man masturbates to a climax. In this slice of America, sex is either sadistic or auto-erotic, but it is never more important than the clam chowder. At the close of the play, after the fight between the faux father and the unclaimed son to see who will win the waitress, Stubbs, his manhood restored, tries to decapitate the colonel with a Civil War saber. The action is frozen, and the moment held in tableau. Johann Callens reads the immobility as an indication that the inhabitants of the diner are "beyond expiration." The cadaverous white couple is, suggests Callens, already from a kind of underworld, from the realm of the just-dead of Sarte's *Huis Clos,* or the frozen-in-time of Beckett's *Endgame* (1997, 227). Homicidal and suicidal, complacent and consumerist, isolationist and imperialist, voyeuristic and oblivious, lying and self-deceptive, approaching a mythic state of death-in-life—this is Shepard's projection of America under the New World Order.

Wallace's vision of America is a history ghosted by unresolved past conflicts, one in which domestic inequities and prejudices play themselves out on foreign soil. In an interview, "Strange Times," she summoned writers

> to imagine, in every detail, the hundreds of new ghosts that our governments are creating in Iraq. We can make these ghosts real. We can open our doors to them, invite them to sit at our tables. We can talk to them about the theories and ideas that have killed them. And we can make a choice not to let their murder go unrecorded (2003, A1).

Her effort to make these "ghosts real" resulted in the play *In the Heart of America*, which opened in London at the Bush Theater in 1994 and moved to the Long Wharf Theatre, where it was directed by Tony Kushner. In 2001, the play was part of a Naomi Wallace theatre festival in Atlanta; in 2003, the Outward Spiral Theater in Minnesota staged it to coincide with the beginning of the bombing of Iraq. Of the plays written in response to the 1991 war, *In the Heart of America* is the most structurally and intellectually complex; its dramaturgy bears comparison with Kushner's works and Caryl Churchill's early plays.

Wallace's play opens with a crippled Palestinian American woman, Fairouz, searching for her brother, Remzi, an Iraq war soldier who is missing. She tracks down his fellow soldier, Craver, a poor Appalachian, suspecting that the two men were lovers, and tries to convince him to tell her why the military will give her no information about Remzi's disappearance. She finds Craver hiding in a cheap hotel room in Kentucky, and slowly she extracts the story from him. While there, Fairouz is visited by the ghost of a Vietnamese woman, Lue Ming, whose child was murdered in the My Lai massacre. Like Fairouz, she too is searching: her quest is for Lt. William Calley, the real-life soldier who led the massacre. She finds Calley re-incarnated in the person of Lt. Boxler, the commander in charge of Remzi and Craver's unit in Iraq. Through exploring the connections between prejudice and recurrent aggression, Wallace's play shows how the visible violence of war and the less-visible violence of social domination activate and sustain each other. This symbiosis manifests itself in different scenarios of subjection. In exposing this interdependence, *In the Heart of America* moves between the present and the past, takes place in four locales (a motel room, a military camp, another room, and the desert), and breaks its five characters into different couples, triads, and split-stage groupings. At times, one or more characters is watching the others, doubling the act of spectatorship for the audience members, and connecting with the play's suggestion that when violence is committed, people fall into three categories, according to whether they "watch, kill, or die" (96). This insight, so pertinent to the spectacularization of war, is the ethical mandate of Wallace's play.

Each of the play's two acts has eleven brief scenes. The structural parallelism enables a contrast between the two women's quests, the men's experiences of brutality, and the Vietnam and Gulf Wars. Its two-act structure also corresponds to the two halves of the Iraq War, Operation Desert Shield and Operation Desert Storm, with the first part re-producing the anticipation and excitement of the build up to the bombing. Episodic and discontinuous, a performance of *In the Heart of America* requires the audience to take in soldiers, civilians, ghosts, souls, dead parents, inventories of weaponry, and three wars, as well as Appalachian, Palestinian, and Vietnamese culture—all of the heterogeneity that has been flattened out in media coverage or nationalist rhetoric by the urge to produce the us/them dichotomies that conflict requires. This compulsion to first dichotomize and then to dominate is the play's foremost explanation for the persistence of violence. At its most far-reaching, *In the Heart of America* depicts encounters with Otherness—even the Other that is part of the self—as fueled by threat and by fear. As explored by Hegel, Fanon, Levinas, and Butler, among others, the ethical encounter with Otherness subsumes more limited critiques of racism, classism, sexism, and homophobia in order to offer a trenchant understanding of aggression as corporeal, economic, and epistemic violence. Wallace's play cuts deeply into these layers of hostility and self-hatred.

This larger emphasis does not mean that *In the Heart of America* engages with the Gulf War indirectly. Like Peter Sellars's version of Aeschylus's *The Persians* (discussed in the next chapter), the play details the full arsenal of American high-tech weaponry, examining how its wizardry disguises death and injury. As was done by the San Francisco Mime Troupe, it directly counters Bush's plans for a New World Order. But how Wallace names the weapons, which she does in great detail, is quite different. In a fascinating scene, the soldiers, Remzi and Craver, displace their anxiety onto the hope that technologies of death will keep them safe. Remzi recites a memorized list of all the bombs and weapons used against the Iraqis. To his listening squad, the recitation sounds like a calming "lullaby" of all the "ways to kill the human body" (111).

In taking on the complexity of identity issues, Wallace's play reminds audiences how agonizing and divisive such debates can be. They nearly destroy the siblings' relationship: Fairouz privileges her Arab ancestry and her mother's experience of political displacement and violence; Remzi desires assimilation into American national identity. When his sister tries to convince him of the irony of a Palestinian going to war to defend an occupied country, Remzi retorts that he is sick of being a "hyphen," that he is an American before he is an Arab. He tells her, "I am not a refugee. It's always something else with you, always once removed. I am not scattered" (95). Yet, it also seems plausible that Remzi's desire for assimilation is actually a dream of invisibility. He carries within him the guilt he feels for watching in hiding while his sister was attacked by a bunch of school children who demanded to see her "devil's" foot. By the drama's end, Remzi will have emerged into the very visibility he scrupulously avoided: he reclaims his Arab family, falls in love with Craver, and defends an Iraqi prisoner from abuse. The consequence of his search for wholeness and self-acceptance is literally dismemberment: when he and Craver are discovered together, he is so beaten by his fellow soldiers that his bones are scattered and left in bits in the Iraqi sands.

Unlike Remzi, Fairouz and Lue Ming already know how discrimination, especially misogyny, works at home and in the military. In act one, scene five, Lue Ming re-enacts the children's attack on Fairouz, calling her a "dirty Arab," but also "slope," "dink," and "gook," and then explaining how each insult was used in a past American war. Neither of the women seeks the kind of belonging that Remzi does: Fairouz is homeless; Lue Ming is migratory. Though she calls herself an Arab woman, Fairouz cannot really identify with her mother's traditional values and has no desire to embrace them wholly, but she also knows she will find neither love nor friendship in America. Lue Ming wants the man who stabbed her infant daughter four times to confess to his crime, and the soldier who cut off her own long braided hair and kept it as a souvenir to acknowledge his brutality. When Lue Ming appears to Boxler/Calley in the Iraq desert, she confronts him about the civilian massacre of some five hundred old men, women, and children in Vietnam, and the abuse and sexual violations committed. But Boxler/Calley need not confess, he believes, because the war is over and because his celebrity status—with a hit song about his courage—has absolved him. That Calley's brutality has found a new outlet in the Iraq war is exemplified by a "joke" he tells. After eviscerating an Iraqi prisoner and pulling open his rib cage, Boxler, says, he stood in the corpse and waved to his men: "Hey boys, now I'm really standing in Iraq" (129).

Like Remzi, Craver also desires escape: he wants to flee the desperate poverty of his rural family life and the memory of his father working in the mines. In act one, while Remzi and Craver are waiting for the bombing to begin, they acknowledge that they each hope that military membership will give them sense of pride and the chance to protect a way of life. By the time he is back in Kentucky, Craver believes America will be punished by plague or flood for making Iraq into a "body with every bone inside it broken" (130). He is as radically displaced as Fairouz. In different ways, each of the four characters has experienced violence on the basis of perceived difference. They all know economic discrimination, harm against their persons, social exclusion, and the violence that accompanies, as Slavoj Zizek writes, "the very symbolization of a thing, which equals its mortification" (2008, 61). The America of Boxler/Calley either instrumentalizes or excludes the America of Fairouz, Remzi, and Craver. Indeed, as the Conradian echoes suggest, American imperial greed devours its most ardent champions: even Boxler speaks of being "human once" before he became the Kurtz-like Calley.

Wallace's play is interested in how the uninitiated are recruited and incorporated into such brutal practices, how a Calley can always find a Boxler. Act one, scene six, in particular, shows the power of the performative in constructing behavior and forming subjectivity. Here, Lt. Boxler teaches two new soldiers, Remzi and Craver, how to tap deeply into personal pain and transform it into hostility. In this segment, the play enacts the (de)formation of subjectivity through performative rituals and mimicry, practices that are used extensively in combat training. Boxler schools Craver and Remzi in the ways of interrogating an Iraqi prisoner. First, Boxler establishes an us/them dichotomy based on nationalism, reminding the two new recruits that they are "all family here" (110). But he quickly breaks this association down, first by gender, then ethnicity. To establish his authority over them, Boxler calls Remzi and Craver "girls" and "babe," and "Barbies," and he then pushes the men to reveal their family origins. Remzi is a "half-breed, a sandnigger, a stinking Arab"; Craver's father is a "broken-down, coal-shitting piss-poor excuse for an American dream" (112–113). When he playacts the part of the Iraqi prisoner, he continues to taunt the men in order to incite them: he advises Craver to think of the Iraqis as the real culprits in his father's death, and he offers an absurd version of personal and American history:

> If the ragheads hadn't shot our buffalo, we could have swapped them for their camels, and then we wouldn't have needed the coal mines to begin with, and your father would have worked in an auto factory, and he'd still be alive today (114).

But when Boxler suggests that the two are gay, Craver starts to choke Remzi while Boxler urges him on. For Boxler, insulting sexual orientation is neither more nor less important than attacking family origins. It is simply another tool in the arsenal of aggression. But for Remzi and Craver, this form of fueling aggression crosses a line since their sexual orientation is grounds for military discharge.

Here, Wallace's play invokes the miltary's "Don't Ask, Don't Tell" policy, which became law when Wallace was writing her play and was not repealed until Obama took office. Since 1982, and hence during the time of the Persian Gulf War, military policy had decreed that homosexuality was incompatible with military service and persons who engaged in homosexual acts or stated that they are homosexual or bisexual were to be discharged.[11] The Clinton administration attempted to undo this policy, but their efforts were blocked by Congress. As a compromise, the Clinton administration issued Department of Defense Directive 1304.26, which attempted to diminish the number of discharges of gay military personnel through a "DTDA" policy. This "liberal" gesture, however, continued the practice of denying full citizenship to a particular sector of society, and it is within the context of this public discussion that Wallace's play was written and first performed.

In the Heart of America clarifies how de facto discrimination became de jure discrimination in the instance of homosexual men and women in the military, and thus, how denying rights to certain groups is a constitutive practice of state power even within democratic governments. Such a perspective also implies that the lines drawn between democratic and totalitarian governments are permeable and suggests that the rhetoric of absolute difference between the two forms of government is another example of a false binary. In exposing this dynamic, the play anticipates what will become a much larger discussion post 9/11, that is, the incursion on individual civil rights during a time of terror and the fundamental violations of the internationally agreed-upon prohibitions against torture. At the point of its writing, however, that debate had not been as fully articulated, but in combining the attack on Remzi for being gay and the attack on the Iraqi prisoner, Wallace's play makes the connection between civil rights violations and violations of international law. In effect, to the American military and the American government, Remzi and the Iraqi prisoner are the same: threats. Though the military policy does not sanction violence against homosexual servicemen and women and military codes ban torture, the culture in both military and civil society allows the violence to happen. This connection will be even more starkly exposed through the scandal of Abu Ghraib in the second Iraq war.

In the Heart of America addresses how degrees of exclusion are a part of how American capitalist democracy operates. That the victims of the discrimination do not recognize its manifestation in their own lives achingly reveals that they cling to the hope enshrined in political rhetoric about national belonging. Remzi wants to prove that he is worthy of fundamental rights. Such a belief, indeed, delusion—according to Giorgio Agamben in his discussion of "bare life" and Michel Foucault in his understanding of "governmentality"—is a necessary spoke in the wheels of late-capitalist democracies: populations must be controlled, policies administered, and certain bodies cast out for state power to maintain itself. This complex idea is one that I will be exploring in later discussions—especially as it bears on the detention of terrorist suspects in Guantanamo Bay, Cuba—but because it is especially relevant to Wallace's play, it bears an introduction here. Of particular relevance is Agamben's explanation of the not-quite-outcasts (he calls them "homo sacer") whose lives are placed at the furthest point of legal protection.

Agamben comments that the state of exception—the period which is entered into only by a decree issued by the sovereign—exists at the "limit between politics and law," which he calls a "no-man's land." He frames the problem thusly:

> If the law employs the exception—that is the suspension of law itself—as its original means of referring to and encompassing life, then a theory of the state of exception is the preliminary definition of the relation that binds and, at the same time, abandons the living being to law (2003, 1).

For Agamben, certain subjects can be deprived of their rights of citizenship when a state of exception is invoked; these subjects are reduced to a condition of a bare life because they are neither dead and outside the law, nor ontologically counted and hence part of the political community. They live in a suspended state that has been tactically defined. They are not-quite-outcasts.

Foucault employed the term "governmentality" to describe the way that political power administers its populations and goods, but this descriptive definition has expanded, in Judith Butler's usage, to describe the "main way state power is vitalized" (2004, 51). Butler has described how governmentality operates:

> Govermentality operates through policies and departments, through managerial and bureaucratic institutions, and through the law, when the law is understood as a "set of tactics" and through forms of state power, though not exclusively. Governmentality thus operates through state and non-state institutions and discourses that are legitimated neither by direct elections nor through established authority. Marked by a diffuse set of strategies and tactics, governmentality gains its meaning and purpose from no single source, no unified sovereign subject. Rather, the tactics characteristic of governmentality operate diffusely, to dispose and order populations, and to produce and reproduce subjects, their practices and beliefs, in relation to specific policy aims (52).

Whether one exists outside the law (Agamben's homo sacer) or one is the object of the state's tactical and discursive positioning (Foucault's governmentality), both are means of avoiding questions of legality or legitimacy. Both are exercises in state power, exerted through suspending or repositioning the status, and hence rights, of its own citizens.

These theories help explain why it is so significant that Wallace foreground the issues of military service and sexual orientation in her play. In so doing, Wallace moves the audience away from understanding the simple and dreadful fact that domestic prejudices travel with the army to comprehending a more searing indictment: that denying civil rights within the military is not only part of military culture, it is part of civic culture, and it is the root cause of war. This policy acts to legalize inequity—the very source of conflict. Violence against its own members facilitates the conceptual and real violence taken against the enemy. The gay Arab American is exactly the kind of body that must be controlled—"governed"—or expelled from the political community, stripped to a bare life. In Agamben's terms, Remzi is the body that had no rights but is not outside the law; in Foucault's paradigm of governmentality, Remzi's identity can be used or discarded according to "policy" aims. Remzi, because of his ethnicity and sexuality, is disturbingly close to the threatening Other.

In trying to understand how alterity can be encountered in a nonthreatening manner, Emmanuel Levinas has observed that "the Other precisely reveals himself in his alterity not in a shock negating the I, but as the primordial phenomenon of gentleness" (150). By this logic, only those who can allow themselves to be open to gentleness can understand another. Clearly, Remzi, who learns to love his own heritage when he visits relatives in the Middle East, who bathed his sister's injured foot with herbs and spices, who tenderly persuades Craver to eat a fig, who wanted, more than anything, to be fully "American," has the gentleness and the courage to embrace the peaceful possibilities of Otherness. As Wallace's play exposes these invisible and ubiquitous forms of force, it also offers compelling acts of resistance and activism. Fairouz has a ram's horn onto which her brother had carefully inscribed her name. "If you blow on the ram's horn," Craver tells her, "it will make a noise" (146).

CHAPTER 3

THE PERSIANS

ULTIMATELY, GEORGE H. W. BUSH GARNERED POPULAR SUPPORT FOR the Persian Gulf War—especially after the country heard the testimony of a fifteen-year-old girl, known only as Nayirah to the Congressional Human Rights Caucus members. She tearfully described how she witnessed Iraqi soldiers steal incubators in Kuwait and leave the tiny babies to die. One might have imagined that Saddam Hussein's true record of extreme violence against his own people—documented cases of torture, rape, execution, and amputation; the use of chemical weapons against the Kurds in the Halabja attack and Anfal campaign in the late 1980s—would be enough to warrant humanitarian intervention. But these abuses occurred during the time that the United States supported Hussein. Moreover, the Vietnam syndrome discussed in the last chapter manifested itself as isolationism, and the government would need to make a very convincing case that invading Kuwait, hardly a country without resources, was worth American lives. Citizens for a Free Kuwait accordingly hired a PR firm, Hill and Knowlton, whose Washington office was led by Craig Fuller, a Bush advisor and close friend, to help mobilize opinion (Stabuer and Rampton 2005). Hill and Knowlton filmed the testimony of Nayirah (who was later revealed to be the daughter of Saud Nasser Al-saus Al-Sabah, the Kuwaiti ambassador to the United States) and sent it to media outlets. Bush often referenced the invented atrocity as evidence for his humanitarian decision, and some senators cited the testimony as instrumental in their decision to support the war.[1]

No war is conducted without manipulating the facts, demonizing the enemy, and appealing to citizens' fears and patriotism. As Sam Keen has observed, it is necessary to "create the enemy" before we actually kill them: "Before the weapon comes the image...Propaganda precedes technology" (1986, 10). But in the past two decades, a special kind of manipulation and political rhetoric has been applied to the history and people of Iraq. In 1991, George H. W. Bush needed to downplay US involvement with Hussein—there was that pesky photo of Donald Rumsfeld greeting Hussein—and he needed to ramp up Hussein's villainy. Hussein was installed as Hitler's successor—this analogy appeared over a thousand times in print and on television (Kellner 1992, 63)—and the Iraqi people were divided into barbarians or victims. A war of personalities ensured: Bush, the civilized defender of the good, was morally mandated to defeat the brutish dictator who "followed the law of the jungle" (66). As would happen again in 2003, Hussein was alleged to possess extremely dangerous chemical weapons.

Undoubtedly, Hussein was a brutal leader, guilty of the worst crimes against his own people, but he was also a self-interested pragmatist who cut deals with the West. Initially neither particularly traditional nor pious, he discarded his Western suits for Arab clothing when it was politically advantageous. Until 1991, Iraq was viewed as largely pro-Western, with close ties to France. At one time, Hussein was even regarded as moderate: after the Ba'ath Party assumed power, he was viewed as an effective politician who worked to modernize Iraq by promoting literacy, advocating for women's education and universal schooling, and improving infrastructure.

The point here is not to deny the atrocities that Hussein committed, but rather to begin to acknowledge a more complex history of Iraq—and thereby appreciate the psychic state of a people whose lives were at times improved and at times terrorized by the same leader. This is part of the story that Heather Raffo tells in *Nine Parts of Desire* and that Trevor Griffiths offers in *The Gulf Between Us*. These two plays, along with Peter Sellars's revision of Aeschylus's *The Persians* based on Robert Auletta's reworking of the play, offer a portrait of Iraqi history that indicts Hussein's brutality but also condemns neo-imperialism, the West's "rescue" operations in 1991 and 2003, and the period of life-threatening sanctions imposed in between.

The three plays also address how the enemy is framed through media coverage and through political propaganda. What these plays react against is figuring Hussein as a brutal madman whose atrocities *took place in a geopolitical vacuum*. Figuring Hussein in absolute terms not only allowed Western self-interest to take cover under the guise of Western humanitarianism, it also enabled the metaphoric placement of all Iraqis—and soon, all Arabs and Muslims—as willing zealots, bent on the destruction of the West. Ultimately, as all know, framing Hussein as absolutely evil allowed him to serve as a surrogate for the elusive Osama bin Laden.

If we conceive as the War on Terror as not only an attack on those who attacked us but also as a quest without end for American economic primacy and security that is fought both through conventional military operations and through the technologies of image/language management, it is defensible, as I pointed out in Chapter 1, to view the Persian Gulf War as the beginning of this long conflict. Put another way, George W. Bush's decision in 2003 to fabricate a connection between Al-Qaeda and Iraq was well-prepared for by the way that Hussein had already been framed with the same qualities attributed to bin Laden: violent, irrational, and lethal. The politics of personalities (the cowboy Bushes and the barbaric Muslim leaders) trumped any lack of hard evidence (as discussed in Chapter 6) and erased significant differences in political and religious ideologies between Hussein and bin Laden. The national hysteria caused Americans to discard most of their foundational ethical and political principles: the use of proportionate response, a respect for the Geneva conventions, and a rejection of detention without trial and the use of torture. Paul Virilio has linked this "geo-strategic delirium," the constant sense of danger and alert, to globalization, a connection emphasized in works by Harold Pinter, Caryl Churchill, and Tony Kushner. Virilio argues further that we ought to think in terms of "impure war," by which he means asymmetrical warfare that operates via disequilibrium (2008, 8–9). Once some disequilibrium has happened, order must be restored and deterrence heightened. Thus, retaliation of some sort must be pursued; security measures, including those that are aimed at the civilian population, such as the Patriot Act, are enacted, and enemies—the "evildoers"—must be identified (9). Because the disequilibrium is caused and felt both through psychic damage as well as physical destruction, the retaliation and restoration of order must also be pursued through actual and symbolic means. The control of the symbolic, however elusive and ephemeral, thus has played a more consequential role in warfare than ever before. As Jochen and Linda Schulte-Sasse have pointed out, the "reality of politics is being shaped, from the outset, by the imaginary of media images and language" (1991, 71). Central to war waged through media are two tasks: controlling the image and identity of the enemy Other and simplifying the conflict into a binary opposition, effectively censoring historical context or political complexity.

In this chapter, the three plays that I discuss refuse to allow such control and such simplification to go unquestioned. Trevor Griffiths's *The Gulf Between Us* (1992), Peter Sellars and Robert Auletta's version of Aeschylus's *The Persians* (1993), and Heather Raffo's *Nine Parts of Desire* (2003) each render a sophisticated political and psychological portrait of Iraq's history and of the motivations and consequences of UK and US involvement. In doing so, they complement the effort made by David Hare in *Stuff Happens* and by Richard Norton-Taylor in *Called to Account* to comprehend the different desires at work in the Bush and Blair administrations. The three plays also anticipate the discussion undertaken in Chapter 5 where Muslim identity, of whatever national origin, has been tagged as terrorist, thus installing the binaries that perpetuate conflict. Significantly, the three plays all feature women characters as moral agents, rejecting the political uses to which they have been put in both Bush administrations. Implicitly, the plays associate sexism with militarism, an issue that is also taken up in plays by Judith Thompson and Frances Ya-Chu Cowhig. I have gathered these plays together because, despite the fact that Raffo's play was written a decade after Griffiths's and Sellars's, they all address the role of the media in framing the enemy. They also expose the rhetoric of rescue used to justify American involvement in Iraq. Hence, they enact a complicated critique: life under Hussein was unbearable, but American intervention did not bring the relief that was needed.

Bridging the Gulf

Trevor Griffiths was already at work on the play that would form itself around the physical act of building a wall on stage when he watched the 1991 bombardment on television and felt himself "drowning in rage and pity," convinced that the deadline set for Iraq to withdraw from Kuwait was bait (1992, v). His response, *The Gulf Between Us*, premiered at the West Yorkshire Playhouse in Leeds, England, on January 16, 1992, the one-year anniversary of the first attack on Iraq.

The Gulf Between Us opens against the outline of a large Bedouin tent, where the mysterious, protean figure of Rafael Finbar O'Toole is charmed into visibility by a golden spotlight. His opening words are an incantatory reminder that the ground he stands upon, the cradle of civilization and the land of the Arabian Nights, is the "heritage of antiquity" (1). The minute O'Toole finishes his monologue with "God is good," there is a blackout, and the visual is replaced with the aural. In a darkness that starkly opposes the overload of technological spectacle, the audience hears a cacophony of unfamiliar accents. These are ordinary Arabic exchanges from the souk, bazaar, schoolroom, tearoom, and mosque. Out of these unfamiliar words, threads of English appear, first as a lexicon of English words with Arabic roots, then as the voices of first-world leaders, identifiable as George Bush and Norman Schwarzkopf justifying the "punitive use of force against Third World intransigents." The voice-coil transforms into a muezzin calling the faithful to prayer, a moment frozen "grave and pure" until it becomes the wailing sound of an air-raid siren. A moment of deep silence follows, after which "mute cockpit-videos of famous strikes on bridges, buildings, and installations" materialize (2). Finally, the audience listens to an anonymous Western voice defending the action while the sound and images fade.

These beginning moments of *The Gulf Between Us* are worth reflection since they effectively reverse the relationship between media and theatre.[2] Media, in the form of total television, annexes any image it wishes; it pulls all visual signs into itself as it assembles its great pastiche of the pure performing present while it simultaneously dissembles its own constructive practices. Griffiths's play does the opposite, folding technology into the frame of theatrical presentation. As one reviewer noted, the opening "electrifying" minutes reclaim "the bombing of Baghdad from the archives of television warfare and make of it something human" (Milne 1992, 105). The aural element, of voices changing from daily bits of Arabic conversation to first world political discourse in English, foregrounds the act of medial transformation. The audience is subject to a technological transformation of elements, but unlike the homogenized version that marked television coverage, Griffiths's use of the technological recording emphasizes difference and disconnectedness, the sounds of strife, imminent danger, and irreconcilable visions. The final sounds of the recorded coil, the muezzin call to prayer, the siren, and the sounds of the raid, reproduce the cacophony of terror and assault heard on the streets of Baghdad—though not in most televised reports. Since the aural elements were noticeably absent in the televised version of the war, Griffiths's choice to begin with sound, and not only the sound of terror but also the sound of the connection between modern and ancient civilizations in the shared heritage of the alphabet, is a significant way of rebutting a media presentation that largely filtered out complex representations of the vexed relationship between Middle Eastern and Western cultures. It tacitly demonstrates what oversaturated viewers may neglect: that there are absences in the coverage, holes where human voices speak in sounds both strange and familiar.

When the media show ends, the audience is "abruptly plunged" into harsh daylight. Elderly Arab men comb through rubble for personal effects, and a teenage boy, Ismael, already conscripted, is charged with supervising the damaged area. Armed members of the People's Militia arrive, pushing a terrified and weeping bus driver in front of them. Ismael reads the document he is handed, listens to something on the phone, and summarily executes the driver, shooting him in the back of the head.

In form, *The Gulf Between Us*, is a postmodern pastiche that blends the fabular and the naturalistic, the historical and the contemporary. To the extent that media coverage of the 1991 Gulf War emphasized immediacy, brevity, technology, and knowability, Griffiths's play offers the long view of history, stretching back to the venerable history of Arab civilization. In the middle are the dead Iraqi children, exhumed from the carnage, embraced, named. Their real-life counterparts were the women and children burned or simply evaporated when the United States dropped two 2,000-pound bombs on the Amiriyah shelter. The presence of the teenager armed with a cell phone, gun, and soccer ball introduces the discordant note of modernity, a visual recognition, perhaps, of the coexistence of elements of religious tradition and contemporary secularism that the West finds indecipherable.

The beginning of the play, then, is appropriately complex: the audience must make sense of the mysterious O'Toole, the voice coil, the attack, the execution, the juxtaposition of an empty desert and cell-phone modernity. Though the larger share of the play's criticism will be directed against the Western alliance for the "murder of a quarter of a million people... consign[ing] another one or two million to death in the aftermath and bomb[ing] the country back five thousand years" in order to "create a new world order" (vii), the play's opening scene of execution acknowledges the internal oppression imposed on the Iraqi people as well. Ismael, the armed teenage soccer player, is like the youths in Robin Soans's *Talking to Terrorists*, conscripted into movements they do not understand. Further, the cynicism of the regime's use of a shrine that was also known to serve as a nursery as cover for a military installation is criticized—alongside the Western alliance air attack. Griffiths has been praised for a capacity to stage complex moments of history, understanding the range of power dynamics that come together in a moment of important political crisis, and the introductory moments of *The Gulf Between Us* signal that such understanding is at work in this play as well.

When O'Toole reappears and resumes his recitation, he tells the audience that his tale will be a triangular one, of the "Builder, the Gilder, the Minder" and the "Gulf between them" (3). Actually, these characters—Billy Ryder, the Builder; Chatterjee, the Gilder; and Ismael, the Minder—are joined by a fourth character: Dr. Aziz, the only woman character and the moral center of the play. She is, like Atossa in Sellars's play, and the women in Raffo's play, an embodiment of Iraqi feminine strength and intelligence that refutes Muslim stereotypes. By the end of the play, she will offer the most direct and damning indictment of the Western alliance; she is able to voice such a clear and unequivocal judgment because she is the only character in the play not compromised by self-interest. Before her denunciations are uttered, however, Griffiths introduces the audience to the comic characters who are at once the war's parasites, perpetrators, and dupes.

Rafael Finbar O'Toole, whose name invokes a kind of rootlessness or transnationality, is the equivalent of the narrator called the Gukha in Arabic literature (Garner 1996, 385); Griffiths says that he is a fabular creature, someone "doomed to live forever," who is "anarchic, antiauthoritarian, devious, cynical, and compassionate" (386). Fallible in his specific memories, O'Toole manifests some instinct for the good; as a transnational and unaligned figure, he hovers over the action and, chorus-like, points out instances of heroism and occasions for pity. Because he is partly Irish, O'Toole is also lazy, voluble, often drunk, and partially unreliable. He reminds the audience of English imperial prejudices as he bedevils the stolid, working-class Englishman, Billy Ryder. Griffiths bathes O'Toole in a golden beam of light when the character serves his oracular function, but he just as quickly returns him to the company of the ordinary and self-interested.

If O'Toole's origins are unknowable, Ryder's are completely exposed. He is in the Middle East because of a business opportunity. Passing himself off as an expert construction supervisor, Ryder is actually a union bricklayer, attired in Armani and Rolex from his recently acquired cash flow. Ryder wants to make a financial killing during the war and then whisk himself back to early retirement in England. His name suggests the parasitic economy of which he is a part. Inarticulate and uneducated, but suddenly rich, he is a bred-in-the-bone neocapitalist with colonial prejudices. He is, to borrow the title from Griffiths's 1993 play, one of "Thatcher's Children." Ryder's character further suggests that the New World Order is just Armani-clad nineteenth-century imperialism stripped of the guises of Victorian rectitude. Ryder is the trickle-down version of the idea of the New World Order: he believes enthusiastically in profit and corporate efficiency, ignoring his own labor roots and his fellowship with other laborers. In the end, Ryder's political obtuseness interferes with his mercenary economic desires. His bald self-interest, greed, and jingoism cause him to underestimate his Arab employers, and he fails to pull off his great swindle and great escape.

Jean Baudrillard has described the Gulf Was as a competition between a rug salesman and an arms salesman, and something of this spirit is evident in the play (1995, 65). The first act of *The Gulf Between Us* is a comic competition of self-interest, each character linked to self-serving reasons for rebuilding the bombed shrine/crèche. The action is a kind of geopolitical con game, played out not by the strategists, but by their dupes. Ryder wants to rebuild the shrine, make a fast buck, and get out of the Middle East. Ismael wants to look important, avoid the wrath of his violent superiors, and play soccer. The invisible Iraqi leadership want the shrine rebuilt before the world discovers that it is really a crematorium for Iraqi infants and that the leadership is complicit in the deaths of its own people. The leaders of the Western alliance will disavow knowledge that the holy shrine was anything but a disguised military site. O'Toole wants to use the rebuilding of the shrine as a way of negotiating Chatterjee's release from jail. In one of the play's many comic twists, O'Toole reveals that, ever the trickster, he had added a gold tooth to the statue of the state leader, but let Chatterjee take the blame. Because all of these motivations must remain hidden, the first act is comprised of various moments of bullying, lying, trickery, and deception. Like Shepard's drama, Griffiths's play includes action that is both vaudevillian and violent, such as when O'Toole slams Ryder's hand with a brick. Other parts, like Ismael's execution of the bus drive, are simply brutal.

Dupes duping dupes, the characters are each supremely confident in their own powers of self-preservation and ignorant of the larger forces controlling their actions.

In stark contrast to the self-interest and the twisted complicities of the male characters is the figure of the woman doctor, Dr. Aziz. If O'Toole can manipulate and outtalk the others, he is silenced by the stern and straightforward Dr. Aziz. She has come to investigate the whereabouts of the infants and to assure the Iraqi mothers, whose wailing punctuates the play, that they are safe. Dr. Aziz refuses to be deterred, and when she sees the ashes of the children in the shrine, her response, in the form of several speeches, is swift and searing. These speeches, the longest in the play, offer the most direct political commentary. Her first condemnation is for George Bush:

> And I have seen you, Mr. President, with your sensitive expression and sorrowing eyes on my television screen... And I had forgotten, what you will not acknowledge but what the world knows, that yours in a country forged and shaped in brutal genocide (48).

Her second speech is addressed to the Western alliance of the United States, Great Britain, and the United Nations, excoriating them for hiding their brutality behind euphemisms such as "collateral damage." There is, for Dr. Aziz, no explanation commensurate with the disproportionate and indiscriminate violence the West has committed against civilian populations. She looks down upon the charcoal figure of an immolated child, as the audience hears the soft tones of women repeating the names of their children, and she says:

> This will not be justified by invoking the evil of my rulers or the unavoidability of your "collateral damage." This world is full of evil, look at those you bought or bribed or bullied to give you houseroom here, look at those you would restore to their thrones, and tell me how we are worse. As for the unavoidable, how stupid, how very stupid you must think us, to imagine a decent human being believing you for one second, when you have told us and you have shown us your ability to tell the time on a child's wristwatch from one hundred miles, the side a woman parts her hair, the stubble on a man's face. We have a holy place, a place of worship, a place your cameras tell us every day is filled with children, And you send a missile, not a wayward bomb, to burn it up (49).

Nor does Dr. Aziz spare Ismael: his good soldiering is mindless and irresponsible.

Whatever Ismael's role is in the death of the children, by the end of the play he is a marked man. The blame for the execution of the bus driver will be passed along to him, but just as he begins to understand how he has been used by the regime he serves, a fragment of a cluster bomb rips into him. O'Toole eulogizes him as a fallen hero, and like Dr. Aziz, he places blame on the regime for one kind of brutality, but on the Western alliance for a greater one. His final speech explains the serpentine events of the play and lodges its final accusation. Ismael, acting on orders, helped to cover up the bombing of the nursery. But he had been duped when his commander failed to return from the brothel and missed the call saying the bus driver had not relocated the children. He executed the driver to protect his commander while the children were "simply left there, forgotten." There is no doubt that the military had designated the children as human shields; they had built a "control gear in the roof, a known target of enemy guided-fire since Day One" (57). These events, which appeared in Western news reports as the atrocious use of human shields, are described by O'Toole as a "pickle," and audiences may well object to such an understatement. What is most clear is that O'Toole, like Dr. Aziz, has saved his anger for the Western alliance. He poses the ethical question most pertinent to the new technowars led by the United States:

> Whatever happened to proportion, doesn't this sort of thing stretch the credulity a touch, even yours, they could see it was being used for military purposes but managed to overlook—or at least overcome—that it was used as a nursery, oh come on Lord, these men know exactly what they are doing (57).

Which is worse, asks O'Toole, using a shrine and nursery defensively or knowingly aiming a missile at it?

Trevor Griffiths's *The Gulf Between Us* enacts a counter-history to the narrative offered through the coverage of the 1991 Gulf War. Difficult and perplexing, its obscurity stands against the false transparency of narratives created on the spot. O'Toole offers no easy access to the meaning of the events of the targeted shrine; he, and the audience, with the assistance of Dr. Aziz, must labor to unpeel the layers of deception and cynicism, to come, finally, upon the irreducible sight of the results of the West's disproportionate use of violence. With its unreliable narrator, its incorporation of media images into the theatrical frame, and its insistent reminders about the achievements of a rich and ancient Arab culture, *The Gulf Between Us* provides a framework for assessing the war that is largely unavailable through mainstream coverage. While stories such as those offered by the media to explain the war are the quickly devised products of technologies of visibility, which tap no historical understanding or cultural empathy, Griffiths's play, like Wallace's *In the Heart of America*, rejects such a simplistic Manichean worldview, which divides humanity into the civilized and the barbaric. It acknowledges that there is evil in the world, evil at work in the regimes that make puppets of their young and ashes of their children. Corruption and greed and incompetence play their part. And there is evil in the mindless acceptance of trickle-down economic theories that keep working-class citizens, the Ryders of the world, wedded to practices that will never enfranchise them. But, above all, the play asserts, there is the question of proportionate response.

In *The Gulf Between Us*, a long view of history is set against media stories that do little to investigate the complications of the political past or the achievements of a particular culture. Griffiths's play brings the enemy on stage, and the enemies' culture is made familiar. In Baudrillard's terms, the enemy is dehysterisized. Refusing to represent all Arabs as servile or fanatical and thereby excuse the responsibility for patient diplomacy, the play places on stage a reasonable, intelligent, and sympathetic character who reviles both the corruption of her country's leaders even as she rebukes Western hypocrisy. The play refuses the racist interpretation of Arab people as premodern nomads or as irrational fundamentalists. It also shows the allied forces and Iraqi governments as equivalent regimes when they make pawns of their young. And it refuses to allow the dead to be unnamed or made invisible. Griffiths personalizes the deaths of the innocent though the mothers' grief and the recounting of their names against the reluctance, in the Western media, to offer any extensive coverage of the damage inflicted on the Iraqi people or on the environment.

Most importantly, the play denounces the scale of Western retaliation. Through the speeches of Dr. Aziz and her unambiguous ethical presence, *The Gulf Between Us* blasts the false moralism of a nation that uses technological superiority to evade moral responsibility. In the course of the six-week 1991 war, 250,000 Iraqis were killed; by the time the play premiered, the sanctions that would take the lives of thousands more were in place.

THEATRE AS ALTERNATIVE INFORMATION SYSTEM

Peter Sellars, the distinguished auteur/director, decided to produce a Gulf War version of the "first surviving play in the history of Western drama," *The Persians*, in part to promote empathy for the Iraqi people (quoted in Auletta and Aeschylus 1993, 5). Like other writers responding to the Gulf War, Sellars is interested in how modern military and media technology inhibit understanding, and he puts theatre forward as a means of alternative information. His production claimed the highest international visibility of any of the Gulf War plays I have discussed above. It was commissioned by the Salzburger Festpiele and performed in Austria in 1993; from there, it went to the Edinburgh Festival, the Mark Taper Forum in Los Angeles, and the Hebbel Theatre in Berlin (Auletta and Aeschylus 1993, 9). His adaptation was meant to elicit, in his own words, "a more sophisticated level of outrage and empathy to the history of our own lifetimes" (quoted in Auletta and Aeschylus 1993, 8). In a commentary produced for the program notes of the Salzburg Festival's production, Sellars speaks directly to theatre's role in promoting such engaged critique. Aeschylus's play, Sellars writes, was a notable act of courage because it asked the Greek audience to sympathize with the vanquished enemy. In doing so, *The Persians* is a "lodestone" that

> presents us with an emblem of theater's possibilities and responsibilities: the potent combination of first-hand eye witness documentary material, freely interwoven with purely fabricated imaginative material, to create a complex moral discussion that moves simultaneously forwards and backwards (1993, 5).

While there was less objection to Sellars's signature mix of performance styles—the play interpolates Javanese dancing and sign language—many objected to modernizing Aeschylus's language. Sellars's choices in casting, language, and technology unsettle cultural stereotypes and prompt Brechtian acts of spectatorship, especially about the degree to which received information is "profoundly mediated" (Delgado and Heritage 1996, 227). Sellars has suggested that ancient plays, such as *The Persians*, not only provide a "larger perspective," but "speak with honesty and simplicity about very complex issues" against a "culture of distraction that overwhelms us with images" (Lester 2002, 1). He points out the task of theatre in an environment of images:

> That our experience is so profoundly mediated must be shown, used and critiqued all at the same time. These days it's a waste of time, for example, talking about the government, because the government is a minor incidental side-effect of the media empire. Media is what controls the vote in America.... In many of my productions I'm trying very consciously to say, "Wait a minute, what is the position of media in your life? How much direct information are you getting? And meanwhile how much information are you getting from another point of view?" (Delgado and Heritage 1996, 228).

Ultimately, *The Persians* was not a success—no play can speak to the backs of audience members leaving the theatre—but it is a daring failure.[3] Sellars wants to trace the rise and fall of a megalomaniac personality, and in this ambition, his use of Greek tragic form is appropriate. But he also wants to indicate the Western role in helping create the monster of Xerxes/Hussein, and so he inserts commentary about technological menace and Western neoimperialism that does not blend neatly into his presentation of Iraq's problems as internal and dynastic. Because Darius, Xerxes/Hussein's father, harbors ambitions that are equal to Western expansionism, he is partly a creature of contemporary Western geopolitics and partly a product of his own violent history. With this emphasis, Sellars's production attacks the New World Order rhetoric that depicts Muslims as premodern or irrational. Finally, and here Sellars is most successful, he hopes to install greater sympathy for the Iraqis who are simultaneously victims of Hussein and of the war. Sellars's play is most compelling when it focuses on the disproportionate use of the American military arsenal and the damage it caused. Here the character of Atossa, like Dr. Aziz in Griffiths's work, is the ethical center of the play.

Peter Sellars is interested in the dangerous extension of American power, as well as in the psychology at work that enables such overreaching. Sellars's work asks audiences to identify with the enemy—or at least with the enemy's victims—and like Shepard and Pinter, Sellars explores the violence operative in families as a synecdoche for national and global culture. "The fall of a nation is the dysfunction within a family," writes Sellars. "Aeschylus deals with the culture of arrogance, denial and violence, and their long term consequences."[4] However, assessing the "buried inner causes" for which momentous events are but symptoms has been made more difficult, notes Sellars, because "the Gulf War was one of the most censored wars in the history of journalism" (quoted in Auletta and Aeschylus 1993, 7). All the more reason, he concludes, to turn to alternative sources of information and analysis:

> The Pentagon carefully controlled the flow of information to the outside world. One of the things we rarely saw on television in this war with Iraq was Iraqis. Dead or alive. The term "collateral damage" was used to describe dead sons, daughters, wives, mothers, and fathers. The human toll was largely discounted or screened out by ideological or commercial filters. One of the reasons, possibly, for theater to continue to exist in our technological age is as kind of alternative information system that is able partially to humanize the denatured results of our vaunted and costly objectivity (6–7).

Sellars's staging of *The Persians* is shaped around three key interchanges involving the play's principal characters: Atossa, the queen of Persia; her dead husband, Darius, who appears as a ghost; and their destructive son, Xerxes. The first third of the performance takes place immediately before the news of the slaughter of Persian troops; it explores Atossa's growing acknowledgment of culpability. The second is an interchange between Atossa and her dead husband in which the queen levels the accusation that the murderous Xerxes is his father's creation. The third features the long-awaited appearance of Xerxes, bloodied from battle, but in equal measures defiant, mad, injured, and suicidal. Through these scenes, the modernized play replicates

Aeschylus's audacious attempt to create sympathy for the enemy and insight into evil. Some of the explanations about Xerxes, the corollary to Saddam Hussein, are psychologically glib, especially the pat explanation of father-son conflict. More convincing is the portrait of a despot shaped by global culture and Western imperialism as well as by his own personal ambitions and his country's volatile history. *The Persians* is unique among the plays discussed here because it takes place completely within the "enemy" camp. The emergent portrait is of a corrupt regime vying with a relentless superpower—but not in the simplistic terms of villain or hero.

The first moments of *The Persians* give an immediacy to the terror of the Iraqi people caught in the midst of the firestorm; like *The Gulf Between Us*, the play wants to make audible the common cries of ordinary Iraqi civilians, cries that were never a part of the "total television" coverage.[5] In doing so, the play immediately raises the issue of proportional response. The outcry of the chorus illustrates Auletta's modernization of the text, and gives a sense of the "jarring" intrusions of contemporary references that caused some disapproval:

> What is it? What's going on?
> I can't get through on the phone.
> Look! The Hotel's hit!
> The block where I live is on fire!
> The electricity is gone! The power is out!
> Have you heard anything?
> The bridge! The bridge has just been hit!
> The sky a frantic sea of light! The city burning!
> Are we shooting them down?
> Or are they simply destroying us (117–118)?

These interpolations of new journalistic accounts occur elsewhere in the performance: accurate and exhaustive descriptions of the kinds of American firepower used are given as well as a sense of the thousands of corpses—the "desert of bones"—that made up Iraqi casualties. An "almost subliminal aircraft-like thunder" can be heard behind some of the passages, an invocation of hovering danger (Morris, 1993).

The US government's calculated portrayal of Iraqis as fanatical is assailed in the first section of the play. Again, like Griffiths's play, *The Persians* wants to restore the rightfulness of the Islamic claim to cultural prominence. Before learning of the Persian defeat, Queen Atossa and the Persian chorus worry that their plan to "redress the wrongs done to us" in a "holy war" might overstep "some sacred plan" and the "firestorm we raised may suddenly turn and savage us again" (Auletta and Aeschylus 1993, 13, 16). Atossa has secluded herself in the chamber of her dead husband in order to be near his spirit, but her foreboding thoughts and nightmares have begun to make her ill until she realizes that "the agony of my country was beginning to make itself known inside my body, breaking me down, flesh and bone, piece by piece, in order to be born" (20). Her pain causes her to raise questions she had previously avoided, questions about excess and willful ignorance. She wonders if the wealth amassed by Darius has been so extreme that the "excesses" have "become almost like bread" and some "sacred line" has been crossed. Though she agonizes over blaspheming her husband's memory, she must nevertheless ask whether the "golden weight of the power of what we own [is] about to destroy us" (22).

Too, Atossa is concerned for her son. He is the subject of a nearly Foucaldian or Baudrillardian nightmare Atossa has where she imagines the conflict as a fashion show with Xerxes as the centerpiece, until the runway parade is disrupted by a woman in Western garb who begins to whip Darius and savage him. This disturbing image, melding capitalism, celebrity, and violence, inserts a critique of commodity culture that is at odds with the fatalism of Greek tragedy. Sellars pulls the classical genre in two directions: because of Hussein's dictatorial cult of personality, he exposes the hubris of self-aggrandizement, but he also offers a political/cultural critique that exceeds the traditional parameters of Greek tragedy. The question that arises is whether Western commodity culture has taken the place of fate as an irresistible, formative force.

Desperately, Atossa wants to "change the channel," as she puts it, but when she does, she sees Xerxes lying bloody and beaten in the desert with his father standing over him. In an expiatory speech, Atossa admits that she knew the secrets of keeping power, of what was done in the basements of this "palace built of human flesh and veined with living blood" and that her guilt lies in doing nothing (31).[6] She desperately wants the safety of her son and so wishes to make offerings of penance to the gods and to negotiate with the enemy. The chorus tells her that her hopes are futile because the West is merciless: "Experts at applying sanctions/To garotte a county," they'd "like to see us all slaughtered" (33–34). A messenger arrives, interrupting Atossa's self-recrimination, to give an account of the mass destruction inflicted by the enemy but also to tell her that her son still lives. The account includes specific descriptions of the weapons used in the 1991 war and their capabilities: stealth bombers, cluster bombs, antitank missiles, high explosive squash heads, and "Bouncing Bettys." The chorus wonders aloud, "Who are the men that invent such weapons, who spend their days modernizing death?" (44). The advanced civilizations can mask their profound destructiveness by skillful censorship: the screams of the Persians go unheard, and their dead are never counted. Instead, the enemy launches an "endless Technicolor avalanche...a 30 billion dollar production of mass slaughter" (46).

The Persian/Iraqi and Greek/American regimes are thus made co-equal in savage warfare, in expansionist plans, and in denying the actions they have undertaken. Given this equivalence, the character of Xerxes, the allegorical equivalent of Saddam Hussein, appears not as a unique evil, but as the creature of a dynastic, imperial urges responding to the expansionist threat of another imperial empire, one that is culturally alien, technologically advanced, associated with civilization—but willing to leave the Iraqi earth scorched and littered with the dead. When Xerxes finally appears, he feels indomitable simply because he is still living. Now that he has "defied the United States of America, the most arrogant people in the world," he feels fulfilled (Auletta and Aeschylus 1993, 88). Yet, in perhaps a gesture difficult for some audience members to accept because it humanizes the tyrant, Xerxes feels troubled as swollen corpses crowd his thoughts. He slashes open his garment to reveal that he is diseased: the "dead eye of a beast lodged inside me...devouring mind." "I am your sorrow," Xerxes tells his mother, and he instructs her to arraign some other man in the vestments of a king (93).

Because each of the three interchanges asks the viewers to shift sympathies, from Atossa to Darius to Xerxes, understanding their culpability and greed but glimpsing, as well, a capacity for self-remonstrance and sorrow, some American audience members may find the portraits too indulgent. The further insinuation that America has created the despotic urges makes the message even more controversial. Yet, the complexity, the theatrical polyvocality, and interculturalism seek, in Sellars's own words, "a more sophisticated discussion than our television news" that prompts more discerning inquiry. Theatre can prompt such inquiry, Sellars claims, and provoke a difficult self-scrutiny:

> Turn on CNN and you'll see footage of children in an Iraqi hospital saying, "Please don't bomb us," and then cut to Madonna's new boyfriend. In the first days of the Gulf War we had round-the-clock coverage from a hotel room in Baghdad where two reporters couldn't see a thing...But what the planet really needed was a three-day teach-in on Iraqi history. The nightmare in America is that somebody is always sending you a message and we don't recognize it. You may not like the messenger, yes, the building is burning, yes, the World Trade Center is collapsing, yes it's horrifying, but it's also a message. To say it's horrifying is not enough. We have to ask the question—why would somebody be pushed to such an extreme to get this message through? Why was there no other channel left? Can we begin to open other channels so that it's not necessary to take such extreme measures? (1993, 4).

Rescuing Iraqi Women

George Bush argued that a fortunate by-product of the campaign against terror that the United States was conducting in Afghanistan and in Iraq would be the advancement of women's rights in those countries. Conflating strategic interests and humanitarian goals is nothing new in the political rhetoric justifying armed conflict, but the late-twentieth-century record of American tolerance of extreme human rights abuses and unspeakable atrocities, including genocide, has made this conflation not only problematic ethically but also skeptically, even cynically, regarded.[7] Despite these suspicions, the rhetoric of rescue continued to be deployed, and the gendered aspects of increased militarism remained obscured. In this last section, I want to look specifically at the rhetoric of women's rescue that has been used during the wars on Iraq, at how the specific history of Iraq, particularly its status since 1991, has been strategically generalized in order to fit it into the broader narrative of the War on Terror, and finally, at how one instance of cultural intervention, Heather Raffo's *Nine Parts of Desire*, repudiates both the politically instrumental use of Iraqi women's identity and the politically instrumental suppression of the historical facts of Hussein's regime.

It is within the context of a simplified public narrative about Saddam Hussein and Iraqi history as well as within the liminal space of a writer's agonizing personal alliances that Raffo's *Nine Parts of Desire* takes place. In this play, written and enacted by an Iraqi American woman as a solo performance, nine characters describe how varied exertions of domination and control, from Hussein's tyranny to American invasion, have affected Iraqi and Iraqi American women. The work announces itself as an exploration of feminine subjectivity under pressure with its title, taken from Ali ibn Abu Taleb, the husband of the prophet Mohammed's daughter, who observed that "God created sexual desire in ten parts; then he gave nine parts to women and one to men" (Raffo 2006, 7). Sexual desire, however, is the direct subject of only two of the monologues that make up the text; rather, the play examines the subject of desire as political will—both Iraq's and America's—but does so in an insistently historicized context. Ultimately, the play's own desire, according to its author, is to show "how difficult it is to grasp the psyche of people who have lived under Saddam for thirty years with American support, then had a war with Iran, resulting in 1.5 million deaths, followed by thirteen years of sanctions and two wars under American firepower" (quoted in Levantine Center 2008). *Nine Parts of Desire* acts as both a kind of interventionary and documentary theatre, claiming both immediacy and urgency even as it makes a record of what threatens to be erased. It opposes, through its enactment of oral histories, the manner in which mediatized narratives, government spin, and military censorship have themselves become part of the arsenal of techno-warfare and threaten to become a sanitized history of American occupation.

Because the 2003 war in Iraq did not end even after the president declared that its objectives had been accomplished, the Bush administration found itself in need of other benchmarks of progress to maintain both military funding, congressional approval, and public support. Here, the subject of women's rights could be useful. Cited during the 1991 war and raised at the onset of the 2001 campaign in Afghanistan and at the beginning of the 2003 invasion of Iraq, women's rights could be revisited in order to assert progress. Thus, a year after the US invasion of Iraq, on March 12, 2004, in a speech on global women's human rights, George Bush again claimed progress for women in both Afghanistan and Iraq.

Women not only provided a rationale for continued American military action, but they also served as the rhetorical bridge by which to conflate the War on Terror and the war in Iraq, wars united in their common quest to vanquish "barbaric" regimes whose evil particularly manifested itself in brutalizing women. Iris Marion Young has observed, "The Bush administration has repeatedly appealed to the primacy of its role as protector of innocent citizens and the liberator of women and children to justify consolidating and centralizing executive power at home and dominative power abroad" (2003, 10). The strategic appeal of this diversionary narrative was that it turned back accusations that the invasion of Iraq was an instance of American unilateral aggression and in violation of international law.

As the occupation dragged from weeks to years, resulting first in Hussein's capture and execution but ultimately in months of intransigence, violence, and mounting casualties, the actual status of Iraq before 2003 or before 1991 faded from the political conversation. *Nine Parts of Desire* argues that, without diminishing the real brutality of the Hussein years, a focus only on his regime distorts historical understanding and political strategy. Reinstating the larger historical narrative would encompass how various political actors, from the time of British colonial rule to the present American occupation, have been complicit in further impoverishing Iraqi civilians, giving legitimacy to Islamic extremism, and making the most vulnerable sectors of Iraqi society bear the brunt of the violence and deprivations that have ravaged Iraq since 1991. The play, like Griffiths's and Sellars's, assails the disproportionate use of force, the censoring of the Iraqi death toll, and the inhumanity of sanctions.

If it true that the goal of rescuing Iraqi and Afghan women from persecution has been primarily an instance of what Cynthia Enloe, a feminist scholar of international relations, has termed a "statecrafted diversionary narrative," is there even a modest sense in which it has been helpful in calling attention to the real difficulties of women's lives in Iraq? (Cohn and

Enloe 2003, 1198). Here it is important to trace the assumptions and implications of the rescue myth and then to resituate, as Raffo does, the lived exigencies for Iraqi women.

The rescue myth relies on several crucial assumptions: the first is the monolithic view of Muslim men as receptive to terrorism and Muslim women as receptive to democracy; this myth relies on a strategic demonizing of Muslim men and a view of Muslim women as transcendent beings who live outside history. Asserting a false homogeneity among all who follow Islam (as well as conflating Arab with Muslim identities and disregarding the differences among Arab nations), the myth suggests that Muslim women are somehow more knowable than Muslim men and are an accessible part of the human community. Women can be reached and convinced of the desirability of Western values (here coded as "freedom" or "democracy") and be grateful for access to them. Their status is by turns malleable and frozen, but most of all it is *indebted*.[8]

The second assumption is that Iraqi women have no capacity for leading or orchestrating their own political interventions. Because this is the rescue myth at its starkest, it calls for the kind of feminist critique that emphasizes agency within exigencies. It also calls for the development of the kind of "multiple critique" that moves beyond essentializing identity in order to produce a "multilayered discourse" able to "engage with and criticize the various individuals, institutions, and systems that limit and oppress them" (Cooke 2000, 160). The myth of incapacity, the one that rationalizes rescue, is one such essentializing gesture. It is attached to Western notions that identify Muslim women as passive because they are veiled, where the "image of the veiled woman encapsulates for the Western observer all the coercion imagined to mark Islamic culture" (Cooke 1997, 102). Lorraine Adams has called the overexposed image of the veiled Muslim woman the "burka effect," a term that captures the kind of reductive, ahistorical, and politicized rendering of women's lives that Raffo wishes to unsettle (2008, 12). While it would be wholly inaccurate to deny the operation of a strong patriarchal culture or to ignore the serious instances of violence against women in many Muslim countries, some objection must be registered against the Western conflation of Islam with both sexism and female acquiescence. As Drucilla Cornell has observed, the "identification in the U.S. media of freedom with unveiling reinforces the simplistic view that the Muslim religion and freedom were radically at odds" (2005, 108).

The third assumption is that the difficulty of life in Iraq, particularly for women, is wholly attributable to the excesses of Saddam Hussein and in no way caused by American foreign policy; this myth works to dissemble US and other strategic interests in the region. It erases the substantial history of American support for Hussein, particularly in the 1980s. It also refuses to engage with the real costs and ethical complexities of imposing sanctions: if the United States worked to contain Hussein, it nevertheless deepened the poverty endured primarily by women and children.

Assembled from the countless interviews Raffo conducted over a period of eleven years and across four continents, *Nine Parts of Desire* engages all of these myths through its presentation of characters who are composites of the women she met and observed. Seven of the nine characters speak directly to the issues enumerated above; this is supplemented by a transhistorical figure of mourning and an Iraqi American who, like Raffo, reflects on how the Iraqi invasion is understood in the United States. These nine fictionalized composites act as social analogues able to offer "a point of entry into the larger social and economic processes" (Khan 1998, 463).

Raffo's play, then, treads on very complex, even incendiary political ground. It may, in fact, legitimately be faulted for an insufficient presentation of domestic violence. Perhaps because the play so wants to resist the political use value made from narratives of male control in Muslim households, it insufficiently treats the documented reality of such dynamics. Nor does *Nine Parts of Desire* present the pressures of "Islamism," that highly politicized anti-Western movement that has emerged as a powerful ideological force and that regards political violence as compatible with the teachings of Islam.

Raffo plays all of the characters she created for *Nine Parts of Desire*. These nine fictionalized composites of Iraqi women range from the highly secular to the highly traditional, and her capacity to embody each of them is itself an ethical argument for the political possibilities of empathy. Raffo transforms herself from one character to another by re-draping an abaya, a traditional black robe-like garment worn by both men and women in Iraq.[9] With this cloth, Raffo can summon the modern and secular as well as then ancient and religious, and her presentations range from a covered Bedouin woman to a sensual artist, from an aged exile to a young child. In this variety, the play exerts another tacit argument about the way that the lives of Iraqi women are presented one-dimensionally; it demands instead that these women be viewed as distinct and individual, with varied attitudes toward Islam, toward the Iraqi leadership, and toward men. However, *Nine Parts of Desire* also insists that this understanding be contextualized within Iraqi history rather than solely be viewed through the highly mediated lens of current global political and socioeconomic pressures.

The set design is divided into three playing areas: a small pool of water signifies a river and the ancient Mesopotamian history of Iraq; an open space invokes an artist's studio, a doctor's office, a child's room, and an expatriate's home; and a path alongside a side wall becomes the site of the bombed Amiriyah shelter. Aspects of Iraq's long history are signified in crumbling tiles, layers of mosaics, bricks, books, carpets, and sandbags (Raffo 2006, 66). The play opens with the figure of a woman mourner and closes with the figure of a woman street vendor who sells for a pittance the last works of another character, a recently killed artist. Through the set and this framing device, Raffo announces her themes: grief so long that it seems to have become generational and mythic, and pain that hovers between despair and resistance. This experience of grief and pain is bound not only to the war's violence but also to a particularly gendered experience of poverty, restriction, degradation, and censorship. Indeed, Nanna, the vendor, pronounces, "Our history is finish," at the play's close. In the course of commemorating the losses endured by Iraqi women, *Nine Parts of Desire* recounts events from 1963 to 2003, asking the audience to piece together a history of modern Iraq that has not been part of most mainstream news coverage.

Huda, a political activist living in exile in London, is the character who gives a backward glance at Iraq before the 2003 occupation. This neglected history includes a record of some liberties for women under various governments, including Saddam Hussein's, as Iraq positioned itself as a more secular Middle Eastern nation. Huda, whose name means "enlightenment," is a remnant of the period when Iraq women were among the "most educated and professional in the Arab world" (Elia 2006, 157). Now in her 70s, Huda lived through the Iraqi liberation from British colonial rule. After the July 14 Revolution in 1958, which overthrew the Hashemite monarchy, she supported the brief period when Brigadier Abdul Karin Qassim led the nation (1958–1963), courting ties with the USSR. During this time, she would have witnessed the rise of prominent women's groups, such as the League for the Defense of Women's Rights. The progressive Personal Status Laws, which were introduced in 1959 when Huda would have been in her early thirties, would have affected her directly since they transferred the decision-making authority on a number of issues that affected women, such as divorce, child custody, and inheritance, from the religious scholars, the ulama, to the civil administration (Brown and Romano 2006, 52). But with the deposition of Qassim in 1963, Huda was identified as a dangerous "leftist," and with other intellectuals and artists—"communists"—she was imprisoned for two-and-a-half months by the Ba'aths, the party in which Saddam Hussein rose to prominence. She recalls the brutality of detention: torture, rape with electronic instruments, child beatings. Even before Hussein achieved absolute power, he and his party excelled in sadistic practices: Huda recounts the story of a woman forced to listen to her three-month-old baby being devoured alive after being put into a bag of starving cats (Raffo 2006, 51). Along with others, Huda faked a passport and fled.

Huda's role is to illuminate the deeply uneven mixture of horrifying repression and temporary moderation that characterized Hussein's leadership and the American tolerance of him. When Hussein was Iraq's vice president, some women's rights were curbed while others were retained, since women's involvement was necessary to achieve rapid economic growth. In fact, under the Ba'ath party, an effort was made to combat female illiteracy; at one point, every woman between fifteen and forty-five was required to attend classes at local literacy centers.[10] Changes were also made to the conditions under which a woman could seek divorce and in regard to inheritance and to polygamous marriages. These reforms reflected the Ba'ath party's attempt to modernize Iraqi society and to supplant loyalty to extended families and tribal society with loyalty to the government and ruling party. These programs attracted the attention and praise of the West: UNESCO, for example, recognized Hussein for his creation of an effective public-health system.

After he attained the presidency in 1979, Hussein was deemed an acceptable political partner since he seemed to offer a moderate alternative to the rising fundamentalism in Iran. In 1984, for example, Donald Rumsfeld met with President Hussein even after it was reported that he authorized the use of mustard gas and a nerve agent on Iranian soldiers.[11] Though Hussein began his presidency by ordering the execution of his political opponents, his aggression was underestimated and his internal brutality tolerated. Under the Reagan administration, Iraq was the third largest recipient of US assistance (Galbraith 2006). In 1989, the first Bush administration doubled its financial credit to Iraq even after Hussein's mass extermination of the Kurdish people in the Anfal Campaign became known. Those that later decried Hussein as barbarous for gassing his own people—Rumsfeld, Cheney, Powell—citing this as a reason for going to war, had all been in the government fifteen years earlier when political intervention might have made a difference to the Kurds.

The character of Huda is meant to reinstall this forgotten history when Iraq was considered a politically and commercially viable partner to the West. When Hussein began to turn away from Western practices and embrace Islamic and tribal traditions, it was a move to consolidate his internal political power, wholly in keeping with the man who would simultaneously modernize and brutalize. Hussein's suppression of women's rights grew as the Iraqi economy constricted and as the need for him to embrace a less secular identity arose. Prior to 1991, Iraqi women had one of the highest standards of rights and access in the Middle East. By 1998, the Iraqi government reportedly dismissed all females working as secretaries in governmental agencies; women's travel was legally restricted, and formerly coeducational high schools were required to provide single-sex education only. By the later years of Hussein's government, the majority of women and girls had been relegated to traditional roles within the home.

Just as strenuously as Huda condemns Hussein's abuses, she also criticizes the hypocritical politics of Arab neighbors and of the United States. The Arab countries knowingly treated "him like a buddy," even while Hussein and his sadistic sons brutalized women with impunity. She repeats the stories of Iraqi women who were forced into prostitution by Hussein and then beheaded because of it. She so vehemently opposes Hussein, that when she is living in London, her liberal activism is confounded. While she has joined others protestors who rallied for peace in Vietnam and in Chile, she could not march against the American invasion of Iraq. However aware she is of American neoimperialism, she believes there must be foreign intervention lest Iraq be in a state of "permanent repression and cruelty" (Raffo 2006, 22).

Huda represents the vexed position of liberals wanting to address the enormous human rights violations that occurred under Hussein and who reluctantly assented to foreign intervention, taking a gamble on the West. Believing as she does that Iraqis are powerless against Hussein's efficient brutality, Huda nevertheless concludes that the current American "liberation" feels more like "masochism" (51). She excoriates the half-measures America took to curb Hussein after the first Gulf War. After 1991, Huda says, the Iraqis were ready to mount a wholesale rebellion against Hussein and depose him, but America failed to support the dissidents. Thirteen years of intense suffering during the embargo, Huda goes on to say, made Hussein stronger and the country more "backwards and religious" though "funny enough, Saddam he was never religious." Middle-class people sold books on the street to eat and the isolation mentality "gave the fundamentalists their legitimacy" (40). The largest mistake America made, Huda concludes, was to support "Saddam all of his life."[12] Thus after the 1991 war, Iraqi women were so "shell shocked," Huda reports, that "they go backwards, the girls abandon their education" and take to "wearing the veils. Their grandmothers are more liberated than them" (39).

Raffo provides a contemporary analogue to Huda in the figure of the Iraqi doctor. Though unlike the secular Huda, she wears the abaya, she is equally modern in her education and accomplishments. The doctor speaks to the environmental and health damage caused by chemicals used during that conflict, observing that while once Iraq had the best medical facilities in the Middle East, the war has destroyed them. Now she works in Basra where children drink polluted water and play on sites where the radiation released is 84 times the safety limit. With few supplies to treat known diseases, she confronts new abnormalities, struggling to diagnose babies born with multiple genetic malformations and children with new forms of cancer. The doctor is pregnant, and she dreads the birth of her own child, fearing the possibility of disease or disfigurement. At the same time, her husband, injured in the war, remains at home, unemployed and despondent. "We won't survive it," says the doctor, leaving the "it" to refer to calamities past and future. Calling Iraq the West's "experiment," her despair reinforces Huda's view that it is deeply unrealistic to expect such a profoundly traumatized citizenry to quickly regroup and form an effective, democratic government.

Just as Huda serves as the play's historical memory, Umm Ghada is *Nine Parts*' conscience. Her monologue is the ethical centerpiece of the play, performed along the theatre's side wall, in close contact with the audience, whom she addresses directly. As a self-appointed guardian of the dead, Umm Ghada begins her passionate witness by saying that she consigned her own name to oblivion after the American bombing of the Amiriyah shelter on February 13, 1991, killed 403 people, one of whom was her daughter.[13] Now her sole purpose is to be Umm Ghada, the mother of Ghada, in order to refuse to allow her child's life to be erased. As she points a flashlight directly at audience members, she informs them that they are touring the bombed shelter, and she points out smoked figures etched into the ceiling, the charred remains of vaporized humans. Umm Ghada was inside with nine members of her family when the shelter burst into flames, and though she somehow found her way out, her children did not. The only body she recognized was that of her daughter, and since 1991 she has lived in a trailer—her "witness stand"—outside the shelter. She has assembled a collection of photos of pilgrims who have visited. Inside the shelter, she calls attention to the bits of skin and hair stuck into the walls, the handprints from people who lay in the top bunks. She describes how some were boiled to death from burst pipes while others were fused together when the room became an oven. In halting but accusatory English, Umm Ghada discounts utterly that the military was unaware of what it were bombing: it was done on purpose, she says, because the United States assumed the shelter was a military communication center and so dropped two bombs on the roof, the first to drill a hole, the second to explode inside (Raffo 2006, 31).

In changing her name, Umm Ghada has redefined the rest of her life as understandable only in relation to loss. In deciding to live at the site of her children's death, to make her home amidst the grave, Umm Ghada chooses to be forever attached to their moment of disappearance. She says of herself, "I am attached like I will die if I leave" (34). Derrida might read Umm Ghada's decision as he does Blanchot's testimony: as choosing the death-sentence of witness, of the "necessary but impossible abidance (*demeurance*) of the abode (*demeure*)" (Blanchot and Derrida 2000, 16). Ever concerned about the "endless problem" of witness through language, Derrida speaks of the "fatal and double impossibility: the impossibility of deciding but the impossibility of *remaining* (*demeure*) in the undecidable" (16). Thus, in a radical sense, to be the witness that Umm Ghada has committed herself to be is a decision to live forever in the instance of death in order to arrest it somehow; to keep death—or at least its next moment, which is oblivion—"in abeyance" (11). While Derrida illuminates the nonplus of living in the instance of death in order to stave off annihilation, he clearly does not write as a woman—often a figure of waiting—or, more especially, as a mother, one whose identity is bound as much to loss as it is to preservation. The abode of the womb is nothing if not possibility and preservation, and when it has been quickened and then vacated, one becomes a mother, however long that child breathes, and even when it does not. Every gestation bespeaks the impossibility of deciding anything more than the willingness to abide with another. Thus, Umm Ghada is described as a "woman of great *stillness*"; she is, moreover, "proud" and "peaceful" because of her ability to live halted in the moment of her child's death rather than consign it to insignificance (Raffo 2006, 30). However excruciating and even potentially futile her actions may seem—her abaya forms a "black hole" that she stands next to (Raffo 2006, 30)—Umm Ghada offers an image of a moving and potent maternal vigilance.

The image is also politically empowering; it enacts a feminine subjectivity that transforms passivity into activism. Globally, the figure of the Stabat Mater has become not only the face of grief but also the face of political resistance. "Motherism," Miriam Cooke observes, is a "multi-faceted strategy of resistance in postcolonial war, and its literature is no longer a mere social fact; it has become a resisting act" (1995, 25). Umm Ghada is the Iraqi equivalent of Cindy Sheehan, camped outside of George Bush's ranch after her son's death, or of Argentina's Madres de le Plaza, mothers who coalesce around the common cause of their children in order to "intervene in a public space that largely denies women access or participation" (19).

The intervention is particularly important because technologized and mediated warfare has so drastically altered the relationship between the spectator and the scene. The sanitization of suffering that is part of the arsenal of techno-warfare is also the subject of another monologue: that of the Iraqi American character, known only as the American. Here Raffo suggests the consequences of such denial for Americans. This character, an autobiographical stand-in, cannot watch the television coverage dispassionately; she cries out the names of her Iraqi family members as a prayer for their survival. Holed up in her New York apartment, she becomes incensed at the manifestations of American solipsism and hypocrisy: the feel-good news reports of rescuing miners while not even an estimate of the number of Iraqi dead is given; the Amber Alerts to protect against sexual predators while the responsibility for Abu Ghraib gets passed to the lowest ranks; the psychiatric expertise sought in America for even a single trauma while Iraqis live among constant assault and violence. The callousness derives, the American suggests, from the common experience of watching atrocity amid daily routines of narcissism: getting a pedicure while the television blares, going to gym to "work out to the war," or to the bar to "drink to the war" (Raffo 2006, 46). The Iraqi, the Other, is part of the daily media flow, the suffering flattened out on the screen amid stock and weather reports.

These characters—Umm Ghada, the Iraqi doctor, the American cousin—are developed only in relation to the moment when death has arrested their future. The death of the child, the medical deformities, the attack on family members—these are the moments that freeze the characterizations, offering the audience a sense of painful first-hand experience that stands in distinction to the decorporealized information of the televised spectacle. In showing forth this anguish and grief from a clearly feminine/feminist consciousness, the play tacitly claims that this perspective can exert its influence, though this claim is significantly bracketed by the death of the play's most actively subversive character, Layal.

Fundamentally, the frozen testimonies that Umm Ghada and the others offer address Judith Butler's concern that after 9/11, "mourning can only be resolved through violence" (2004, xix). While in the United States a laudable attempt was made to grieve and to memorialize publicly every person who died in the attack on the World Trade Center towers, and a similar effort is made on many nightly newscasts to show the faces of fallen American soldiers, those on the other side remain anonymous. Butler fears that this obliteration can "authorize us to become senseless before those whose lives we have eradicated" (xviii). Such obliteration surely leads to renewed violence, but it also leads, for all involved, to a slippery ethical calculus where some lives are deemed grievable and others are not. If one is willing, as Butler argues, to accept mourning and the loss it involves, that willingness may affect something transformative that can be expressed in terms other than rage or vengeance (22–23).

In *Nine Parts of Desire*, however, the play's most vibrant character, Layal, a seductive and beautiful artist, clever, independent, and intelligent, cannot save herself. Layal's life is the logical culmination of the forces the play has described: a mixed history of women's rights, a mixed environment for creative expression, Hussein's tyranny and secularism, the growth of fundamentalism, the American-led attack and occupation. Within these dynamics, Layal lives by complicity and subversion. Significantly, Layal is the only character to die in the play, but not at the hands of Hussein: while during her lifetime, the Iraqi regime raped and used her, it is an American bomb that kills her.

Layal produces artwork at the behest of the Hussein regime as a means of survival. Her story, like Huda's and Umm Ghada's, has a direct connection to Iraqi history. Like other tyrants, Hussein exercised strong control over the arts, both by offering commissions and squashing dissent. As the Iran-Iraq War ended, with nothing like the overwhelming success he had imagined, Hussein directed the erection of monuments to Iraqi victory and Iraqi martyrdom. Under his cult-of-personality regime, the only safe subject was a flattering picture of Hussein himself, and these pictures produced the groundless histories that Hussein wished to have circulated. Choosing between imprisonment or forced flattery, Iraqi artists sought ways to speak around the strictly controlled system and produce independent, even subversive works. Some Iraqi artists, such as Aryan al-Sayed Khalan, who had been imprisoned and had his tongue slashed, developed an interstitial poetics (Sachs 2003). Convinced that Iraqis could read between the lines, he and others developed a densely symbolic aesthetics to conceal their real pronouncements about tyranny and repression. Others, such as Lutifiya al-Dulayami, wrote analogically; her novel, *Seeds of Fire*, describes a woman graphic artist whose work situation illuminates the production of propaganda. In Miriam Cook's assessment, this kind of writing "seems to suggest that during the war the woman artist may find at the very heart of a totalitarian system the key to its undoing" (1995, 23).

Raffo's heroine, the "sexy, elegant, fragile, resilient" Layal, subverts the commissions she receives by producing art that witnesses and memorializes the transgressed female body. While she is financially able to emigrate, her flight would mean leaving Iraq without dissident artists and abandoning her own unique role as a painter. Layal believes in her own charmed powers of self-preservation since she is adept at manipulating the same sites—bodies and images—that the regime coerces. Despite the repression, Layal paints nudes, using her own body as a stand-in for every abused woman, offering it as a medium for inscribing that woman's tale protectively onto canvas. In contrast to the false monuments to martyrdom, Layal takes on pain and risk. Like Umm Ghada, she has given herself over to her own kind of death sentence; commending her own body as the place where the wracked pain of the Other can be made visible and known. She knows, ultimately, that the cost of complicity is death, but complicity is the only avenue toward something akin to artistic freedom. That is the deal Layal knowingly makes in order to produce a painting of a "woman eaten by Saddam's son," a beautiful university student whom Uday, the son, saw and desired and beat (Raffo 2006, 13). Had the young woman kept silent about the beating, she might have lived, but she did not and so the son "stripped her and covered her in honey and watched his Doberman eat her." In Layal's painting, the girl, Philomel-like, has been transformed into a branch's blossom, forever out of the reach of mad, barking dogs. "You see," says Layal, "nobody knows the painting is her but I believe somewhere she sees" (14).

Though the defiant Layal asserts that she reveals something "in her trees, her nudes, her portraits of Saddam," her dissidence is not well-understood, and the cost of her testimony is psychically damaging (15). Knowing she is looked upon as a "whore" for painting Hussein, she scoffs at the notion that she could stop and be "safe." In her third monologue, Layal has passed from defiance to a deeply traumatized, even psychotic state. The protracted unsettlement of living on the cusp of complicity and subversion and the cost of being the battered body inevitably empties her resources. If the game has turned sadomasochistic, it is because one cannot remain untouched by the terms to which one has agreed. And so Layal admits that she seeks out her oppressors: "Always I run to them crying, begging, take care of me, they love me to run to them begging, so they can have me." Layal goes on, "If I am not afraid, then there is no feeling. I have been raped and raped and raped and raped, and I want more because they see me, they know me as I am, and that is freedom" (49). Here the myth of rescue is revealed in its most desperate, delusional, and suicidal form. Layal's compromises never result in the freedom she seeks.[14] When Layal accepts a new commission, this time by the occupying American forces, she agrees to replace Hussein's portrait with one of Bush, all the while still feeling herself judged as a whore. She decides, however, to drop her usual veil of transparency and write in English, "Bush is Criminal." In this declaration, made in her fourth and final speech, Layal ventriloquizes the agonies of the women she has painted and repeats snippets of monologues already heard. She conflates her pain with that endured by Iraqis under both Hussein and the American occupation: the bodies of lovers under surveillance by Hussein become the bodies fused together at Amiriyah; Uday's prostituted women and America's targeted victims merge as one. Layal cannot forever entice and then elude the powerful men who protect, then abuse her, but in the end, death comes impersonally. Her final gesture is a curse on America: "You have our war inside of you like a burden, like an orphan," she says. "And we tether you to something so old you cannot see it. We have you chained to the desert, to your blood" (35)

Nine Parts of Desire enacts the use value to which the lives and bodies of Iraqi women have been put by all sides. What, ultimately, does the play say about the possibilities for resistance or agency? One might argue that each of the women depicted demonstrated, along with Umm Ghada, the possibilities of "third space" politics. For Homi Bhabha, a "third place" is one of supplementarity that "registers a site where resistance can be enacted from within," and by the end of the play, each of these women has abandoned the solidity of an uncomplicated identity position to reside in one with less clear-cut affiliations or uninterrogated allegiances (1990, 208). The political agency that the play and characters claim is the ability to disrupt the brutal but predictable imaginary of domination. Against the menacing energy of exploitation, the "great stillness" of Umm Ghada, her witness, and her invitation to mourn stands in rebuke.

HOW THE WAR SHAPED THEATRE; HOW THEATRE SHAPED THE WAR

None of the theatre works I have discussed so far amassed anything as large as the audience that tuned into CNN or some other news outlet to watch the 1991 Gulf War. None held the viewers' attention for so long or used technology to claim special access, by force of relentless visibility, to the "truth" of the war's events. No play could produce a narrative as quickly as those made on the spot by news anchors or embedded reporters. Those plays that appeared almost immediately—*Back to Normal* and *States of Shock*—did not disrupt the euphoria felt by most Americans for whom the military victory was a moment to savor. No theatre audience rivaled in number the masses who gathered for ticker-tape parades. And if there is one irrefutable legacy for political art from the Gulf War it is this: no critique can ever again act independently of media-generated images. Political theatre, in the information age, will always be a restaging of what has already been seen.

It is not possible to overemphasize this last point. The 1991 Gulf War was the key event in ushering in an era of media spectacularity that substantially changed the way that information is shared and knowledge produced. The old saying that truth is the first casualty of war held as true in the Gulf War as in any other conflict, but the difference here is that the manner of instantaneous, real-time technological transmission privileged visibility to such an extent that it acquired the status of fact. Technology guided what we saw but presented itself as neutral and objective. Somehow we believed that information transmitted via the lens of a machine is without bias or self-interest. This same codification applied not only to information technology but to technologically enhanced weaponry. Accuracy became synonymous with impartiality; mechanical launching somehow removes human agency and human intention. The belief in a disembodied, objective technology as a means of waging war and in a disembodied, objective technology as a means of seeing it are demonstrably false beliefs, but they are ones that have secured a firm hold on the public imagination. In failing to recognize that technology always remains an ideological tool and that thinking about it as neutral and objective is to ignore its aesthetic/polemical packaging, we have become liable to Walter Benjamin's warning that "all efforts to render politics aesthetic culminate in one thing: war" (1936, epilogue).

But if the technological age is marked by spectacularity, it is also marked by disappearance. Every subject covered by the media has a short shelf-life since it is a medium that depends crucially on newness and immediacy. This fact has produced certain generic conventions. One can quickly list the emergent "technowar style": brief but in real time, technowars use highly developed weapons systems, censor casualties or other brutal acts, and enlist the media as coproducers. The reportorial style can also be described: driven by breaking news that was instantly aired, and by the competition between networks to be first with breaking news, Gulf War reportage was incremental, subject to revision, reliant on continuous narrative by reporters who became celebrities, less concerned about accuracy than about immediacy, and given to human interest/heroic myth stories. In the tedium between bursts of activity, panels of "experts" attempted to frame, though not necessarily historicize, the unfolding events. The blueprint for waging a successful technowar was laid down in 1991 and largely followed in the bombing raids on Afghanistan and in the 2003 Gulf War. The reporting style also left its mark; though, as I will discuss later, both military and political strategists and media management became more savvy about spectacle management.

Here the particular strengths of socially engaged theatre emerge to claim a singular role. More than other forms of critique, politically engaged theatre can employ its own understanding of semiotics and performance in order to call attention to the constructedness of media presentations. These performances can expose the incompleteness, subjectivity, or partiality of news reportage; they can illuminate the limits of spectacularity, and they can critique the forms of narrativization that underlie instantaneous coverage. Theatre with an awareness of the prevailing media culture can disrupt the closed circle of passive consumption and enabling desire. Certainly *Back to Normal* took on the new model of technowar reportage, emphasizing in particular the news organizations' need to find a story or invent one in order to win ratings. Every play discussed drew on the audience's memory of what had been televised already: the sounds and sights of American firepower lighting up the night sky. But the plays never left these sounds and sights unframed: they were connected (in Shepard) to scenes of indifferent consumerism; they served as the backdrop that opened onto frightened Iraqis (in Sellars and Griffiths); or they offered a false assurance to naive American soldiers (in Wallace). The Gulf War theatre thus addressed the contradictory desire of the new media both to place its spectators in a very specific milieu—close to the action, with thrilling immediacy—but also to "liberate" them "from space and time" (Fischer-Lichte 1992, 19). Where instantaneous transmission collapses both time and space boundaries, and round-the-clock coverage brings every event into the private world of individual viewing, even as it filters out portions of information or context, theatre, conversely, demands that "production and reception are concurrent processes" that happen within a community, relying on the material and corporeal, not just the visible (20). Theatre requires community, and it insists on context.

It is not only its intimate understanding of what constitutes the performative that defines political theatre's contribution to political critique. In addition to this vitally important capacity to interrogate signs and call attention to the performative process, there is theatre's insistent concern for making connections between the present moment and its anterior causes and likely consequences. In short, the Gulf War theatre helped expand the debate, inserting the kind of critique that both extreme nationalism or extreme dissociation avoided. A review of some of the perspectives offered by the Gulf War theatre makes the case for its contribution to democratic debate. Against the false emotionalism of "feel-good" television interviews (injured children; parents of slain soldiers) as well as the hysteria of mass displays, several theatre pieces attempted to make room for more authentic kinds of empathy and cross-cultural understanding. This effort stands in direct opposition to the purposeful demonizing of certain leaders or the wholesale dismissal of populations as backward, fanatical, and irrational. The three plays discussed above each place the "enemy" on stage . Each play offers a reasonable, sympathetic, intelligent figure or figures (Dr. Aziz, Atossa, the women of *Nine Parts*) who revile the corruption of their country's leaders but also rebuke American hypocrisy. Each woman raises the question of the morality of the West's disproportionate response. Each calls attention to the murderous capacity of technology described so frequently in terms of surgical accuracy and precision that its death-dealing purpose is lost amid the admiration for its impressive assemblage. All three plays also invoke the history of the ancient Persian civilization in order to counter depictions of this culture as inherently barbaric. They each include a moment when an ethically persuasive character demystifies the politics of the New World Order as a moral program.

CHAPTER 4

FROM THE RUINS OF 9/11: GRIEF AND TERROR

AFTER THE TWIN TOWERS CRUMBLED TO THE GROUND, THE cinders drifted northward and seaward. Handfuls of dirt taken from Ground Zero were blessed and buried in place of incinerated bodies, and New Yorkers knew that they'd breathed in the ashes of the dead. The taking of life took one hour and twenty minutes; the loss of life totaled 3,021 dead; 2,792 of those died in New York City. The 9/11 date has come to act as a dividing line in the American historical consciousness, separating a prolonged age of innocence from the new and dreadful knowledge of vulnerability. Ultimately, this profound threat to national self-conception would be used to produce a rhetoric that divided the globe into allies and enemies. By exploiting the language of grief and fear, a rationale for defense through pre-emptive action was devised. In this chapter, I discuss works that were written in the immediate aftermath of 9/11. Plays by John McGrath, Anne Nelson, Neil LaBute, and Alexandra Gerstem-Vassilaros and Teresa Rebeck each attempt to register the horror of the event and to begin to describe the "new normal."

More than a third of the world population saw the attack on the twin towers at the time of its occurrence, and millions more watched the subsequent events unfold, drawn into the loop of rebroadcast images and repeated commentary. A searing, often traumatic image can recall virtually each one of the major incidents that have taken place since the terrorists bombings: the bombing of Afghanistan; Osama bin Laden's elusiveness; the arrest of John Walker Lindh, the "American Taliban"; Colin Powell at the UN; Bush and Cheney making the case against Hussein for harboring weapons of mass destruction and being linked to Al Qaeda; Tony Blair "sexing up" the Iraq dossier; the attack on Iraq in 2003; the toppling of Hussein's statue; saving Jessica Lynch; the "Mission Accomplished" speech; Hussein's hanging; Guantanamo; Abu Ghraib; Lynndie England; the hooded prisoner; torture; waterboarding; Cindy Sheehan's vigil; the Iraq surge; the blue thumbs of those who voted in Iraq's democratic election; the plan to focus again on Afghanistan; Osama bin Laden's compound and the reaction to his killing. These images became the site of knowledge production, replacing reports, analysis, or testimony, though the knowledge produced was often contestable. While Roland Barthes's contention that "from a phenomenological view, in the photograph, the power of authentication exceeds the power of representation" (2000, 76) has been challenged by Photoshopping and other techniques that can alter the original, the power of images to retain some evidential value remains, even if it has been degraded. On the other hand, the power of images to enchant—to traumatize, mesmerize, shock, provoke—persists despite skepticism. It is too soon to write a consensual history of the War on Terror, but one challenge will be to examine how events were justified (or assailed) on the basis of narratives spun around images.

But there also seems to be something about the 9/11 attacks that resists memorialization. Don DeLillo, in an essay entitled "In the Ruins of the Future," writes that "the event itself has no purchase on the mercies of analogy or simile. We have to take the shock and horror as it is" (2001, 39). Whether DeLillo is right or not, the fact is that what is popularly spoken of as the "tragedy of 9/11" did not produce a grand "master work," such as Pablo Picasso's painting *Guernica* or W. H. Auden's poem "September, 1, 1939." The astuteness of DeLillo's observation is supported by how difficult it has been to commemorate the site of the attack or to reverence the dead. On the one hand, in the hours and days following the attacks, New York became a city of impromptu shrines, posted pictures of the missing, and hand-crafted expressions of grief. Art critic Arthur Danto observed that by the end of the day on September 11, New York had been transformed into a "ritual precinct, dense with improvised sites of mourning." He concluded, "I thought at the time that artists, had they tried to do something in response to 9/11, could not have done better than the anonymous shrine-makers who found ways of expressing the common mood and feeling of those days, in ways that everyone instantly understood" (2005). Yet, the fact that no memorial was quickly erected at Ground Zero speaks to the intense desire to produce a work of substance that can and will accommodate the myriad emotions that September 11 produced. Any such plans to memorialize the dead pose daunting architectural and social challenges: how does one build a commercial sector/commemorative site over a crematorium? "History decays into images, not stories," Walter Benjamin observed, but he did not anticipate so many images, so instantaneously dispersed and widely seen, so numerous, viral, and impossible to collect (2002, N11).

And so the question remains about why the aesthetic responses to 9/11, particularly in theatre, have not (cannot?) meet the needs and expectations of the pained and stricken American community—and given the ethnic and national demographics of those killed in the attacks, of the larger community of mourners. Does this "national tragedy" in fact resist tragedy and all that tragedy means: pathos, illumination, recognition, catharsis? Have we stultified our own creativity and empathy by our insistence that 9/11 was an "unimaginable," "incomprehensible," and "unprecedented" event? Did 9/11 become so quickly layered by other discourses—the language of victimization, heroism, vengeance—that responding it to the event per se became impossibly entangled in sentimentality, jingoism, and opportunism?

On the other hand, perhaps we should be wary of grand terms such as "tragedy," and of art that demands "contemplative immersion" and "concentration," since, as Benjamin recognized, this kind of aesthetic posture privileges a partial, elite view even as it obscures ideology. If we are, as *The New Yorker* art critic Peter Schjeldahl has observed, a "culture that is insulated against worldly realities by persnickety aestheticism" (2000, 94), it may be salutary to stop looking for the master work that can impose some interpretive order on the attack. Terrorist attacks still loom, and so another question must be addressed: how does one use art to respond to an "exceptional" event when the event may be repeated, if not in scale, then in frequency, and seems not to have an endpoint?

Director Richard Foreman suggests the role of the artist is not to find answers to such questions but "simply try to plumb the depths of what's really happening, what's really 'there' on all levels." He continues:

> Art is made out of the way human beings can process terrorist attacks, global capitalism, prejudice, stupidity—not the things themselves but the way of processing them. Art is the machine that processes the negative material. I don't think it should or will change because of terrorism, no matter how powerful the momentary image (a negative idol) it creates in our consciousness (2004, 6–7).

The fruits of this processing, according to Foreman, are compassion, detachment, and mental energy, qualities that would surely have helped work through the trauma of 9/11 (6).

Sadly, there are no conclusions reachable here: the time to produce something consoling, explanatory, ethical, and true that might affect how America responded to the attacks was closed down quickly. On network television, as Robin Anderson reports, the cry for war started just a few hours after the attacks, and within a month the United States began bombing Afghanistan (2006, 203–204). What happened, as is now widely known, is that the Bush administration used the nation's intense grief and raw emotions to pursue an unrelated goal—regime change in Iraq—and to legitimate an open-ended war on terror. On September 11, 2001, just twelve hours after the attacks, President Bush announced, "The search is under way for those who are behind these evil acts" (2001). He signaled how the war could be expanded: "We will make no distinction between the terrorists who committed these acts and those who harbor them" (2001). On September 15, at the first meeting of national security experts, Saddam Hussein's name was already raised when Deputy Secretary of Defense Paul Wolfowitz argued that the time was apt to pursue additional targets. On September 25, 2001, Secretary of Defense Donald Rumsfeld announced Operation Enduring Freedom, the name for what had now officially been declared a war, though Al-Qaeda was new kind of enemy for the American public: a deterritorialized group committed to religio-political goals. The United States began bombing Afghanistan on October 7, 2001; by December 17, heavy American air-strikes pummeled Tora Bora, killing hundreds of Al-Qaeda members (and many civilians), but Osama bin Laden escaped apprehension. Some sixty Al-Qaeda members were taken to Guantanamo Bay, and the Afghan war was declared a victory. Fourteen months later, the United States bombed Baghdad.

As this chronology attests, dialogue and reflection that opened briefly after September 11 was quickly closed down. The oft-repeated question, "Why do they hate us?" was not immediately defensive, jingoistic, or smug, though it quickly became so as demonizing rhetoric and images inserted themselves into the national conversation, taking root where critical inquiry about America's history in the Middle East or about the teachings of Islam might have produced fuller understandings. Soon nothing could be said that did not pass a patriotic litmus test, and so Susan Sontag's objection to how the press and government were "infantilizing" its citizens drew quick condemnation. She said:

> The voices licensed to follow the event seem to have joined together infantilize the public. Where is the acknowledgement that this was not a "cowardly" attack on "civilization" or "liberty" or "humanity" or "the free world" but an attack on the world's self-proclaimed super-power, undertaken as a consequence of specific American alliances and actions? How many citizens are aware of the ongoing American bombing of Iraq? And if the word "cowardly" is to be used, it might be more aptly applied to those who kill from

beyond the range of retaliation, high in the sky, than to those willing to die themselves in order to kill others. In the matter of courage (a morally neutral virtue): whatever may be said of the perpetrators of Tuesday's slaughter, they were not cowards. (2004, 28–29).

It is true that Sontag's comments were published less than two weeks after the attacks and they touched a nerve, but her desires—that public dialogue itself not be hijacked, that there be some effort to understand the political motivation behind the attack, and that we avoid doing further harm by cloaking the event in empty sloganeering—were offered in the interest of a "mature democracy." Dissent is quelled in part, Judith Butler reminds us, by "shaming tactics" that produce what "will and will not count as a viable speaking subject and a reasonable opinion within the public domain" (xix).

In the months and years that followed the attacks, theatre searched for forms through which to sift through the ruins. In the following chapters, I examine how particular forms emerged and particular issues gained prominence. Documentary theatre grew more prevalent, as if theatre needed to present facts, stories, and issues that were ignored in the media or at odds with nationalist rhetoric. Issues around the prosecution of the war—extraordinary rendition, hidden prisons, indefinite detention, torture, the incursion on civil right—and around the effects of the war—on the environment, on civilians, and on the soldiers themselves—are the focus of important theatrical pieces. However, in comparison to as vast and complex a play as Tony Kusher's *Homebody/Kabul*—which was four years in the writing and overtaken by the World Trade Center attacks, and which I will discuss in the final chapter—theatre about 9/11 seems to have been written on a smaller scale. Several theatrical pieces—Anne Nelson's *The Guys*, Neil LaBute's *The Mercy Seat*, John McGrath's *Hyperlynx*, Craig Wright's *Recent Tragic Events*, and Steven Berkoff's poetic monologue *Requiem for Ground Zero*—are all set on or shortly after 9/11. Others, such as Theresa Rebeck and Alexandra Gersten-Vassilaros's *Omnium Gatherum* and Culture Clash's *Anthems: Culture Clash in the District*, take place in the days that followed. As a group, the works have little in common, but each is in tacit conversation with some part of the public codification of 9/11. In this, they interrupt the dominant rhetoric of 9/11 as an attack without cause or precedent and reclaim it from indecipherability. David Simpson, in his important book *9/11: The Culture of Commemoration*, argues that "9/11 has a past that we can rediscover, a present that we must monitor, and a future we can project" (2006, 13). Theatrical works produced in response to 9/11 contribute to this analysis and in so doing provide a record of the immediate fear and grief and how quickly it was co-opted.

WHERE WERE YOU ON 9/11?

> It is my hope that in the months and years ahead life will return almost to normal. We'll go back to our lives and routines and that is good. Even grief recedes with time and grace. But our resolve must not pass. Each of us will remember what happened that day and to whom it happened. We will remember the moment the news came, where we were and what we were doing.
>
> —George W. Bush, address to Joint Session of Congress, September 20, 2001

In her book *Precarious Life: The Powers of Mourning and Violence*, Judith Butler raises the question, "If we are interested in arresting cycles of violence to produce less violent outcomes, it is no doubt important to ask what, politically, might be made of grief besides a cry for war?" (2004, xii). George Bush's speech to the Joint Session of Congress on September 20, 2001 enshrined 9/11 as a historical divide, and set forth a logic to rationalize the very kind of instantaneous vengeance that Butler warned against. The speech stoked the nation's raw emotions. In it, Bush strung together a concatenation of loaded terms –danger, freedom, grief, anger, resolve, justice—to legitimate an instant retaliation as well as a wider military response. Speaking in the first-person plural, Bush presented himself as having taken the measure of the nation's mood and so feels himself obliged to bow to national consensus. "Tonight, we are a country awakened to danger and called to defend freedom," he stated. "Our grief has turned to anger and anger to resolution. Whether we bring our enemies to justice or bring justice to our enemies, justice will be done." To explain why America was attacked, he recited a catalog of American virtues that the enemy envies and hates: our freedom of speech, of religion, of assembly, of democracy itself. He elided historical differences and contexts to claim that the terrorists "follow in the path of fascism, Nazism, totalitarianism." Bush then addressed what ordinary Americans should do now that the world has changed. He advised his countrymen to "live their life," "uphold the values of America," continue to participate and have "confidence in the economy" and "pray." As "long as the United States of America is determined and strong," the president assured, "this will not be an age of terror." Such assurance came mere seconds after he had put the world on notice: "Every nation in every region now has a decision to make: Either you are with us or you are with the terrorists."

Bush's speech laid out three key questions through which to understand what had just happened to America: how has 9/11 changed my world? Why were we attacked? What should be my response? In his speech, he dwelled on the first, simplified the second, and usurped the third. The September 20 speech emphasized loss, grief, outrage, and solidarity—embodied in the special guests of the evening, the widow of one of the men who helped down the third plane in Pennsylvania and Prime Minister Tony Blair, who had flown across the Atlantic to be present—but erased any historical complexity or American culpability. And though the president began by stating baldly that the nation was at war, he essentially asked nothing of American citizens except they go about business as usual. Patriotism was defined as compliance and consumerism rather than sacrifice.

Each of the 9/11 plays listed above raises and answers at least one, if not all three, of Bush's questions. They begin by describing what the character was doing when the attacks occurred. In Anne Nelson's *The Guys*, Joan, a Manhattan editor, recounts getting a call from her father in Oklahoma telling her to turn on her television set. In Craig Wright's *Recent Tragic Events*, a first date is interrupted by one character's anxiety over her missing sister. In John McGrath's *Hyperlynx*, Heather, a member of the British MI5, is walking through the park on September 11, thinking about recent protests around trade summits. In Neil LaBute's *The Mercy Seat*, it is September 12, and a man who has been having an affair with his boss wonders whether he should seize the opportunity to let his wife and children think that he died in the attack. Steven Berkoff's performed verse considers the viewpoints of those in the planes and those in the buildings. From this common beginning, the plays diverge to tell different stories, but it is worth pausing over the significance of the shared narrative framework.

In *Precarious Life*, Butler comments that in the United States "we begin the story by invoking a first-person narrative point of view, and telling what happened on September 11" (2004, 5). It is an obvious opening gambit, but it is one with both personal and political implications. Clearly, in the personal realm, especially to New Yorkers, but also to others across the nation and the globe, the narrative that begins with "I was [where] on September 11" is an attempt to fix, in place and time, the moment when the world was felt to have changed irrevocably. It also inaugurates traumatic narratives of personal loss and grief, or, alternatively, of vicarious sorrow and helplessness. The exchange of these stories enfolds small, individual moments into the swelling tale of national tragedy, making the loss both common and particular. Yet, in this political narrative, the "I" at the center of the story resists any position except that of the attacked, the victim, and the innocent. Politically, the September 11 story requires such a narrative framework, Butler suggests, because to back the story up, looking for what caused the attack, would be to transgress the limits of the "sayable," the limits of what is permissible in the public domain during a time of shock and grief (2004, xvii). Within this framework, the United States as the victim of violence is entitled to draw the lines the president ultimately did, dividing the world into those with the terrorists, and those with us. And pundits and politicians are allowed to berate those such as Susan Sontag who transgress what is "unsayable."

In Nelson's *The Guys*, one of the two characters, Joan, opens the play in just this fashion, recounting where she was and what she was doing when the twin towers were hit. But later, in one of the direct-address monologues, Joan comes close to violating the boundaries of the sayable. During a trip to Argentina immediately after the attacks, she recounts her anger and bitterness when she hears a woman whose son was one of the disappeared say she felt "glad" about the attacks because "American imperialists had it coming." Joan is furious that comments such as the one she overheard proliferate, and that the massacre of the civilians inside the towers is so denigrated. She believes that "everything the Argentines were saying was about their own war twenty years ago" (2002, 30). They are drawing misplaced comparisons, Joan thinks, rather than recognizing the uniqueness of the attack on America. Joan asserts, "It's about us," but she then pauses before delivering the final line of the monologue: "Isn't it?" (30).

In this small reflection, Joan enunciates the tensions—and interpretive challenges—that emerged immediately: to whom did the 'tragedy" belong? And would the experience of 9/11 make America more isolationist and vengeful, or, through the experience of global solidarity at the time of the attacks, more connected and co-operative? Didion, in her essay on September 11 observed that, for a while, the latter was happening, that Americans were "making connections between the political process and what happened on September 11."[1] Similarly, Ariel Dorfman, in his collected essays, *Other Septembers, Many Americas*, expressed hope that having gone through the horrific process of knowing the bodies of their loved ones had disappeared forever, incinerated in the blasted towers, the "inhabitants of the most modernized society in the world may be able to connect, in ways that have been unthinkable before September 11, 2001 to the experience of so many hitherto inaccessible planetary others" (2004, 9).

It is not only in the interest of global conciliation but also in the interest of national well-being that the rhetorical stance of the first-person account of September 11 be scrutinized. Butler contends, "The ability to narrate ourselves not from the first person alone, but from, say, the position of the third, or to receive an account delivered in the second, can actually work to expand our understanding of the forms that global power has taken" (2004, 8). Her comment should not be taken to suggest that the healing process of speaking about and listening to a first-person account of trauma and loss should be abandoned—this is the process that Nelson's play so affectively reproduces, a point I will return to below; it is to remind us that even this enormously important process can be taken over by public formulations about what is sayable and thinkable.

John McGrath's *Hyperlynx*, as the title suggests, emphasizes the connectedness between the 9/11 attacks and other global events. *Hyperlynx* was the last play that John McGrath, the founder of 7:84 and author of some 60 plays, wrote before he died in 2003. He had started it in response to the Genoa riots, where about two hundred thousand protestors assembled at the 2001 G8 summit; some four hundred were injured and one killed in clashes with the police.

Hyperlynx begins with Heather Smithson headed to a meeting where she will discuss her new assignment: she is being taken off the Iraq/Afghanistan desk to head an infiltration operation that will spy on antiglobalization protestors. The two-act play is split between how Heather views the world before and after she learns what has happened in New York. For Heather, who is nearing retirement, her new assignment poses a dilemma since she has sympathy for the young idealists and direct knowledge of how corporations, especially agribusiness and pharmaceutical firms, have manipulated safety and trade regulations. She also knows how governments—her own, but also the US—have sought to discredit the protestors through negative media. In the opening lines, Heather, while admitting her role in authorizing assassinations and torture, believes the ground beneath her work has shifted, and she is about to become "a border guard for the new global empire" (2002, 9). The remainder of the first act's monologue deals with Heather's anger over governmental complicity with big business and the measures taken to derail global justice issues. She cites instances of genetic food engineering and withholding AIDS medication as particularly heinous examples and tries to figure out how she can gather intelligence that will subvert governmental harassment of the antiglobalists.

By act two, an hour-and-a-half later, the attacks have taken place, and Heather is desperate to contact her son, Tony, an investment banker in the United States on business. She is infuriated that obvious warning signs about Osama bin Laden have been overlooked, even as she is disgusted by Islamic fundamentalism. But she also recalls a conversation with an Afghani apprehended during the bombings of the US embassies in Africa who told her how the Arab world "spits" on democracy as nothing more than market capitalism. Now that "the suicide bombers have certainly given a whole new dimension to anti-globalisation protest," Heather is unsure of how to proceed with her plan to unmask governmental co-option (47).

The play is static; as a stripped-down monologue, it does not draw upon the range of theatrical traditions that have marked McGrath's earlier drama. The main character is not particularly sympathetic: we are never sure why she joined the MI5 or how she rationalized her earlier, admittedly brutal role. The ending—her daughter turns down a lucrative job and resolves to marry a Palestinian—is forced, and the characterizations of her children (daughter a left-wing martyr; son a complacent businessman) are pat. While the monologue is supposedly a conversation with herself, it is essentially a lecture on corporatism. Despite these numerous shortcomings, the play makes connections that other works have not about globalization and the protests over workers' rights and trade. McGrath's play reiterates much of the analysis offered by thinkers, such as Noam Chomsky, who contend that, while the 9/11 attacks were heinous acts, Western state terrorism played a part in fueling Al-Qaeda's fury. It edges toward Jean Baudrillard's controversial view that, while terrorism is immoral, so is the new and single world order of globalization, and that they are not separate from each other: terrorism is the shadow of globalization (2002, 12).

Neil LaBute's *The Mercy Seat*, set on September 12, does not offer anything like McGrath's intellectual meditation on terror and corporatism. Instead, LaBute offers a morality play. *The Mercy Seat* is the story of a married man, Ben, who has been having a several-year affair with his boss, Abbey. The play opens on Abbey's place, which is covered in a light film of dust, and Ben is seated near the window through which the drifting ash of the attacks is visible. The television is blaring, and his cell phone rings incessantly (surely the most realistic picture of 9/11 households), but Ben does not answer it. He is in the midst of considering whether to fake his own death and start a new life with Abbey, who is out looking for some havarti cheese for Ben. When she returns, her first words, and the opening lines of the play are, "Save it." The reference is to Ben's cell-phone battery, but the play's moral struggle is encapsulated in this Beckettian aphorism. Ben's personal decisions—whether to "save" his marriage, "save" his daughters the heartbreak of a divorce by letting them think he is dead, "save" himself of having to make a choice between two women or to render an honest accounting of his life—are each at the tipping point precisely because he is "safe"—having stopped by his mistress's apartment instead of going to work. When the towers fell, he was getting a blow job.

By the end of the *Mercy Seat*, we know where the characters were on 9/11, but the question of how to respond to 9/11 is still not answered. Significantly, Ben is seated back on the couch where he was when the play started, a voyeur on the suffering outside. In this pronouncedly unheroic play—a theme raised in the drama when Abbey tells Ben he is no Audie Murphy, a cultural reference that escapes him—the issue pursued is how the moment of 9/11 revealed ourselves to ourselves. C.W.E. Bigsby, in his study of LaBute's drama, reprises actual stories similar to Ben's: there were numerous instances of spouses cashing in on the death of partners who never existed or were still alive. Some, such as Carleton McNish, actually went through a memorial service in order to receive over $100,000 from charities. Others saw smaller opportunities for gain in the disaster: false claims were submitted, including nearly three hundred thousand for air conditioners and vacuum cleaners (2007, 104). Apparently, some 40 women spent 9/11 trying to get through to the new Yves Saint Laurent store on Madison Avenue to make sure their $2,500 silk blouses were being held on reserve (Callens, 2003, 69). The president's advisors—Wolfowitz, Cheney, and Rumsfeld—saw 9/11 as an opportunity to "cash in" on regime change in the Middle East.

It would diminish the play, however, to read *The Mercy Seat* only as a parable about government opportunism. Rather, LaBute, who dedicated the play to David Hare, and who has affinities with the theatrical traditions of David Mamet, Harold Pinter, and Wallace Shawn, is interested in the formation of individual subjectivity by historical and social forces, though he clearly rejects determinism. His characters are interpolated, as Louis Althusser would term it, within social forces, forces they can only inarticulately explain, like the arrivistes in Pinter's *Celebration* or the salesmen in Mamet's *Glengarry Glen Ross*, but they still have the ability to choose other, better selves. This is essentially the moral dilemma facing Ben: which self will he pick? The moment of truth is not incidentally related to 9/11—as Ben prefers to see it, calling 9/11 his "meal ticket"—but eschatologically. When Ben cannot tell Abbey how he feels about 9/11 and the whole "morality" thing, it is not because the catastrophe is undescribable, but because Ben's ethical consciousness is stagnant. Wanting it all, he has been happy not to choose between his wife and his boss/mistress. His physical attitude, sitting in the same place on the sofa, unanswered cell phone in hand, unable to leave the apartment, provides a visual trope for his frozen conscience. But the attack has suddenly provided a moment of unexpected, low-risk opportunity, and so Ben deliberates. If Abbey will leave her home, better job, larger income, and pension, and flee the city to live illegally under assumed names, he will allow his family to think he died in the attack. He defends the view in accidentally religious terms:

> Doesn't mean I'm not torn up about this, that it doesn't, you know, cover my soul... It "moves" me, if course it does! But we gotta look at the implications here, What it means to us, our future (2003, 15).

Lest the audience fail to connect Ben's cynicism and opportunism with part of the American national psyche, he does so in the very next speech:

> Do you honestly think we're not going to rebound from this? And I don't just mean you and me, I'm saying the country as a whole. Of course we will. We'll do what it takes, go after whomever we need to, call out the tanks and shit, but we're gonna have the World Series, and Christmas and all the other crap that you can count on in life. We do it every year, no matter what's happened

or is going on, we still go to the movies and buy gifts and take a two-week vacation, because that's-the-way-it-is. (Beat.) I'm not making light of anything either. When I say that, or making excuses for what we decided...you know...this is not about that. I'm saying the American way is to overcome, to conquer, to come out on top. And we do it by spending and eating and screwing our women harder than anyone else (16).

He goes on to say that while 9/11 is a national disaster, it will fade from attention the "next time the Yankees win the pennant" (16), an observation that sounds cynical but has been borne out in the diminished attention to the victims of the Asian tsunami, the Katrina hurricane, and the Haiti earthquake.

The Mercy Seat works against two constructions of 9/11: one, that the world changed the moment the plane hit the side of the building, and, the other, that the American response was one of quiet heroism to the unbelievable horror. Indeed, report of the 9/11 Commission was entitled Heroism and Horror, and its lucid presentation of the many factors affecting the first responders reads as an understated account of uncommon bravery. Nevertheless, the double construction—9/11 as exceptional and as heroic—was a narrative put to political use. David Simpson addresses this instrumentalization in his book *9/11: The Culture of Commemoration*. He notes that from the start, 9/11 appeared as an "unforeseen eruption across the path of a history commonly deemed rooted in a complacent steady-state progressivism," and within two years, the fall of the towers justified the invasion of Iraq through a process "marked by propagandist compression and manufactured consent so audacious as to seem unbelievable, except that it happened" (2006, 4). Part of this propaganda involved "framing"—the double entendre intended—the dead as uniformly heroic. More needs to be said about such presentation, and the discussion below about Nelson's *The Guys* will revisit this subject, but as a beginning it is useful to recall that however much the intention behind the brief comments in the *New York Times* "Portraits of Grief" series was to avoid elitism and honor each individual loss, what emerged was a photo gallery that tacitly affirmed democratic values and the opportunities associated with American capitalism.[2] For Simpson, the framing in these "portraits of grief" became, in its endless reproduction and recirculation, less an archive of loss and more a piece of evidence for legitimating the political and military response. "The dead," Simpson writes, "have been framed for the purpose of justifying more deaths" (88). That is why, he reminds us, we see only pictures of some of the dead—never of Iraqi casualties and seldom of slain American soldiers. Moreover, the portraits of grief that appeared in the *Times* were never distinct from the paper's economic self-interest. Howell Raines, then editor, explained that the *Times*

"Pulitzer sweep" happened because the writers were going at a "dead run to cover the fast-breaking news of the post-9/11 period" and a group of editors and reporters "invented the Portrait of Grief series," which became in effect a "national shrine" (quoted in Simpson, 39). Tom Englehardt's description of media and government and military planning as the "ur conglomerate" of the 1991 Persian Gulf War shows itself in Raines's language: his paper's commercial success overlaps its patriotism which is at one with nationalist rhetoric. "Instrumentally," as Simpson has concluded, "each facilitates the other" (40).

Simpson begins his book by asking the question, "Who has an interest in claiming" that the world changed with 9/11 (1)? LaBute answers this question: everyone. *The Mercy Seat* contests the portrayal of 9/11 as a representative occasion of the selfless and sacrificing American character. Rather, the play depicts the avaricious and amoral Ben as a man for whom 9/11 opened doors. When Abbey tells Ben about following a woman who is posting pictures of her missing loved one, he refuses either to imagine his wife's desperation about his whereabouts or to think of how he might aid the truly bereaved. Handing out candy bars, he tells Abbey, won't do any good, and it will blow his cover and their chance for happiness. In *The Mercy Seat*, America's exceptionalism is not the democratic values that are practiced by its quiet heroes and productive citizens, it is the economic, personal, and political opportunities that are available to those who will seize them. Theatre critic John Lahr has noted that LaBute feels drawn to restoration comedy for its depiction of amorality and privilege, of "well-to-do people with time on their hands, who go around hurting each other, doing things that are pretty unpleasant, just because the opportunity presented itself" (2006, 12). In *The Mercy Seat*, 9/11 is one such opportunity.

Various reviewers have compared LaBute's play to Edward Albee's *Who's Afraid of Virginia Woolf?* and rightly so since Abbey and Ben are as accomplished and vicious sparring partners as George and Martha. But in these latter-day American icons, each of whom also have pilgrim names, there is little vestige of whatever brought them together. In the dry hours of their dwindling affections, Abbey and Ben are as greedy, cruel, and assaultive as George and Martha but without the latter's painful awareness of what their games and fabrications cost. LaBute's title suggests, with cruelty and irony, that 9/11 might serve these two self-absorbed characters as a mercy seat: as a place of atonement and grace. As much as it is about no-cost opportunism, *The Mercy Seat* is also about the possibility of salvation, as long as salvation is a conscious, ethical choice. Abbey—who has felt herself demeaned by her own hypocrisy, by Ben's indecisiveness, even by a humiliating style of lovemaking—finally makes a stand. She will sacrifice everything only on the condition that Ben call his family and tell them he is alive. In finally recognizing and refusing her own complicity, Abbey makes a moral choice; she is the character who can leave the apartment to see what harm has befallen her coworkers, to walk among the bereaved and through the devastation. Like Albee's play, LaBute's is a state-of-the-union play, both politically and sexually, one that calls out for a thorough self-reckoning—about our illusions, our insularity, our freedom, and our amorality.

LaBute's examination of selfishness and sacrifice intersect with one of the most dominant discursive formations that rose up around 9/11: the assertion that all the dead victims were heroes. Certainly, the police, firefighters, and coworkers who reentered the inferno or put the lives of others before their own deserve to be called heroic. But the slippage between the first term, victim, and the second, hero, becomes problematic when the agency and choice involved in heroism is nullified. As Simpson has observed: this "desperate urge to assure us that these deaths were not in vain, that they were exalted and dignified sacrifices in a great cause, does service to no one—to neither the dead nor the living. It is an inhibition on inquiry, an effort to foreclose attention to the historical circumstances in which they occurred" (2006, 49). Jean Baudrillard takes this argument a step further. While not denying the suffering and death that 9/11 brought about, he points out the speciousness in reasoning that if we contend that "the voluntary martyrdom of the suicide bombers proves nothing," then "the involuntary martyrdom of the victims of the attack proves nothing either." Like Simpson—and LaBute—Baudrillard protests using the victim's deaths to build the case for war, saying there is "something unseemly and obscene" in making such an argument (2002, 24).

Nelson's play *The Guys*, written in just nine days and performed within two months of the attacks, is therefore all the more remarkable for how it avoids trivializing the notion of heroism. Its simple presentation—performatively, linguistically—rebukes the hyperbole of the speech Rudolf Giuliani gave at about the same time the play premiered, when he declared that Ground Zero will be remembered as great battlefield some thousand years hence (quoted in Simpson 2006, 47). Instead, the play, a surprising hit, offered the moving experience of what can be accomplished by listening attentively to stories that served no other purpose than to mourn the dead.

"New York. My beautiful, gleaming...wounded city" (Nelson 2002, 7). Such are the opening words of Nelson's play, set 12 days after the attacks. It is an important work for several reasons, not least of which is how quickly it appeared, and how well it captured the raw, personal grief before it became woven into a national narrative with a political end. Because both grief and memorialization would quickly be politicized and thus foreclosed, *The Guys*, like the impromptu memorials that sprang up all over New York, initially provided a site for deeply felt pain before such emotions were directed into behaviors (such as President Bush's infamous "go shopping" advice) and before other sites were constructed, such as the viewing platform that Mayor Giuliani opened on December 30, 2001, inviting all Americans to come and experience "all kinds of feelings of sorrow and the tremendous feelings of patriotism" (Lentricchia and McAuliffe 2003, 103). Without making too large a claim about its therapeutic value, since the period allowed for dialogue, and questioning was closed down by the decision to go to war, it is fair to say that the achievement of this drama was to honor the grief-stricken without appropriating their loss. This accomplishment relied on three important factors. The first was Nelson's insistence that images of the attacks be excluded from the staging. The second involved providing a place for and a vision of community—of fellowship forged through shared loss—that did not encourage the community to transmute injury into insularity and hyperpatriotism. To this end, the play's emphasis on ordinary duty, as opposed to exceptional heroism, was key. The third was to find a way to particularize grief without installing a collective narrative that immediately politicized the pain or referenced views coined in the media. In this, Nelson's insistence on bare staging kept the focus on one character speaking and one listening, and on their shared effort to say something true.

The play is autobiographical: it is the story of a writer who assisted the captain of a firehouse in composing eulogies for firefighters who died in the World Trade Center attacks. Joan, the play's writer, observes there was no feasible sequence of events that would have brought Nick, the captain, into her life, but after "September 11th, all over the city, people were jumping tracks" (2002, 16). The story derives from Nelson's own account of the play's beginnings. A journalism professor at Columbia, Nelson heard that a fire captain needed help, and she volunteered her services. Later, she was seated at a charity function next to Jim Simpson, the artistic director of *The Flea*, a theatre located near Ground Zero. In the course of their conversation, he asked Nelson to try her hand at writing a play based on her conversations with the captain. *The Guys* was first performed on December 4, 2001, with Simpson's wife, Sigourney Weaver, in the role of Joan, and Bill Murray as Nick. The play has been performed in 48 states since 2001, and it was restaged at The Flea in 2006 in commemoration of the fifth anniversary of the attacks. Like Tony Kushner's brief play *Only We Who Guard the Mystery Shall be Unhappy,* Nelson's play became a vehicle for star-turns, with well-known actors taking parts in the New York and Los Angeles productions.

The Guys is staged very simply, and indeed the simplicity is the source of its strength. The two characters sit in arm chairs and talk. Joan prompts Nick to describe his men, and as he does so, she forms his words into moving tributes that accurately describe the dead even as they preserve Nick's voice.

Occasionally, Joan breaks the fourth wall to speak directly to the audience. There are no images of the planes crashing into the towers, no scenes of the wreckage, and no portraits of the dead firemen. Nelson wanted the play to "give comfort through language," and so she guarded against the audience being retraumatized by visual images. She also resisted the enchantment of the visual, the pull the visual has on viewers that draws them into the excesses of the image. The lives of the men who have died and the empathetic witness Joan offers to Nick are the focus of the play, and in service to the expression of direct emotion, Nelson spends little time on causes or consequences. The captain is stunned and sorrowful, but mostly he is anxious to provide solace to his men's families and to affirm the meaningfulness of the firemen's lives. In the main, Nelson guards against introducing anything that would dilute the expression of raw grief and real compassion. There is, then, no plot as such, just stories exchanged, though by the end of the play, positions have been reversed: Joan is distraught and Nick is consoling.

The play does in fact begin with the first-person narrative Butler discusses as culpable for narrowing the focus of the event into something egocentric and divisive. But in Nelson's play, the first-person narrative is used to establish Joan's helplessness and to indicate how even for those close to Ground Zero, experiences were immediately screened. Joan recounts that her father called her from Oklahoma to tell her to turn on the television, and so she "joined the witnesses of the world" and watched the second plane hit. But *The Guys* reevaluates the term "witness" as much as it does "heroism" since its performance modeled not the scopophilia of watching a spectacle but the empathetic witness necessary to interrupt the endless loop of melancholia and repetitive trauma. It also depicts the distress that comes with listening and entering into the pain of another. Arguably, *The Guys* is considerably less accomplished than other works that express immediate grief, such as John Millington Synge's *Riders to the Sea* or any of Euripides's plays. *The Guys* lacks their poetry and ritual, and clearly does not wish to invoke fate, but in performance, its plainness is its virtue, standing in contrast to the empty rhetoric or ready-made clichés that were already saturating the public. Nelson raises some complex issues: how does one mourn an absent body? How can individual merit be recognized amid so many casualties? How can the grief-stricken begin to understand that an event so personal will be dispassionately dissected or cynically manipulated? The play implicitly acknowledges how images of the dead stand in for the absent, irretrievable body, and also how those same images can be made into codes for a way of life rather than a particular, precious life. It does not explore these issues in depth, as if to pursue these larger issues would be disrespectful to the work of mourning, but it does raise them subtly. Mostly, *The Guys* succeeds on communitarian and activist terms. It validates storytelling and deep listening as important processes for working through trauma, and it does so without imposing a political agenda on the act of speaking. While the play gestures toward the ultimate need to understand the collective trauma through some historically informed lens, it retains its focus on individual pain, refusing to mythologize it into heroic terms that deny its ordinary particularity. It shows that listening has a cost: that vicarious trauma can occur as one opens one's self to another's pain. But in its delicate and honest depiction of how sentimentalism or empty empathy—Ann Kaplan's term for empathy that does not cost anything (2005, 21)—are counterproductive to both individual and national healing, *The Guys* suggests that relief from pain requires an interdependency that is itself a civic virtue.

If *The Guys* offered a forum through which empathetic listening quelled some of the anguish felt after the attacks, another play, *Omnium Gatherum*, which premiered at the Humana Festival in Louisville in 2003, allowed its spectators an evening of unexpected comic relief through a different kind of listening: one where they might well be overhearing themselves or listening with new ears to opinionated drivel passed off as thoughtful analysis. Coauthored by Theresa Rebeck and Alexandra Gersten-Vassilaros, *Omnium Gatherum* derives much of its charge from recognizing how the guests at an exclusive New York dinner party parody public figures from Martha Stewart to Edward Said. Although written in advance of the reality shows that focus on social climbing/celebrity culture, it employs much of the same manic energy, as the talk around the dinner table veers between pondering and pandering. The common man is represented by the fireman who is also the only person to have done anything beside think about the unanswerable questions of religious discord, imperialism, and terrorism. These global divides are replicated in miniature by the small antagonisms that arise among the rest of the guests, all of whom have been chosen by the hostess/social arbiter to add a social frisson to the evening. The differences between the conservative writers and radical scholars, the vegans and carnivores, men and women, blacks and whites are, however, soothed over by exquisite food and lots and lots of liquor. The play is more farce than parody, especially when the audience learns that the evening's pièce de résistance is the final guest: an actual terrorist—and real violence threatens to erupt. Fortunately, the dinner party seems to be taking place in an other-worldly spot between heaven and hell, and at least one of the guests is already dead, so little harm can be done, and the play, surprisingly, turns its reverence for food, travel, talk, and, most of all, company into something close to life-affirming. It seems that the blessing offered at the start of the meal—of gathering "in the hope of understanding and fellowship"—is partially realized (2003, 13).

Even Mohammed is included in the final image: he eats appreciatively while the others dance.

Omnium Gatherum is a clever but slight work that veers between two poles: the need to face ourselves and the need to face the enemy. It succeeds at facing ourselves: all the guests are revealed as self-contradictory and self-interested but reconcilable members of the human race, but the portrait of the enemy is wildly domesticated. He abandons ideology for a good meal, and though it is this dream of common humanity that brings as much relief as the witty barbs and comic characters, it does little to really understand incommensurable difference. On a small scale, *Omnium Gatherum* wants its spectators, however different their lives may be from the gathering of the chic guests, to come to the same conclusion about sitting down with each other. But though the play talks about radical differences, it offers diversions, not solutions. When a stalemate is reached or anger erupts, another dinner course is served, and tempers are appeased. While *Omnium Gatherum* makes no claim about solving global crises, it implicitly suggests that any culture, religion, or government that silences dissent is not a guardian of freedom.

Each of these plays attempted to interrupt the hypernationalist discourse that grew in response to 9/11. But nothing could halt the will to retaliate, since any measured response was overshadowed by the menacing figure of the terrorist and the hysteria of the anthrax scares. Both the terrorist and the terrorist event exist simultaneously in the realms of the symbolic and the real, and in the week following 9/11, the question of the real and the symbolic arose again, in deadly form. From September 18 and for a few weeks afterward, dust that fell from letters mailed to several news and media outlets and to two senators was found to be anthrax, a deadly chemical. Ultimately, the FBI concluded the anthrax scares were the work of an American microbiologist, but the letters included the language of the terrorists: "You cannot stop us. You die now. Death to America; Death to Israel. Allah is Great." In a profound sense, it did not matter if Al-Qaeda had sent the anthrax that killed five people and infected many more: terrorists benefited from the hysteria. However much the guests at the *Omnium Gatherum* dinner party made the alleged terrorist feel welcome, nothing could eclipse the menacing face of the terrorists. That face belonged to two men: Osama bin Laden and Mohammed Atta. Facing them and the terror they instill is the subject of the following chapter.

CHAPTER 5

FACING TERROR

> Reality and fiction are inextricable, and the fascination with the attack is primarily a fascination with the image.
> —Jean Baudrillard (2002, 28–29)

AMERICAN PROPAGANDA LEAFLETS DISTRIBUTED THROUGHOUT AFGHANISTAN depicted a rictus-faced Osama bin Laden, half-flesh, half-skeleton. Though the caricature was meant to warn Afghanis not to shield the terrorist, it depicted the Al-Qaeda leader as a terrifying shape-shifter. His elusiveness, invisibility, and terrifying mutability intersected with the most profound concern that terrorism cannot really be fought or ever met face-to-face. His death in 2011 inspired further fears of perpetual retaliation.

In contrast to the near-mythic status of bin Laden, other experiences in the war have an unsettling banality. Journalist Ghaith Abdul-Ahad, reporting for the *Guardian*, describes a morning in Fallujah, Iraq, when he found himself in the company of a Yemeni man who had come to join the insurgents. They were joined by other insurgents who, upon learning that the writer was not a Muslim, asked, "Why don't we kill him" in the same tone, as Abdul-Ahad describes it, as "Why don't you have a cup of tea?" (Hoyt et al. 2007, 95).

These two anecdotes encapsulate the prevailing anxiety about terrorism: on the one hand, it is elusive but ubiquitous; on the other, it is close by but deceptive. Because we cannot be sure of what is "real," the real is actually enlarged by projections of the imaginary. In this formula, there is an awful complicity, as Jean Baudrillard recognized when he wrote, "At a pinch, we can say that they *did* it, but we *wished for* it" (2002, 5). Baudrillard is characteristically ambiguous and provocative here, leaving unspecified how we wished for it: was it through our global political designs? The new imperialism of globalization? The imaginary, in film and television of disaster scenarios? Regime change? Or more simply, is it impossible, as Baudrillard suggests, not to anticipate our destruction because "no one can avoid dreaming of the destruction of any power that has become hegemonic to this degree" (5)?

James Der Derrian has commented that most approaches to terrorism focus on either its psychological dimension or its organizational structure and, therefore, important aspects of its motivation and execution are insufficiently examined, especially its connection to the imaginary (2009b). He contends that the terrorist event of unpredictable, randomized violence depends "more on the intangible power of menacing symbols than on techniques of physical violence to achieve their goals" (73). Der Derrian gives the name "mytho-terrorism" to this new and lethal blend of the imagined and the real, and it is notable that the "imagined" is in the past tense, since terrorism builds its power on latent fears and catastrophic scenarios as much as it does on an unexpected act of physical violence. "Mythology and terrorism fuse when imagined solutions to intractable problems are pursed through new or unconventional rituals of violence," Der Derrian writes, and perhaps what is "new" about twenty-first century terrorism is its manipulation of past memories or cultural images of the horrific, which have been circulated through media, accessible on the Internet, and archived in films (73). In the contemporary experience, a sense of the surreal occurs because the terrorist act takes spectators out of time. Like Henri Bergson's notion of the *duree*, where various states of time are psychically experienced simultaneously, September 11 plunged its captive viewers into an awful déjà vu of a disaster scenario even as it froze the present moment of the horrific (the falling man; the plane's nose in the building) and fast-forwarded to a sense of an irrevocably damaged future. This temporal simultaneity or timelessness is the result of an aesthetics of shock, an "agro-effect" as Edward Bond might term it. Or it shares the aesthetics of the Theatre of Cruelty in which Artaud's dream that viewers would see his "real body bursting into fragments/collected under 10,000 notorious looks as a new body which you'll never be able to forget."[1]

To think about timelessness is to think about the sublime both as the effect produced on viewers and the motivation of the actors. Mytho-terrorism, Der Derrian points out, is propelled by forces that are "eschatological and millenarianistic: that is, they join redemption, social change, and cathartic violence in the pursuit of a new era" (2008, 74). Frank Lentricchia and Jody McAuliffe have identified analogous preoccupations in the romantic dream of awakening the world through transgressive art, and thereby transforming it. Indeed, many critical theorists and philosophers—from Terry Eagleton to Paul Virilio and Jean Baudrillard—have spoken of the excesses of the terrorist act in terms applicable to both religious and literary imaginations, arguing that it is dangerous to overlook the ritualized, aesthetic character of this kind of political violence. Agreeing that historic rationales need to be supplemented, Baudrillard contends, "No ideology, no cause—not even the Islamic cause—can account for the energy which fuels terror" (2002, 10). As opposed to material explanations of terrorism, the approach that combines the analytical resources of aesthetics, religion, and trauma studies comes closer to understanding something that goes beyond economic or political grievance. Terry Eagleton has noted:

> Terrorism is not political in any conventional sense of the term and as such poses a challenge to the left's habitual modes of thought. The left is at home with imperial power and guerilla warfare, but embarrassed on the whole by the thought of death, evil, sacrifice, or the sublime. Yet these and allied notions... are germane to the ideology of terror as more mundane or material conceptions (2005, iv).

Eagleton explores the "affinity between terror and the sacred" because "terror begins as a religious idea, as indeed much terrorism is today; and religion is all about deeply ambivalent powers which both enrapture and annihilate" (2). It is not, however, difficult to connect the two views: the romantic artist substitutes his own creative power and his larger sense of the intrinsic force of the imagination for the ambivalent power of the sacred. The romantic artists, like the follower of Dionysus, will surrender to rapture and nihilism. Der Derrian agrees that on the borderline where rational and irrational uses of violence meet, the "intelligibility of terrorism is more likely to be discerned by a mythical reading than by a rational analysis" (2009b, 74).

One might think that after 9/11, theatre artists would produce works that draw on their understanding of aesthetic categories, such as the sublime, or their familiarity with literary antecedents that engaged thematically, even if not formally, the experience of terror, cathartic violence, revolutionary irrationality, religious fervor, ethical transgressiveness—of life *in extremis*. But in the main, the theatrical response to terrorism has not attempted something like John Adams's 1991 opera, *The Death of Klinghoffer*, which reimagined the 1985 terrorist killing of a Jewish American businessman, Leon Klinghoffer, by hijackers from the Palestinian Liberation Front. For understandable reasons—particularly the obscene scale of the attacks in the United States—restaging the violent and excessive aspects of terrorism risks retraumatizing victims and spectators. Then there are the daunting challenges of representing the event without diminishment or aggrandizement or trying to find an equivalent response to what Karlheinz Stockhausen controversially called the "greatest work of art that is possible in the whole cosmos."[2] Despite these difficulties, several playwrights have attempted to understand the mentality of the terrorist and the dynamics of terrorism. Allan Havis's *Three Nights in Prague* imagines the time spent in Prague by

Mohammed Atta, one of the hijackers. Robin Soans's *Talking to Terrorists* constructs a typology of the figure of the terrorist/freedom fighter. Their approaches are opposites of each other: Havis's play tries to imagine Atta's psyche even as it probes the rumored meeting between Atta and a member of the Iraqi government; Soans's play, a montage of politicians and insurrectionists, wants to comprehend the political motivation beneath terrorist activity. Representing terrorism as a new kind of conflict and the anxieties that it fuels and draws upon is undertaken in two plays by Caryl Churchill: *Far Away* and *A Number*. These works take an indirect approach, but as always, Churchill finds potent theatrical equivalents for dread and violence, the most salient features of terrorism. Together, these four plays take up the fundamental questions about terrorism. Who would be drawn to suicide terrorism? How does the terrorist act mesmerize its executor? What is the social profile of a potential terrorist? How does terrorism terrify?

Frank Lentricchia and Jody McAuliffe close their book, *Crimes of Art and Terror*, by imagining a dialogue between the nineteenth-century German playwright Heinrich von Kleist and the twenty-first century Egyptian hijacker Mohammed Atta, one an artist who commits suicide and the other, a suicide pilot. This pairing follows the pattern they used throughout their study, in which they juxtaposed case studies, taken from both fictional and the real sources, in order to shed light on the intersections of aesthetics and terrorism. Their closet drama attempts to imagine the experience of sublimity that both transgressive art and terrorism provoke.

In the conversation between von Kleist and Atta, each man recounts an achievement of limitlessness, that is, of the sublime. Von Kleist, who has drawn his lover, Henrietta Vogel, into the murder-suicide pact, recounts the artful care with which they arranged themselves in a shallow trench. He fires a shot through her left breast and then puts the pistol inside his own mouth because "this is where my voice originates." He shoots, and time slows immeasurably so that he can feel and know each transformative instant of his action:

> I drop the pistol at my feet, rest my hands on my knees, and feeling the one-third ounce piece of lead impact the bone behind my uvula, I clench my teeth so tightly, they will need an iron lever to pry my mouth open to find the cause imbedded in my brain, because I have nothing more to say. From the moment she and I sat down together, I know I am dying and my vision is complete (2003a, 167–168).

Atta's response also describes how time slows and stops:

> In the instant the nose (not the wing) of the plane touches the tower I have time to travel to Jerusalem, rise into the seven heavens where I speak with

angels, prophets, and Allah, visit the fiery Gehenna, and return in time for my obliteration. I have no desire outside of this moment. We concur that the end of time is all (2003a, 168).

For both men, the experience of sublimity is an experience of completeness. For von Kleist, the artistic vision can never be complete while he is alive; for Atta, the moment of death is a sacred wholeness that allows him to abandon all other desires. Eagleton describes the sublime as a "rhythm of death and resurrection as we suffer a radical loss of identity only to have that selfhood more richly restored to us. These fearful powers blot us out into a kind of nothingness, yet like God this is a fertile rather than a barren void, since to suffer the loss of all of our distinguishing features is to be granted an epiphany of pure selfhood" (2005, 44). The ecstatic unloosening of life's grip, the unbound spirit now limitless and whole—these are the seductions of sublime self-sacrifice. How can we comprehend such consciousness? Clearly, only partially or analogically, but Lentricchia and McAuliffe's work makes the desire comprehensible and recognizably within the realm of human emotion and aspiration.

Some might argue that while it is unethical to characterize the suicide terrorist as a barbarian or inhuman monster—though undoubtedly the act is monstrous—it is also wrong to romanticize a criminal. Turning innocent humans into cargo carried by an assault vehicle is clearly criminal and deeply immoral, but it is not an action taken in a social void. Eagleton, like Lentricchia and McAuliffe, reminds us that "terrorism and the modern democratic state were twinned at birth," though in "the era of Danton and Robespierre, terrorism began life as state terrorism" not a "strike against sovereignty by its faceless foes" (1). If there is an intimacy between terrorism and the modern democratic state, it accordingly demands that the line demarcating the barbaric from the civilized be reinspected. For Eagleton, the difference in conservative, liberal, and radical views about the relationship of civilization and barbarism is epitomized in how magnificent sites, such as Chartres, are regarded. The radical, he suggests, concludes that Chartres was built on an exploitation that in the end was not worth the cost; the conservative is skeptical about the extent of exploitation, and the liberal decries the mistreatment but thinks the end result was worth the cost (14). "The same goes for political terrorism," Eagleton contends:

> It is not a matter of offering Osama bin Laden a seat in Parliament, but of granting justice to those who might otherwise exact a terrible revenge. Justice is the only prophylactic for terror (15).

Until (or if ever) such justice can be achieved, the terrorist and the terrorist/ artist continue to disrupt the prevailing order through gestures that demand complete attention and therefore rationalize terrorism's tactics. The thinking, according to Eagleton, proceeds along these lines:

> At the root of your so-called reason, so terror proclaims to orthodox political society, lies the ravenous unreason of greed, power, and exploitation, none of which can be rationally justified... and this so-called rationality deploys an ungovernable violence in its defense, In rejecting rational politics, we shall expose the violence at the root of your civilization (55).

So far, two reasons for suicide terrorism have been suggested. In the first instance, suicide terrorists feel the pull of ultimate meaningfulness (experienced as a kind of completion) by willingly surrender to an immense moment of signification. In the second, terrorism assails hegemony. Both explanations assume a high degree of political awareness and conscious commitment. But what experiences would form such political consciousness—what precedes political convictions? These are the questions that Allan Havis and Robin Soans take up.

Allan Havis's 2003 play, *Three Nights in Prague*, attempts to understand how a young person chooses to become a suicide bomber and, even more particularly, what this person's mind looks like after it has committed itself to this path. The achievement of Havis's play is to depict a mind that becomes so saturated with a religious/political viewpoint that it is impenetrable, even to itself. The play begins with a prologue that is drawn from the text of Mohammed Atta's actual 1996 will. He steps forward to announce what he wants to happen after his death:

> I am Mohamed El Amir Awad El Sayed. I believe that the prophet Mohamed is God's messenger and God will resurrect those in their graves. I want my family and everyone who reads this will to fear Almighty God and don't fall to deception and to follow God and his prophets. I don't want any women to go to my grave at all during my funeral. In my memory, I want all people to do what the prophet Ibrahim told his son to do, to die as a good Muslim (186–187).

What follows does not unfold in chronological order: it is an account of three nights Atta purportedly spent in Prague, meeting with an Iraqi consulate official, Ahmed al-Ani. This meeting was supposed to have occurred in April, five months before the attacks, but subsequent intelligence has concluded that the meeting did not take place (Crewdson 2004, 29). Havis is interested in two issues that were topics of intense speculation: what kind of person is motivated to become a suicide bomber? And what would a meeting between an Iraqi official and an Al-Qaeda member look like, especially given the insistence by the Bush administration that the two were intimately connected?

Three Nights in Prague was staged in four venues, but as Havis describes in his introduction, there was a reluctance to produce a play as potentially incendiary as a portrait of the lead suicide bomber. Few can argue, however, against the view that Atta remains a fascinating, even hypnotic, personality, due in large part to the vast circulation of his portrait. His face—unsmiling, intense, vacant-eyed—commands as much interest as any other portrait from 9/11, and except for those of Osama bin Laden and Saddam Hussein, Atta's visage is the most recognizable. For many, Atta's face is as much a portrait of evil as the faces of the World Trade Center victims were portraits of grief, and those of the firemen, portraits of heroism. We are, then, regardless of the actual events in Prague, back in the realm of mytho-terrorism, asking what kind of child grows up to be Atta. *Three Nights in Prague* attempts to dramatize a psychohistorical explanation of the War on Terror by exploring what aspects of personality and background made someone susceptible to bin Laden's mission, but also, albeit implicitly, why Americans were so ready to give credence to a fairly unlikely alliance between Al-Qaeda and Iraq.

One thing Atta is not, in Havis's play, is a psychopath, and research by political psychologists has shown that few suicide bombers are, since weeding out the mentally unbalanced is critical to achieving the mission's objectives. Atta, arguably, fits into a group that Emile Durkheim classified as an "altruistic suicide."[3] The purpose of Atta's visit to Prague, in Havis's imagination, is to convince the Iraqi consul to join the attack against the United States by providing biochemical weapons, a transponder, or cash. The consul, a real person named Ahmed al-Ani, argues that Hussein is not interested in collaborating with the "stateless, lawless, and friendless" bin Laden, whom he believes hates "all Arab governments, except the Taliban" (2010, 186–187). Moreover, al-Ani objects to any similarities posed between the two leaders: Hussein is a "brilliant tactician" whereas bin Laden is a "hypocrite" who preys on the weak and "fucks sheep" (206). He also highlights the differences between the way each side practices its religious beliefs: al-Ani says he laughs at religious zealots. But though he scorns Atta's belief in paradise and the virgins awaiting him there, he cannot unsettle Atta's cold religious conviction.

Three Nights in Prague attempts to imagine an unproven event that nonetheless became part of the intelligence that Douglas Feith, then undersecretary for defense, supplied to the US Senate Intelligence Committee. If the Prague visit had been proven, Cheney, in particular, would have had his *causus belli* and evidence of what he claimed were direct ties between Hussein and Al-Qaeda (Blanche 2004, 15). In the pained atmosphere after 9/11, Americans sought desperately for explanations, and some 70 percent believed the Hussein was involved in the attack (17). Though this meeting was later discredited, and Atta was shown to have been in the United States during the time he was supposedly seen in the Czech Republic, Cheney never backed off his insistence on the connection until he was out of office. Havis's play portrays some of the self-evident inconsistencies of a link between Hussein and bin Laden. Other than a mutual hatred of the United States, their political/ideological goals diverged, but these differences were covered over in an American attitude of Arab culture as undifferentiated. The Middle East was depicted routinely as a place where the "cynical elite" vie with the fervid "Arab street" (Lynch 2003, 83). But there is strong evidence—such as the fatwah issued by Yusuf al-Qaradawi and other leading moderates condemning the September 11 attacks as contrary to Islam—of nuanced attitudes toward America even as most Arabs are concerned both about American imperialistic designs in the Middle East and its support for Israel (87). Moreover, as Marc Lynch discusses, although Arabs were deeply concerned about the toll taken on the Iraqi people by American sanctions after 1991, that does not mean they failed to recognize Hussein's role in brutalizing his own citizens. Media coverage and government bellicosity flattened out this more complex portrait of Arab attitudes.

The pertinent question of Havis's play, then, becomes not, What would a meeting between Al-Qaeda and Iraqi representatives look like? but, Why are Westerners so willing to believe in such an alliance? While historical alliances between enemies have often been brokered, the case of bin Laden and Hussein is evidence of a fairly unbridgeable divide. Osama bin Laden singled out the Ba'ath regime in his condemnation of Middle Eastern governments and strongly objected to the invasion of Kuwait, and he also saw Hussein as in the way of establishing an Islamic caliphate (Bapat et al. 2007, 273). Their mutual wariness precluded a shared commitment to wage war against the United States and its allies. As one group of scholars puts it: "Although both Saddam and bin Laden may have been better off with an alliance, neither side was able to cooperate due to the inability of both sides to trust each other" (274). In *Three Nights in Prague*, there is only one scene of the ten in which al-Ani and Atta share the stage, and in it they are consistently in disagreement despite al-Ani's remonstrance, "We have to find how to trust each other, Atta" (Havis 2010, 203). Atta replies that he trusts only Allah. This impassive extremism exasperates al-Ani, and he tells Atta to stop talking "like a fucking ghost" (203). Atta does not wince; he leaves telling al-Ani that he is a coward.

If this scene demonstrates how little effort Americans have taken to understand the differences between religious perspectives and political ideologies, the rest of the play attempts to come to grips with Atta's service to the cause. Perhaps one of the most interesting aspects of Havis's play is that Atta offers little in the way of political propaganda to convince al-Ani to support the cause; his arguments are put forth on the basis of a collective Arab and

Muslim identity and on the basis of the purity of the mission itself. That this is the case sheds light on why a Western emphasis on individual desire and individual agency does not go far in understanding a highly affiliated sense of self. The sense of the self as inextricable from the collective is attached to a specific historical and political milieu, and for Muslim youths, much of this milieu is one of economic and cultural stagnation if not actual deprivation and humiliation. While this profile seems to fit many other suicide bombers, especially the Palestinian suicide bombers and the discouraged young Saudi men whom Lawrence Wright profiles in *My Trip to Al Qaeda* and *The Looming Tower*, it does not describe the lives of Atta and other 9/11 leaders, many of whom were older, employed, and educated. Mark Sageman, a psychiatrist who studied the profiles of four hundred Al-Qaeda members, found that three-quarters of them come from comfortable middle-class and upper-class homes, with 63 percent having attended college (Sageman, 2004). As he observed, these were "the best and the brightest."

By the time Atta travelled to Prague, he had dedicated himself to restoring the Islamic caliphate, the stated goal of Ayman al-Zawahiri, who was bin Laden's second-in-command (Post 2008, 17–18). In committing himself, Atta would have had to "navigate a hierarchy of values in tension" within himself and with others, and in Havis's play, we see these values challenged by all he meets (28). Al-Ani criticizes them directly: he attacks bin Laden's plan, the glorification of martyrdom, the promise of a reward in paradise, the formulaic religious language, the self-abnegation. In each case, as Atta rejects the criticism, he seems something of an automaton—he does not need sleep, he does not make mistakes, he defends the suicides, and he refuses to acknowledge that his plans will kill innocent children. If someone knew him for 20 years, he would still be a stranger, Atta says, because he has no personality. The point is compelling. He appears to have entered the psychological phase of deindividuation in which group norms dominate individual wants. He has reached the end point of negotiations about whether or not to engage in suicide terrorism, and he has accordingly "re-narrativized" all questions in order to achieve "a total resolution" (28). The young man who studied architecture and engineering in Germany and who was described as polite, intelligent, studious, serious, and elegant has disappeared.

But perhaps not completely: such seems to be the revelation of the scenes in which Atta summons a prostitute to his hotel room because he feels permitted to have some pleasure. Here Havis's story becomes complex, not only because of various circles of espionage and distrust, but because of Atta's own secrecy, even to himself, about the nature of his sexual desires. Atta has asked Pavel, a poor Czech who works for al-Ani, to bring him a clean young woman, and in the first scene, the audience meets Dolni, who is actually Pavel's teenage son. We learn later that Dolni is critically ill and needs an expensive operation, and that his father, who knows that Dolni is gay, has sent him to Atta. Both father and son seem to know that Atta may be repressing his own homosexual desires. What is indisputable is that Atta despises women. Dolni successfully seduces Atta, flattering his vanity, but also invites Atta to think of him as both a son and a daughter. In the meantime, while Dolni is with Atta, his father waits downstairs, sure that no sexual act will actually occur. He explains the situation to al-Ani:

> Atta is with a "young woman" who is not "a woman" so he can still feel clean. To his God—Allah—there is no woman in that hotel room. And Allah is happy. Everyone is happy (2010, 213).

In this invention, Havis is borrowing from rumors that Atta's elegance tended toward the effeminate, and that he was a closet homosexual, though others have noted that the absence of women in his life was not at odds with cultural practice.[4] Havis also borrows from suggestions that Atta and his father were at odds, and in one scene, he has Atta confide in Dolni that his father taunted him for being girlish. Pavel and Dolni seem to be able to negotiate Atta's mixture of repressed desire, self-deception, paternal hatred, religious observance, and entitled martyrdom. Havis's point is that Atta's ideological adherence has smothered even the most fundamental self-knowledge. By the end of the play, Atta has shown a human weakness: he wants Dolni to leave the country with him, but Pavel protects his son, and Atta kills Pavel. The play ends with two acts of "love": Atta "loves" Dolni as the wife/lover/son/daughter he needs and so plans to take him into the paradise of sacrifice. Pavel truly loves the son, and despite the ruse of pandering his own flesh and blood, sacrifices his life for his child. Corporeal, human love prevails over mysticism and self-delusion. When Dolni calls the police to say, "This awful monster from Cairo—Mohammed Atta—killed my dear father. And you will do nothing about it" (226), it is his loss that is most felt. It is the true voice of loss that is heard over all of the voices of political strategy, religious ideology, impoverished scheming, and even psychological self-hatred.

The answer to the question of what made Mohammed Atta into a suicide terrorist is not at all conclusive; it is psychologically layered. Unlike the one-dimensional cartoon of fanaticism, Havis offers a nuanced portrait showing Atta's vulnerable youth, his secret self-loathing, the sense of humiliation at the hand of Westerners, the influence of the highly charismatic bin Laden, the gradual acceptability of suicide for the cause, the promise of a rich afterlife, his immersion into such a strong collective identity, and the final point of no return. The specific contribution of Havis's play is not whether or not a meeting in Prague took place, but rather the presentation of what seems unthinkable—the choice of one's own death, and the rationalization the death of others.

If Havis's play attempts to open up the excesses of the terrorist mindset, Robin Soans's *Talking to Terrorists* does the opposite: it tries to explain how one man's terrorist is another's freedom fighter, and it grounds the violence in the twin incitements of poverty and political exclusion. As a verbatim play, one taking directly from recorded interviews, *Talking to Terrorists* should not have a pre-determined thesis: the point is to see what emerges from the research. But documentary drama involves a process of selection and presentation—and hence requires some guiding principle. While this issue is one that will be examined in greater depth in the following chapters, it immediately raises the question of how the advantages and liabilities of an entirely (or largely) imagined theatrical piece compare to the advantages and liabilities of one consisting of public utterance and verifiable events.[5] The answer is case-specific: documentary works like those produced by London's Tricycle Theatre simplify an unwieldy amount of complex material. Other works make audible unheard and unseen voices. *Talking to Terrorists* wants its audience to understand what drives people to commit acts of terrorism; it seeks politically and psychologically credible explanations for this particular kind of violence. Seeking for such rational explanations is the play's strength—and its weakness.

The two producing companies, Out of Joint and the Royal Court Theatre, initially asked David Hare to write the script. He declined to participate because, as he said in an interview with Jenny Hughes, "The moment at which somebody is willing to kill themselves for what they believe is very obscure to me, I don't understand it...I basically didn't want to do that as I felt in advance that I wouldn't succeed, unless I knew I had something to explain about that subject" (quoted in Hughes 2007, 160). Soans did agree to the project, and he and his collaborators conducted interviews around the world. The finished piece juxtaposes the stories of violence committed by state agencies and terrorist groups in Ireland (IRA and UVF), Kurdistan (PKK), Uganda (NRA), and Palestine (AAB).[6] Just as the members of the banned groups are anonymous, the politicians who dealt with the crises or were affected by acts of violence are left unnamed, and the comments of various minor, but real people, are woven in between. The title of the play is taken from a comment made at the play's beginning that "talking to terrorists is the only way to beat them" (Soans 2005, 25).

What does a documentary project about terrorism bring to the subject that an imagined work does not? Posed this way, the query suggests a binary that is not truly defensible. Separating the "real" from the "imagined" or "symbolic" or "mediated" or "virtual," as I have indicated previously, is not possible, and it is an especially reductive move when applied to a phenomenon such as terrorism. On the continuum of "happened" and "fabricated," documentary theatre positions itself closer to the end of factual occurrence. However, critics such as Stephen Bottoms have objected that "unmediated access to 'the real' is not something the theatre can ever honestly provide" (2006, 57). He goes on to suggest that the theatrical self-referentiality that documentary theatre tries to avoid is

> precisely what is required if they are to acknowledge their dual and thus ambiguous status as both "document" and "play." Without a self-conscious emphasis on the vicissitudes of textuality and discourse, such plays can too easily become disingenuous exercises in the presentation of "truth," failing (or refusing?) to acknowledge their own highly selective manipulation of opinion and rhetoric (57).

Bottoms particularly cites Soans's play as glossing over crucial historical and political distinctions among those identified as "terrorists" and using the testimony of several "experts" to prop up a neat psychological explanation about why people become terrorists. Bottoms's views are not only persuasive, they can be extended further. The absence of greater specificity in the construction of the terrorist typology is disturbing. While political psychologists such as Jerrold Post have traced commonalities among terrorists, they also have been careful to point out the differences among terrorism that is political, terrorism that is criminal, and terrorism that is pathological.[7] Their taxonomies are discrete, and Post is especially careful to trace terrorist motivations in terms of nationalist/separatist reasons, social/revolutionary causes, and religious/extremist affiliations. Additionally, there is little acknowledgment in the play about how information technologies have changed global terrorism. Post, for example, insists that a crucial part of understanding terrorism is understanding the distinction between acts that wish to cause substantial violence and acts that are attention-seeking. Finally, *Talking to Terrorists* does not engage sufficiently with suicide terrorism, and it is a fair question to ask whether or not the 9/11 bombers fit into the profile the play establishes. The "mythic" half of "mytho-terrorism" is unaddressed in *Talking to Terrorists.*

While the play does not sufficiently account for the proliferation of terrorism because of mass-mediated images, it builds its persuasiveness on the assertion that what the audience is seeing, gathered from off-the-record comments, is real and true. Four essays on verbatim/documentary theatre are included with the script of *Talking to Terrorists*, and all of these commentaries emphasize authenticity and accountability.[8] The play's direct connection to public events was underscored in the Royal Court's production, which featured a program cover depicting a man carrying a heavy bag on the way to the London Underground. The July 2005 bombing of the London Underground occurred just one week after the London staging of the play, deepening the sense of the play's prescience.[9] Indeed, perhaps one of the reasons why Michael Billington hailed the play as an important theatrical event was its relationship not only to what was happening around the world but also to what was occurring in Great Britain. And certainly its message—that terrorists can be engaged in rational discourse—is reassuring.

In *Talking to Terrorists*, Soans chose not to identify directly the public figures the play includes, though they are fairly easy to recognize, especially in Great Britain. Many audiences would know immediately that S.S.1 is Mo Mowlan, the secretary of state for Northern Ireland, and that S.S.2 is Craig Murray, the British ambassador to Uzbekistan, especially given the notoriety of his second marriage to an Uzbek belly dancer. While it is a defensible dramatic choice to try to keep their celebrity offstage, it is fairly impossible, given the media attention they have received. While Soans's play constructs a typology of terrorists, it is less successful in presenting what motivates the politicians who respond to the terrorists. The Mowlan and Murray figures each introduce one of the play's two acts—Mowlan arguing for direct engagement with terrorists; Murray objecting to selling the British soul for "dross" through the use of torture—and they represent dissident opinions within the political establishment. There is nevertheless something unpersuasive about the imposed anonymity: while it may work to humanize the terrorists, it does not make the easily recognizable politicians equally anonymous or "universal representatives of their organizations" (Innes 2007, 439). Christopher Innes argues that having the unknown terrorist share a stage with the unnamed politician levels them, that "their anonymity also signals that the vilified terrorists and the state authorities are interchangeable (both being reduced to acronyms); and this parallel treatment of government and terrorist organizations underlines a thematic parallel, since one section of the text relates to official violence: terrorism conducted by governments, assassination as policy" (439). I would contend that no such leveling can occur, and that the well-known stories of some, like the kidnapped envoy of the archbishop of Canterbury, Terry Waite, have greater emotional pull, a point made by Innes's account of the positive reception the actor playing the envoy received. The belief that blocking out a name will disturb information abundantly available in the media or on the internet is naive.

From its April 2005 premiere at the Theatre Royal in Bury St. Edmonds to its London production at the Royal Court, *Talking to Terrorists* played at some ten British venues, and for some, it offered a "practical demonstration on stage" of how "terrorism might be defused by talking and listening" (Innes 2007, 440). This formula may seem to be the same as that offered in Anne Nelson's *The Guys*, and in fact the play does suggest that the terrorist is first a trauma victim. Whether Irish or Kurdish, Nigerian or Palestinian, the arc that the play traces is largely the same: the experience of violence and political oppression in their youth led the men and women to join terrorist organizations; their subsequent experience of imprisonment and isolation gave them opportunity to reevaluate their affiliations. Some, such as the IRA and UVF men who converse in the prison library as they are working on university degrees, come to see each other in more humane terms. Others, such as the Nigerian woman who recounts her life of a child soldier, begin to see themselves as pawns of the group they serve. If these stories offer hope, others do not, such as the girl in Bethlehem who is glad that on 9/11 Americans felt the pain that was all too familiar to her. In the final analysis, the face of the enemy depicted in *Talking to Terrorists* is far less frightening and intractable than that imagined either by Havis or by Lentricchia and McAuliffe. The play attempts to install a broader historical perspective about terrorism that is straightforwardly political and sociological, and it rejects the rhetoric of absolute evil. The stance it takes—that communication is possible and necessary; that terrorism is a rational choice—is certainly a more desirable narrative, but its comfort may be as much of a construction as imagining the suicide bomber sharing the stage with the politician.

Terrifying Familiarity

In the final scene of her 2000 play, *Far Away*, Caryl Churchill offers a surreal view of the world ravaged by battle: the warring forces are ethnic, professional, animal, and environmental. Portuguese car salesmen fight Latvian dentists; the French align with the cats; the Venezuelans aid the mosquitoes; the river takes sides. The absurd possibilities initially sound incredible, but they point to a dystopic future of endless conflict among unpredictable, multiplying alliances where the human, natural, and animal worlds all vie for dominance. No settlement will be reached for nothing but dominance is at stake.

The terror that terror produces, Baudrillard's phrase for the replication of the same from the same, is not only the definition of terrorism, it is also the definition of cloning. Both terrorism and cloning generate something—fear, violence, an organ, a sheep, a person—from something smaller. Leveraging symbolic power, like scraping cells, produces something disproportionately greater than the original. Three airplanes produced a ten-year war; the number of people who died on 9/11 (2,995) grew to include over 6,600 military coalition deaths in Iraq and Afghanistan, over 100,000 Iraqi deaths, and an undetermined number of Afghani deaths, estimated between 13,000 and 32,000.

In *A Number*, written in 2002, Churchill abandons the nightmarish, disjointed, surreal dramaturgy of *Far Away* to produce a quieter work about a father talking with his son. The calm is, of course, misleading, and what gradually unravels in the play is a deeply disturbing—terrifying—story that conjoins new fears of biotechnology with old ones of egoism, broken families, damaged selves, and lost chances. The hitch in the family drama is that there is more than one son, in fact there is an unknown number, since they are clones.

The play premiered at the Royal Court under the same director, Stephen Daldry, as *Far Away*. Read in tandem, these plays perform the twinned anxiety about monstrous difference and ubiquitous similarity that has come to define terrorism. Both *Far Away* and *A Number*, despite vastly different styles and tone, articulate the panic that comes with no longer being able to know what is "real." The visible world is unreliable as a known entity; the body is no longer a witness to itself; familial, tribal, or any other kind of bonds are unstable. Ideological warfare has become "terror against terror," and, if Jacques Derrida is right, our response has not killed the virus of terrorism or inoculated ourselves against it. It has developed, in fact, into an autoimmune disorder.[10] Neither *Far Away* nor *A Number* name terrorism as its subject, but both stage its psychic state even as they gesture to its causes and consequences. Churchill followed these plays with two others that are more overtly political (*Drunk Enough to Say I Love You* in 2006 and *Seven Jewish Children—a Play for Gaza* in 2009), underscoring the nature of the earlier critique.

Terror's Production Line

In *Far Away*, the riveting centerpiece of the play is a parade where row after row of manacled prisoners, each wearing a different, outrageously ornate hat, march across the stage, transforming it into a grotesque runway show. Like some prelude to a nightmarish Wimbledon or Kentucky Derby, this moment of epic spectacle interrupts an otherwise intimate, three-character drama in order to showcase some 50 or more prisoners heading to their execution in one-of-a-kind designs. This wordless scene occurs midway through the second act, inserted between the conversations of two hat makers on the verge of romance who discuss low wages, corrupt management, and the ephemerality of their work. Except for a few references—that all but a few hats get burnt with the bodies (2000, 31)—the hat makers, Todd and Joan, are more concerned about their rights as workers than the fate of the hat-wearers. As is often the case in Churchill's plays, the dialogue is elliptical and obscure, suggesting both ignorance and evasiveness. When Churchill abruptly shifts to the parade, it is impossible for an audience member to look with anything but helpless fascination at a display of economic and social disjuncture that is most disturbing precisely because the amazing hats are so diverting and the prisoners are so ordinary. In part, we've never seen anything like it; in part, we've seen it all before.

Such, of course, is the common experience of spectatorship in mediatized postmodernity. On the one hand, there is the "breaking news"—that sudden compelling moment of the new that demands attention—and then there is the already seen—the blitzed story, the podcasts, and YouTube clips—that turn almost every event instantaneously into a rerun. Such is the paradox of the "unprecedented" but "already imagined" disaster of 9/11. The nature of mediated information—its instantaneity, volume, and reach—generates an image pile-up that seems to produce inversely proportioned knowledge and insight. There are several ways to chart theatre's response to public theatricality, one of which is documentary or verbatim theatre such as *Talking to Terrorists* and the works discussed in the next chapter. At the opposite end of the spectrum from documentary theatre, Churchill's *Far Away* is without plot or clear references; its mysterious, elliptical presentation puts into play fragmentary bits of dialogue that raise, albeit most indirectly, issues of conflict, identity, knowability, partisanship, production, consumption, and violence. And while unlike a documentary drama, the obscurity remains at the play's end, the audience leaves the play with a strong sense that the drama just witnessed is "brutally in synch with the troubles of the world at large" (Als 2008, 132). *Far Away* speaks especially to the insight that theatrical performance can offer about public performance. Specifically it addresses the status of visible evidence in the public sphere; the connection between visibility, commodity, and social control, and the link among image, regressive identity politics, and war. The through-line that connects these issues is the unstable relationship between the newly visible—what I will call the evidentiary—and the already codified—the image. Spoken evidence plays, verbatim theatre, and quasidocumentary plays—works such as Gillian Slovo and Victoria Brittain's *Guantanamo: Honour Bound to Defend Freedom* or David Hare's *Stuff Happens*—attempt to supplement or recontextualize the public record of events by explicitly invoking them. *Guantanamo* exposes a situation that has been censored, ignored, or underrepresented, while *Stuff Happens* takes what has been represented in the media—the available pronouncements by major political figures—in order to disclose the unarticulated but operative ideology behind it. These theatrical works concur that information and judgment are compromised through mediatization and seek therefore to provide a fuller account or a more coherent analysis of the facts. Churchill's play, on the other hand, engages the War on Terror not by direct reference but by a combination of faux realism, spectacle, and enigma.

I have tied this power of the image, both iconic and transient, to the events of 9/11 not to install that date as an originary moment, but as a consolidating one. If, as in Chapter 2, we trace the epistemological and, ultimately, ontological effects of image dominance on the public sphere to the first Gulf War in 1991, the first technowar, and then think quickly about how other instances of "global media crisis orchestration" appear randomly until "crises" became the regular, rather than exceptional, component of media coverage, it becomes clear why Der Derrian insisted on adding a third term, "entertainment," to the military-industrial complex. He describes how networked technology has affected evidence and knowledge, noting that while it provides

> new global actors the means to traverse political, economic, religious, and cultural boundaries, how war is fought and peace is made are reapidly changing. Indeed, the rise of global media makes it ever more difficult to maintain the very distinction of war and peace. For the moment, the "West" might enjoy an advantage in surveillance, broadcast media, and military technologies; but the "Rest," including fundamentalist terrorist groups, non-governmental organizations, and anti-globalization activists, have tapped the political potential of networked technologies of information collection, transmission, and storage (2009b, 253).

Der Derrian's description of grasping distinctions between the "incidental, accidental, and intentional" acts of war goes some of the way to describing the epistemological challenges for spectators who themselves inhabit a speculative world. In the first scene in *Far Away*, the child, Joan, comes to her Aunt Harper to say she cannot sleep. It is two in the morning, in a rural area, and we learn that Harper has recently taken Joan in. When Joan reveals that she heard a shrieking sound and went outside to investigate, her aunt puts her off, giving her half-explanations. The dialogue's structure of incrementally revealed statements by one character that are met by diversionary remarks and half-truths until it is impossible to stall the truth is replicated in *A Number*. Both Harper and Salter (the father in *A Number*) evade, defer, or recast the explanations they offer. Incrementally, the audience learns that the noise was not an owl, but a human screaming and that Joan saw her uncle "bundling someone into a shed" from a lorry (2000, 14). Slipping on the blood-stained ground, Joan peers unnoticed into the shed, where she sees more people with blood on their faces and her uncle hitting a man and a children with a metal stick. Her aunt counters each of these partial revelations with a variety of parental responses: the child should not be out of bed; the child did not see things accurately; the child misinterpreted what she saw. In *A Number*, when Bernard/B2 tells Salter that the information he has acquired about the clones does not fit with his father's explanations about his mother's death, Salter also lies and then must modulate the lie again when B2 says something more. Both adults attempt to thwart the quest for the truth by making sweeping generalities: Harper tries the psychology of guilt and heroism: the child will put everyone's life in danger if she talks about what she saw, and Joan must see that her aunt and uncle are "part of a big movement" to "make things better" (2000, 20). Salter repeats that B2 is the "one he wants" and tries to convince him to sue the doctors for stealing his identity.

We are not far, in Churchill's arcadia, from the suburbia in Harold Pinter's *Ashes to Ashes*, where Rebecca wondered what her husband was actually doing to the workers in his factory. Like Pinter's own disturbingly enigmatic dramas about countenancing mass violence, Churchill's play is interested in the language that evades fact and justifies atrocity. Harper's plain speech, like her dress, seems normal and reliable. But like Pinter's brutal businessmen in *New World Order* who feel pure when they torture dissidents, Churchill's ordinary farm aunt believes that she is one of the people "who are putting things right," and that her "soul will expand right into the sky" for doing her "little bit" (20–21).

Harper instructs Joan to believe her explanations rather than what she has seen. To prove her point that the visible is not consonant with the evidentiary—that the one who observes is not automatically the one who witnesses—Harper explains that what appears to be the image of human trafficking—the lorry full of people—is really the image of clandestine escape. It is not what Joan "imagined [she] saw in the dark" (13). The truck is not conveying the captured; it is liberating the victims. Importantly, the audience following the dialogue is split between believing the child and believing the aunt. Importantly, Harper's explanation would not work if the audience member could not picture the very image that Harper describes. We bring to the theatre images of trucks crammed with illegal immigrants, crossing from the south, driven by those who would exploit their poverty and desperation. But we also bring images of American rescue: the same trucks carrying men and women to safety. In Churchill's play, it is not clear what side Harper is on. It is disturbing that she defends the husband who has bloodied a child, but she seems kind to her niece who is, perhaps, too young to know what is going on in the dark shed.

The structure of feeling that the drama produces invokes the anxiety attached to the many ambiguities of the War on Terror. Harper's logic—things are not what they seem—is the essence of the terrorized state when white powder might be anthrax and Leeds neighbors might be Al-Qaeda members. Harper's explanation is also the same defense offered in the aftermath of the Abu Ghraib scandal. When the photos of the humiliated Iraqi prisoners appeared, the implicated soldiers "explained" that these pictures of hooded, naked men were merely shots of fraternity-like hazing. Soldiers giving the "thumbs up" to obviously tortured Iraqi corpses were signaling nothing except they were part of the cell phone/Facebook/digital camera culture of posing, and posting. A child beaten with a metal stick; a hooded, naked prisoner—neither are images of abuse. We wish, like Joan, to believe.

Between the first and second acts, years have passed; Joan has grown up and has found a job in a hat factory. Like her coworker, she feels lucky: there are few positions for those who majored in "hat at college" (23). So Joan works away, creating out-sized, original creations in the subsequent scenes, all the while chatting with an emerging love interest, Todd. He has worked at the hat factory much longer than the recently hired Joan, and though Todd concedes that it is one of "the best jobs," he assures her that she'll soon find out that there's "a lot wrong with this place" (23–24). Todd's list of problems includes the grueling production schedule, the pay, the contracts, and possible undue influence from nepotism. By the third day, Todd's comments are solipsistic: a hat some other boy has made that Joan notices is "derivative," and he is "the only person in this place who's got any principles" (27). When Joan challenges him to do something about the inequities, Todd resolves to confront upper management. Spurred on by his conviction that he is on the moral high ground, Todd confronts the manager. By now, Joan clearly admires Todd, and she offers to resign if Todd is fired even though she has just learned that her hat will be preserved in the company museum as the prizewinner for that year.

Joan and Todd's conversation seems, on the surface, to be as high-minded as that between Harper and Joan. Workers' rights have been raised. Action is being taken against managerial corruption. Yet, although their dialogue is interrupted, not a single remark is made about the parade of shackled prisoners forced to wear the hats, their impending execution, or simply their sheer numbers. Like the canteen they do not visit, Joan and Todd have cordoned off the reality of how their livelihood depends on an economy of death. More hats mean more prisoners. As in the first act, Churchill bewilders the audience by failing to provide necessary explanations. But if in the first act we wonder which character is telling the truth, in this one, we wonder why neither character seems to take notice of a truth larger than their own workplace problems. Since the prisoners appear robotic, it also becomes tempting for the audience to split the gaze unequally in favor of the elaborate hats.[11] Not only do their numbers and their lack of affect dehumanize the prisoners, their acquiescence makes it possible to pull them completely into the unreality of advertisement or display.

In the first act, Churchill suggested the way in which images may be managed for purposes of control. In the second act, Churchill's parade further obfuscates the difference between signs that are connected with the live and the real, and signs that are wholly constructed or "hyperreal." What is the connection between the hatted prisoners and the social realm of which they are a part? Do they point to a state previous to the present one (something to do with why they are shackled, why they are being executed)? Or is this an irrelevant question? Is the status of the prisoners less important than the status of the hats? And what should we make of Todd and Joan's disinterest in the prisoners' well-being even as they view themselves as worker activists?

Certainly *Far Away* insists on recognizing the interdependence of spectacle and consumption. Churchill's images suggest that at the very least, the undesirable members of a community can have some use-value in the new world of globalized capitalism. These outcasts can literally be "model prisoners" by serving out their time as mannequins for products that are disposed of the minute they are seen. With chilling efficiency, disposable populations and disposable products are mutually serviceable. Importantly, the economy invoked in *Far Away* relies on spectatorship, as much as it does production and consumption (in fact, consumption and spectatorship are near equivalences). Todd watches "trials" all night long, and then comes to work to make the hats that will be destroyed once they are seen. Just as the economy seems to be driven by the endless production of things to look at and then discard, this description fits the play's legal system as well. Given no sense of why people are put on trial, the audience knows only that their hearings are aired every night. Hence, if the hat economy relies on innovation for no purpose but spectatorship, the legal system seems to exist only to litigate who belongs to the watched, criminal class and who belongs to the entitled watchers. The "trials" establish a time-table for dealing with the nonproductive. In this divided society, the class most at risk is the workers like Joan and Todd who cannot access the safe regions of upper management and fear, to the point of denial, joining the ranks of the mannequin population.

Given this vulnerability, it is possible to make some sense of why Todd and Joan concern themselves with the corruption in their workplace but fail to confront the dynamics that have produced mass executions. At least two possibilities offer themselves. The first, is that neither Todd nor Joan can step outside the close parameters of his or her "wholly administered" milieu. However much Todd and Joan may think they have some agency, the play suggests that their world is the one-dimensional dystopia forecasted by Herbert Marcuse: one that is flattened by consumerism, bureaucracy, and media dominance to the extent that "the very aptitude for critical thinking and oppositional behavior" has atrophied (quoted in Kellner 1998, 391). Hence, the language of "rights" in which Todd takes refuge offers only a simulation of agency, as false as Harper's promise that Joan's life will be raised up if she affiliates herself with the right cause.

The question of agency is broached in the final scene. It takes place several years later, back at Harper's house. There, Todd and Harper are waiting for Joan to wake up; she has apparently been walking for hours, after trying to escape a war. Already, the audience is mystified: how has the apparently progressive Todd become linked to the apparently regressive Harper? The seeming contradiction is insignificant when compared to the meteorite shower of identity politics that Churchill rains down on the audience. The "faux-realism" of the first act gives way completely to the surreal and enigmatic: cats are killing babies in China, and the ants have teamed up with the Moroccans. Other coalitions have formed: the Canadians, Venezuelans, and mosquitoes are allies; the engineers, chefs, children under five, and musicians are another group. Sometimes Latvian dentists seem trustworthy, but who knows for sure? Deer are especially seductive. Crocodiles are always evil. The ultra-certain Harper has lost her bearings: she tells Todd she would like to trust him, now that he is married to Joan and is family, but maybe he really "does not know right from wrong" (42). Finally Joan appears, and the play ends on her long account of her journey back home. Everyone was travelling, she says, so others may have believed she was on a mission, and since on her way back she "killed two cats and a child under five, it wasn't that different from a mission" (43). As if it was not enough that all of creation has split itself into smaller identity groups—nationalities, animals, professions—and formed unpredictable alliances, now the weather has taken sides. All manner of weapons have been deployed: coffee, heroin, hairspray, foxgloves, bleach, and chainsaws. The characters dread that complete catastrophe will happen when one side finally seizes the power to "mobilize darkness and silence" (44), and despite its title, *Far Away* feels very much like the here and now of international terrorism. If there is a play that communicates the anxiety of proliferated images, piecemeal but available information, unpredictable and uncertain alliances, constant conflict that threatens to become an annihilating force, social atomization—all of the fears of the present historical moment—it is this one. In this ending, even more nightmarish than the hat parade, Samuel Huntington's thesis about the clash of civilization has virally reproduced itself to a point that any identification is ipso facto a cry of war. Identity generates violence, and difference is conflict. To the extent that affiliations are formed, they are random, unreliable, inscrutable, and temporary. This is a world of terror beyond ideological terror.

TERROR AT HOME

In the opening dialogue of *A Number*, B2, the 35-year-old son of Salter, a man in his early 60s, is explaining the shock of learning that there are a "number of them, of us" out there. B2's father queries B2 about why he did not ascertain exactly how "many of these things" were extant, to which B2 replies, "You called them things. I think we'll find they're people" (3–4). So begins a play in which the familiar face is no longer that: it is a threatening reproduction, one whose humanity is suspect. Such at least is one reaction to the clone. The clone horrifies us with memories of atrocities of human experimentation and Nazi genocide, and it frightens us with visions of an army of robotic, programmable assassins. But in Churchill's play, the clones are neither: B2 is the wished-for son, the best hope of the father, the reproduction of the parent's best self and the confirmation of the parent's best efforts. He is an object of desire. He is an idol.

The connections between terrorism and cloning are closer than might initially be thought, and they become glaringly apparent when attention is given to how each has wreaked havoc on our faith in the "real." Both terrorism and cloning rely on an array of new technologies, particularly biotechnical and informational, that inspire both enthusiasm and dread as issues of control and purpose hover over their utility and possibility. Like weapons of mass destruction, the techno-scientific innovations pose an "in the wrong hands" quandary that is political as well as ethical. Too, terrorism and cloning share a common image system: both the trope of the double, with its attendant sense of menace, and that of absence, with its connotation of irretrievable loss, are attached to the terrorist event and to asexual reproduction. It is not surprising that the *Tribute in Light*, the double shafts of light beamed at Ground Zero six months after the attack, was ambiguously moving since it reminded New Yorkers as much about loss as about hope. At the time that they were lit, President Bush called the perpetrators "terrorist parasites," using language that conjures up the theft of flesh and occupation of another body that cloning also implies. For W.J.T. Mitchell, the links between terrorism and cloning are evident and traceable; he notes that before 9/11, the dominant news story in the United States was the debate over stem cell research. After the attack, the subject shifted, but the visual imagery connected the attacks to the fear of viral/asexual reproduction. Photos of the fallen girders of the twin towers at Ground Zero conjured the spiral strands of DNA; doubles of Osama bin Laden appeared in popular culture; and cartoons connected stem cell research and terrorism.[12] Both cloning and terrorism, Mitchell notes, have a religious valence: they are or respond to acts of impiety, of appropriating the creator's role. Mitchell explains the operative logic that connects these "twin phobias of our historical epoch":

> The clone and the terrorist are cultural icons linked by the fear of the "uncanny double," the mirror image of the self as its own worst enemy. The

terrorist is the enemy who doubles as a friend or countryman, pretending to be "one of us." The clone is the figure of biological doubling as such, the inverted, perverted mirror image of a parent organism, an artificial simulation or twin of a natural person. The terrorist is the "evil twin" of the normal, respectable citizen-soldier, and the clone is the "evil twin" as such. The "war on terror" therefore is also a "war of images" that draws its vocabulary from the language of epidemiology, of plagues, sleeper cells, and viruses, on the one hand, and from iconoclasm, iconophobia, and holy wars over images on the other (2006).

The figure of the clone, Mitchell observes elsewhere, as a "mindless, even headless repository of spare parts, the reduction of the human being to bare life... all turn out to be handy images for the figure of the terrorist himself" (2005a, 914).

Finally, and most importantly for Churchill, terrorism and cloning are the products of desire. Baudrillard's rebuke, already mentioned—"at a pinch we can say that they did it but we wished for it" (2002, 5)—summarizes the complicity in the attacks and the complicity in creating life artificially. And as with towers, statues of dictators, terrorist cells, torture photos, or cells in a petri dish, our desires—to venerate, to replicate, to destroy—are deeply at odds with each other.

Churchill's plays stage these questions, anxieties, and ethical conundrums. Both *Far Away* and *A Number* begin with similar stories: a trusting child has learned something that he or she cannot comprehend, in part because he or she cannot believe his or her own eyes and in part because some basic bond of familial trust has been broken. In *Far Away*, Joan sees her uncle loading children and adults into a truck; they appear bloodied. In *A Number*, B2 tells his father that he has just learned that there are several clones of him. In both opening scenes, the adults/parents (Aunt Harper and Salter) offer ambiguous explanations and diversionary comments. In these few minutes, Churchill stages the skepticism about visual artifacts, the arduousness of reading signs for what is true, and, conversely, reading the real for what is signified. She deepens the experience of incredulity and confusion by the further experience of disinformation. And then she deepens it further by having the lie come from a trusted source. The latter storyline—family secrets, national secrets—is utterly conventional in fiction and life, but in connecting it with the incapacity to understand what one has seen because the "real" and the "replicated" are indistinguishable, and in further placing both within paternalistic power, Churchill has figured the current state of knowledge and action. She has invoked the challenges of the simulacrum, the ambiguities of mediatized spectatorship, and the complexities of political control.

In both plays, Churchill pursues the pressures of the sociosymbolic network on individual subjectivity and on individual moral action. Like Lentricchia and McAuliffe or Havis, Churchill is interested in the psychic dimensions of power, but she is also interested in individual agency. In *Far Away*, Joan is told as a child that her family is on the "good side," but by the end of the play, Harper's lies have never been exposed, and it is not clear that any good side exists anymore. In *A Number*, the connection between desire and moral action is even more explicit: B2 has been cloned because his father "wanted" a "second chance" at raising the "original" son he had damaged and given away. Gaining access to the right doctor has allowed Salter to start over, and part of the eeriness of the work is not only the replication of the son but also his simultaneous erasure. In *A Number*, questions of identity and replication, of historical erasure, of commodification and desire are illuminated through different pairings. Each of the three sons speaks individually to the father—never to each other or to anyone else—and in this mock-up of a creature's conversation with its creator, the shifting points of view illuminate concerns over selfhood, value, truth, and relationship. Here, Churchill intimates how structures of self and other are never eliminated by technology; if anything, technology complicates fundamental questions of otherness. B2, the "good clone," is unnerved both by what it means to his status as an autonomous, authentic subject to have a replica and what it means to his sense of being a son to have been desired as a replacement child and lied to about his origins. B1, the "original," the child who was always difficult (perhaps) but further damaged by his parents' failed marriage, his mother's suicide, and subsequent neglect and abandonment is enraged by the theft of his identity and the theft of a caring family. Salter, who denies his motivations until he is backed into telling the whole truth, wants a life without pain or regret, which he largely achieves with B2. But Salter cannot completely erase the disastrous years of his life with B1, and when B2 discovers the truth, he reevaluates his father. Salter is now horrible to him, an object of hatred. Yet, while Salter's desire is appalling, it is also seductive because it is so primal: to live without the consequences of mistake and misfortune. And he offers an explanation that also strikes the common cord: he could not cope and so he put the child in "care"; he did not kill him.

Michael, the clone who visits Salter after both his sons are dead, is the uncanny double: he is indifferent to Salter's trauma, physically identical but psychologically distinct from the other sons, and disinterested in a further relationship. He is a living confirmation of Salter's failure. What is most frightening about Michael is that he interjects a third possibility in this Frankenstein story: that the created object will be wholly indifferent to the desires of the creator.. The friendly Michael is at the farthest end of cyborg horror since no clone is meant to detach from the purposes designated by its creator. Michael illustrates the primitive injunction against making images not only because we fall in love with the golden calf of our creation, but also because the creation will disavow the creator. Together, the three sons compose what Walter Benjamin called a "dialectical image," which, as Mitchell explains, captures the "historical processes at a standstill." Even a single clone appears as a "figure of our future" that "threatens to come after us as an image of what could replace us, and takes us back to the question of our own origins as creatures made in the image of an invisible inscrutable creative force" (2005b, 25). Even if Salter is not at the end of his genetic line, he is at the end of influence and connection.

Salter, then, is the modern idolater. He loves the idol he has created, and he fails to see how his audacity is an affront. For him, his actions are a private pursuit of the desires to which he is entitled precisely because he lives in a time and place where what can be desired can be done. His logic is that of a consumer. When B2 tells him that he knows about the clones, Salter immediately suggests they sue the hospital because the hospital has "damaged your uniqueness and weakened your identity" which is worth at least "five million for a start." Moreover, the other clones "belong" to B2; they have been "stolen," and B2 should exercise his "rights" (7). Salter attempts to shift the discussion to the legal sphere in order to avoid the personal realm, but his remarks make the human body into the place where "property rights" are determined, and human identity into an issue of copyright infringement. Salter wants, most of all, for the public sphere to stay out of his domestic idyll. But there is no privacy in the infinitely replicable, digitalized world, and, hence, Salter's isolationist fantasy and his hope for "neutral" technology is self-blinding. All of his attitudes have corollaries, obviously, in Western, particularly American, attitudes and policies. I am not suggesting that Salter be read simply as an analogy of American greed and hubris. Churchill's later play *Drunk Enough to Say I Love You* overtly parodies American attitudes through the character of "Sam"—but the play raises many questions about the limitless expansion of desires that have geopolitical corollaries. Again, in a gesture that invites analogy but does not remain there, the fratricide that happens at the play's end is predictable. Since B1 knows he has been thrown away, he is a humiliated, deprived, angry, and now murderous cast-off. He compulsively seeks and then destroys his father's idol, murdering his double, and, predictably, murdering himself. He is a suicide terrorist.

The feel of terror, the approaches to understanding it in all of its psychic, political, and symbolic dimensions, the attempt to grieve the loss terror created, the self-reckoning that terror demanded—these are what the plays produced in response to 9/11 endeavored to capture and to process. After, 9/11, time spent understanding the particular kind of threat and social upheaval caused by terrorism was cut short by the pressure for retaliatory action. As the next two chapters discuss, the actions taken in the name of security spun the world into an ongoing state of crisis.

CHAPTER 6

WAR DOCUMENTS

> Military action was now seen as inevitable. Bush wanted to remove Saddam, through military action, justified by the conjunction of terrorism and WMD. But the intelligence and facts were being fixed around the policy... There was little discussion in Washington of the aftermath after military action.
>
> —The Downing Street Memo[1]

WHEN GEORGE BUSH ADDRESSED A JOINT SESSION OF CONGRESS on September 20, 2001, Prime Minister Tony Blair was in the gallery, seated next to the First Lady. As 80 million Americans watched on television, Bush looked up at the Prime Minister and declared, "America has no truer friend than Great Britain." This "special relationship" would position the United Kingdom as the primary coalition ally, bringing it into the duration of both the Afghanistan and Iraq wars. This involvement posed significantly different political challenges for Blair's government than it did for Bush's administration. An account of these political challenges—and the ways they were manipulated and sold to the public—is the subject of two documentary plays: David Hare's *Stuff Happens*, which opened at the National Theatre in London on September 1, 2004, and *Called to Account*, edited by Richard Norton-Taylor and devised by Nicolas Kent for London's Tricycle Theatre, where it premiered on April 19, 2007.

What these plays depict is that while the American public was grieving and much of the world was grieving along with it, the Bush administration decided not to waste the opportunity the 9/11 crisis presented. The facts conclude that the Bush administration regarded "regime change" in Iraq through a pre-emptive strike as something saleable to the American public in the wake of the attacks on the twin towers and that very early on the Blair government concurred and co-operated. It is clear why Bush found the moment propitious. On September 15, 2001, the US Senate had approved, with a lone dissenting vote, a bill authorizing the president to use all necessary force in combating terrorism (Spring and Packer 2009, 127). With this latitude, Bush sought no further authorization from Congress and began the military campaign against Afghanistan, Operation Enduring Freedom, on October 7, 2001, with the stated aim of capturing or destroying Osama bin Laden and Al-Qaeda and removing terrorist activity.[2] Indeed, the Congress's willingness to allow the government to do whatever it deemed necessary to protect American security produced a second bill barely three weeks later. On October 26, 2001, Bush signed the USA Patriot Act (Uniting and Strengthening America by Providing Appropriate Tools Required to Intercept and Obstruct Terrorism Act of 2001), easing restrictions on intelligence-gathering in the United States. Within just a few months, the administration and the Pentagon declared the Afghanistan campaign a success, although bin Laden would not be found and killed until 2011.

Despite significant protests around the world before the start of the Afghanistan campaign, the war garnered significant public support in the US. Moreover, as Douglas Kellner has observed, the Afghanistan war, especially in comparison to the 1991 Gulf War with its media images of precision bombing and the liberation of Kuwait City, was more hidden, in part because the Pentagon had grown more savvy about how to restrict coverage and control information (2005, 42). While the war in Afghanistan is now the longest waged in US history, in 2001, Operation Enduring Freedom was deemed a success. The Bush administration concluded that the retaliatory action had sufficiently weakened Al-Qaeda so that America could turn its attention elsewhere: Iraq. The rationale seized on was a supposed connection between Saddam Hussein's alleged weapons of mass destruction and the threat of terrorism. Indeed, the intelligence about Mohammed Atta's meeting in Prague with Iraqi officials, discussed in the last chapter, was one part of a dossier of misinformation, false evidence, and manufactured connections that characterized how Bush and Blair defended the invasion of Iraq as a legal operation. How this false information developed is one subject these plays explore, but along with it comes the more pertinent question: why did the American public so willingly buy into two wars that have caused over 5,500 in American casualties and over 100,000 in Iraqi and Afghani deaths, cost close to a trillion dollars, and diverted attention from simmering domestic problems?

The answers to these questions show themselves not only in the issues that the Iraq War plays address, but in the forms the plays take. One of the lingering questions about the build-up to the invasion is whether the American public should been quicker to see through the arguments the Bush administration made. Kathleen Hall Jamieson, in her thorough and judicious review of public statements made by members of the Bush administration, concludes that there were so many "verbal leakages, Freudian slips, and shifts in the burden of proof" that the country should indeed have spotted these stratagems and understood the lack of hard evidence about Saddam Hussein's weapons of mass destruction (WMDs) (2007, 249). Explanations for this national blindness range from grief and fear over the 9/11 attacks to the public's ignorance about the neoconservative plan to install a new political and economic order in the Middle East. Perhaps the most salient explanation, however, was the degree to which US citizens were gripped by a belief in the *exceptionality* of this event. Widely repeated expressions of incredulity were as often articulated as those of terror, rage, and grief, entwining the sense of deep victimization and historical privilege. Thus self-blinded, Americans overlooked many moments of obvious disconnect between evidence and action, between decision and values, and took themselves further from the path of legitimate self-defense and understandable outrage. In response, theatre (as well as other media) turned to the documentary mode. One kind of critique offered through documentary drama is a self-directed reckoning, one that also insists that, while contextualization, connection, and historicization have always been necessary to the public good, they have now attained the heightened status of a civic duty. Though this responsibility is more arduous than it has ever been before, it is all the more pressing.

PUBLIC MISTRUST AND DOCUMENTARY THEATRE

In retrospect, it is possible to see the Bush administration's plan to remap the Middle East by using the shock of 9/11 to pursue the pre-existent goal of regime change. This plan, according to former treasury secretary Paul O'Neill, was openly discussed at the very first National Security Council meeting a mere ten days after the inauguration (Leung, 2004). There were, however, clear warnings against the plan even as it was being hatched. For example, Brent Scowcroft, the Republican national security expert who had worked with the president's father, went on national television on August 2, 2003, to warn against going into Iraq. Scowcroft offered an unambiguous caution: invading Iraq "could turn the whole region into a cauldron, and thus, destroy the war on terrorism." A retired general, Scowcroft advocated letting the United Nations inspectors conclusively determine if Saddam Hussein possessed WMDs (Prados 2004, 1). Given the clarity of his message, and the authority of his opinions, why would this straightforward conclusion go unheeded?

One obvious answer is the aggressive marketing of the idea. When questions began to be raised about the three most pressing questions—was there a provable link between Al Qaeda and Hussein? Did Hussein have WMDs?

Should the UN inspectors first be given the time to make an assessment?—Vice President Cheney called out the questioners. He attacked their integrity, declaring that those who suggested that the intelligence might have been manipulated were themselves "opportunists" engaged in a "dishonest and reprehensible" political ploy (2005a). Even after it became known that the administration manipulated the evidence—first by setting up the Pentagon's Office of Special Plans, a group assembled by Deputy Secretary of Defense Paul Wolfowitz to provide its own intelligence reports to the president (Hersh 2003), and later by omitting the briefing CIA director George Tenant made in September 2002 that Hussein did not possess WMDs—there was no recanting (Blumenthal 2007). In his final press conference in 2008, with historically low approval ratings, George Bush, in his own self-parodic syntax, stated that "not finding weapons of mass destruction was a major disappointment," but he would not go as far to say that pursing the War in Iraq was a mistake based on a lie.

Political deceit was not the only cause for public distrust: on May 26, 2004, the *New York Times* offered an overdue (and to some, self-serving) apology about its coverage of the Iraq War. In its own words, the *Times* found "a number of instances of coverage that was not as rigorous as it should have been." Reporters relied too often on Iraq defectors for information, the "apology" explained, and editors failed to require substantiation. Furthermore, the paper did not follow up on the veracity of reports from some Iraqi scientists, and it did not challenge administration claims about evidence that Hussein had acquired aluminum tubes as components for making nuclear weapons fuel. Admitting it had succumbed to "rushing scoops," the *Times* vowed to intensify its aggressive reporting of the government's "pattern of misinformation" (New York Times Editors, 2004). Nevertheless, the sense, as David Hare has stated, that "journalism is failing us," which had already rooted itself in the public perception about news coverage during the first Gulf War, was even more strenuously felt (Hammond and Steward 2008, 62).

The 2004 *Times* apology was not its first: in 2003, it found that one of its reporters, Jason Blair, had frequently falsified, plagiarized, or otherwise misrepresented information in nearly half of the stories he had written in a six-month period, from October 2002 to his resignation in May 2003. In fact, Blair concocted some of the most emotionally charged stories published during the first months of the Iraq War, including one in which he claimed to have interviewed two wounded marines at the National Naval Medical Center in Bethesda, Maryland, though no such meeting occurred. Blair's writing was as riveting as it was false: long on vivid human-interest narratives and short on facts. The *Times* subsequently promised to tighten its fact-checking procedures and to create a "public editor" to enable readers to raise question about news sources and conclusions. In its extensive self-investigation and public mea culpa, the paper described the journalistic fraud as a "low point" in its 152-year history and assured its readers that such incidents would be far less likely to happen again, since an "ethics refresher course" would be instituted (Calame 2006). Thus, both in hard news coverage and in human interest stories, the *Times* was unreliable.

A "profound betrayal of trust" succinctly describes the feeling among American citizens about the lack of veracity in the executive branch, competence in the intelligence community, and accuracy in news organizations. Other events—the scandal at Abu Ghraib, torture at Guantanamo, the fabrications in the Jessica Lynch story, the excessive payments made to military contractors, especially Halliburton—deepened the public's sense of disempowerment. In retrospect, these revelations about governmental duplicity, military abuse, and self-serving news organizations seem to have provided the public with hooks on which to hang their deep, but perhaps inchoate, feelings of cynicism and skepticism. Such feelings, as I indicated earlier, accrued because of the way in which the unified national—and global—grief and outrage over the 9/11 attacks had become fervently jingoistic as sensationalized news coverage abetted government fear-mongering. As the discourse of American patriotism through American unity entrenched itself, the possibility of dissent grew weaker, with fewer outlets to register objections about the war itself. It is now possible to measure the duration of this xenophobic national monologue: in its most intense form, it lasted about 20 months, from September 11, 2001, until George Bush made the strategic error of his "Mission Accomplished" speech on May 1, 2003. Meant to showcase American military might, the spectacle of Bush triumphalism quickly became a self-inflicted wound. By changing the terms of the war, Bush saddled himself with the need for an entirely different vocabulary, one that described the conflict in terms of lasting safety and stability, and he had to find new signposts of the successful reconstruction of Iraq. Since it was impossible to make the quick exit from the 1991 Iraq War, the troops remained, with growing casualties and costs. As the emptiness of Bush's claim that the "battle of Iraq is one victory on a War on Terror" became increasingly obvious, a place opened up for criticism that was not automatically rejected as unpatriotic.

Significantly, theatre responded less with the impassioned vitriol of pieces such as Tony Kushner's *Only We Who Guard the Mystery Shall Be Unhappy*, a brief work that imagines Laura Bush reading "The Grand Inquisitor" to dead pajama-clad Iraqi children, and more with works that attempted to fill in the information gap and provide a public venue for debate.

This resurgence in documentary drama resulted in a wide array of styles and production values, from the strict verbatim theatre of the "tribunal plays" to the hybrid theatre of *Stuff Happens*. All were motivated by the desire to offer a counter-response to the government's rhetoric and the media's depthless coverage. These dramas were "doing history," creating and performing their own first-hand observations or enacting the testimonies based on interviews they had conducted. In short, as the public realm appear to be increasing fictionalized, theatre purposefully defictionalized itself.

The following list is not exhaustive, but it includes the more prominent works of verbatim/documentary theatre about Iraq. Two theatres dedicated to political theatre were important in developing and staging works about Iraq: the Tricycle Theatre and the Culture Project. In London at the Tricycle Theatre, artistic director Nicolas Kent staged three important tribunal plays: Richard Norton-Taylor's *Half the Picture* (1994), *Justifying War* (2003), and *Called to Account* (2007) as well as Victoria Brittain and Gillian Slovo's *Guantanamo* (2004). In New York, the Culture Project plays, presented by founder and artistic director Allan Buchman, included *Betrayed* (George Packer, 2007), *A Question of Impeachment* (2007), *My Trip to Al Qaeda* (Lawrence Wright, 2007), and *In Conflict* (Douglas Wager, 2008). Culture Project's ongoing *Blueprint for Accountability* presented panels of experts on different subjects intermixed with readings, forming a hybrid form of testimonial theatre. Five other significant documentary plays are David Hare's *Stuff Happens* (National Theatre, 2004); Robin Soans's *Talking to Terrorists* (Royal Court, 2005); Gregory Burke's *Blackwatch* (National Theatre of Scotland, 2006); Philip Ralph's *Deep Cut* (Sherman Cymru, Cardiff, 2008), and Jessica Blank and Eric Jensen's *Aftermath* (New York Theatre Workshop, 2009). While there are numerous other examples of documentary plays, some developed primarily for regional theatres, the works identified above were chosen because they became more broadly known. Some were produced at prominent theatrical venues; some played in multiple locations; and some were televised, broadcast, or paired with journalistic pieces, and hence gained wider notice and larger audiences.

Writers of documentary plays also cite the record of government manipulation and media unreliability, concluding that the public needs as many vehicles of alternative information and discussion as can be found. Soans, for example, has observed that we are living in

> an age where virtually nothing "does what it says on the tin": photographs are faked, television competitions are won by people who have not entered; articles in newspapers turn out to have been entirely fabricated; weapons of mass destruction cannot be found in Iraq... The normal channels of reportage where we expect some degree of responsibility and truth are no longer reliable (quoted in Hammond and Steward 2008, 17).

Hare's view is blunter: verbatim theatre does what "journalism fails to do" in part because post 9/11 journalism is in "some sort of ethical crisis" about how it "came to be so complicit the regime" (quoted in Hammondand Steward 2008, 63). Perhaps the most telling examples of the conviction that live performance offers more insight than that gained through print and media are Lawrence Wright's *My Trip to Al-Qaeda*, George Packer's *Betrayed*, and Norton-Taylor's tribunal plays. These writers, all professional journalists, concluded that the news pieces they wrote could not adequately communicate the stories they were most interested in telling. In Packer's words, he "wanted to do justice to the texture of life among Iraqi interpreters in wartime Baghdad in a way that can't be conveyed in a news article or even a feature story" (Packer 2008, xii). Despite what might appear, then, to be the tight confines of documentary drama, it has risen to the forefront of political theatre, filling gaps in public records, possessing an unexpected elasticity in its staging, and accumulating a documentable record of effective outreach.

DOCUMENTARY THEATRE AND ITS RELATION TO THE REAL

While what these "public-event" plays contributed to the larger discourse about the legitimacy of Iraq War is the later focus of this chapter, it is important to begin by examining how they understand their documentary function. The broadest common denominator among them is that some portion of the text has a real-life, word-for-word corollary; it is the reason, for example, why Judith Thompson's *Palace at the End*, which concerns public events—the arrest of Lynndie England; the suicide of David Kelly—but is comprised almost entirely of imagined monologues, is not included here. But even within the boundaries of verbatim theatre, there are a range of choices: the dialogue may be redacted from a single source, such as inquiry, or taken from a range of public statements and interviews that were made without direct reference to each other. Other information is obtained from more private sources, such as diaries, emails, or off-the-record conversations with staff assistants. At times, the characters who appear on stage are instantly recognizable public figures; at others, they are purposefully unknown citizens whose stories express the dilemma of being less the agent of politics than its object. Effectually, no documentary theatre omits the larger story of macro-level political decisions, but the choice of how to reveal this context—and how much to reveal—is one reason that these theatre works vary widely in tone and subject.[3]

Patrice Pavis, writing in 1998, traces the re-emergence of documentary theatre in the 1950s and 1960s to media domination, defining the genre as "plays composed of nothing but documents and authentic sources selected and assembled according to the playwright's sociopolitical thesis" (Pavis et al., 110). Pavis offers two models: plays that reuse public sources but arrange them as a critique of the original event, and plays that offer a "combative montage," reassembling fragments to mount a critique of a prevailing sociopolitical model. While Pavis's definition does apply to some of the works discussed here, others go beyond the exclusively factual by interweaving fictional scenes, and some authors would prefer to describe their works more as a collaborative search for truth or as an occasion for unheard voices than as an argument based on a "sociopolitical thesis." As a subset of documentary theatre, verbatim theatre is a term most applicable to theatre works that are truly transcribed utterances. The term is used more flexibly, however, to point to works that are based on interviews or public records, but may be edited and performed in a variety of ways—hence Norton-Taylor's admission that he does not know whether to call himself a journalist, playwright, or editor (Luckhurst 2008, 206).

Whether the final text is a completely verbatim account of someone else's words or one that intermingles actual and invented sources, documentary theatre, "*by its very nature*," writes Derek Paget, "problematizes the activity of 'truth-telling'" (2004, 50, emphasis original). Documentary theatre, then, though never without its own bias, is deeply interested in exploring the gray area in the spectrum of political revelation, examining how halfpictures and half-truths may be offered as legal truths and political facts.

This dynamic of self-reflexively re-presenting the real makes documentary theatre a dramatic analogue to postmodern practices of metafiction and montage. It shares in the attributes that Linda Hutcheon has described as "histortiographic metafiction," fictions that represent the past but that are "intensely self-reflexive" (1998, 122). With its emphasis on the means through which knowledge of the past is obtained and transmitted, historiography calls attention to how something is accorded the status of an event, and how, in turn, events are transformed into facts or truths. In so doing, historiography gestures toward the textual, discursive, and situational dimensions of historical knowledge. Historiography therefore engages questions of methodology, medium, verification, the plurality of truth, and the question of authority. By highlighting the constructedness of a historical record, historiography takes as ethically axiomatic the need to expose and reveal its own bias and methods. The same impulse is at work in a metafictional narrative and its drive to expose the apparatus underlying its construction. Like Brecht's epic theatre, which attacked both the implicit "neutrality" of verisimilitude as well as the obscured ideology of Aristotelian theatre by using defamiliarization techniques, postmodern montage attempts to provoke a similarly critical awareness about both the status of the artifact and the operations of power. Montage—whether in Andy Warhol's silk-screens of celebrity images or Barbara Kruger's photomontages—does not reject verisimilitude but instead appropriates it in order to confront and discomfit the spectator via replication and recontextualization.

Documentary theatre is similarly appropriative and metafictive. Like historiographic metafiction, it calls into question the authority of received accounts of truth and fact even as it calls attention to its own methods and biases. Simply remounting the event, even if the set replicates the exact details of the original place and the language is verbatim, places the spectator in a position of a doubled critical consciousness. Reframed, verisimilitude becomes a strategy through which to counter the relentless visibility of real-time media and its tacit claims of authenticity. Norton-Taylor's tribunal plays function along the lines of a frame narrative whereby the internal story (the replicated trial whose main storyline is already known; the media event that has already entered collective memory) is remounted but within a frame of "new" material (the testimony that was given but did not receive as much coverage; the parts of an event the media ignored) that operates meta-diegetically. Hare's *Stuff Happens* also uses frame narrative, though in his play, these frames in the inter-scenes are fictional. In these works, as in historiographic metafiction, the spectator becomes aware of the telling as much as the told. In short, story is exposed as discourse.

So far, then, I have been examining how documentary art reframes, recontextualizes, and thereby reopens the already seen and heard media event for a second look, a different interpretation. Yet, because media events are so pervasive, their capacity to install image and narrative is met with skepticism, and the question arises of how documentary theatre deals with both image domination and public suspicion about the images. Such, says Slavoj Zizek is the "de-materialization of the 'real life,' and its reversal into a 'spectral show' that makes it seem as though "real social life has acquired the features of a staged fake" (2002, 14).

Clearly, no event and no response stands outside the global postmodern condition. For many, this condition is so rhizomic, decentralized, profit-driven, privatized, image-managed, and unregulated that it is as impossible to oppose it as it is to stand outside of it. Jean Baudrillard's essays express some of the darkest predictions about globalization, technological development, and virtual reality. Those who disagree with Baudrillard, such as Christopher Norris, point out that if we accept Baudrillard's "contention that we now inhabit a realm of purely fictive or illusory appearances," then "truth-claims no longer possess the least degree of operative (i.e. persuasive or rhetorical) force" (1992, 14,15). Douglas Kellner, writing extensively about the effect of media on the American political economy, modulates these viewpoints; he has suggested that while it is necessary to recognize the impact of media spectacles, their effects are variable.[4] While Kellner's rejection of cyber-determinism is consoling, it nevertheless remains unclear how citizens can understand the ambivalent semiotics of images and make judgments amid the ping-pong game of their exchange.

This is where current documentary theatre places its marker. Perhaps an even more telling and specific formulation about the milieu in which documentary drama operates is Jane M. Gaines's description. She states that the phrase "new image war," which has been used to describe the current conflict, needs to be elaborated: it is both a "war imaged" and a "war against images." While this is the environment for all cultural production, documentary art insists on a connection with the "real historical material world," Gaines states, and it combines source material, aesthetics, and purpose by using "the world to transform the world." For this reason, documentary art, as a type of politically engaged art connected to the shifting historical circumstances, must deal with its own ephemerality (2007, 46). And it must also deal with the complexity of social reality in which contradiction is a given. Nevertheless, its fundamental and defining feature is that it is *through* contact with the world that documentary theatre is made.[5]

David Hare has suggested that contradiction motivated his writing of *Stuff Happens*, since he was fascinated by why a supposedly clever man, Blair, was so outpaced by a supposedly stupid one. While that observation will be discussed further below, *Stuff Happens* is the one play in the list above that is obviously positioned within an imaged world. In fact, because almost all of the characters are instantly recognizable, it is difficult to keep the work from veering off into parody. As discussed below, while the play seems to be offering a behind-the-scenes look at how the Iraq War was put into motion, its dramatic energy relies almost entirely on the figure of Colin Powell, who, unlike Bush, Blair, Cheney, and Rumsfeld, escapes becoming pure caricature. The point here is that it is not possible to circumvent the massive effect of media on the theatrical representation of public figures, but it is possible, as Hare's play demonstrates, implicitly to acknowledge that inescapability while constructing a performative apparatus that produces more than parody. In addition to the behind-the-scenes interchanges, which are based on verifiable sources, Hare includes scenes the public has already seen: Bush and Blair standing together in Crawford, Texas, is one example. In *Stuff Happens*, then, the wholly imagined (the frame and inter-scenes) is juxtaposed against the real-but-unseen and the real-already-screened. The latter may, through media proliferation and repetition, have entered the realm of the simulacrum, of the "unreality" produced via excessive exposure, but the performance can use even this dynamic to produce a complex spectatorial position. The audience member, exposed to a gamut from the fictional to the screened, adjudicates the truth arising from this composite. Consequently, the engine of Hare's drama is both its tragic hero emplotment and its collage of the imagined and the seen; the tension between these invites the viewer to think critically about surface and depth. Perhaps the best description of this complex spectatorship is to note that while parody invites viewers to revel in the surface imitation—to enjoy the "play" of imitation—"appropriative art," such as Hare's play, asks the viewer to look at and through surfaces more critically.

While *Stuff Happens* deals most with mediated knowledge, all of the documentary plays are in tacit conversation with issues already disseminated in the public realm. Along with dealing with how audiences have already been shaped by the information they have absorbed and with their suspicions about spin and disinformation, documentary plays must establish their authority and veracity. This issue of trust and integrity may be broached through the work or through the venue. Some plays enact integrity by calling attention to their own constructedness. Several, such as Hare's *Via Dolorosa* and Lawrence Wright's *My Trip to Al-Qaeda* are author-performed monologues, offering a kind of informed political travelogue. Other plays include "author-figures," such as the theatre researcher in Gregory Burke's *Blackwatch*, a character who stands in for the creative team who developed the play. When Douglas Wager adapted Veronica Latty's book of interviews with returning Iraq veterans, *In Conflict*, for the stage, he included videotaped projections of Latty talking about her process. In *Talking to Terrorists*, the interviewer does not appear but is implied. George Packer's play, *Betrayed*, on the other hand, does not included a stand-in for Packer, but it stakes its veracity on the author's reputation as a journalist for *The New Yorker* and the public acknowledgment that the characters are composites of Iraqi translators personally interviewed by the author. Because *The New Yorker* published Seymour Hersh's exposé of the abuses at Abu Ghraib, as well as other important investigative reporting by Hersh, Wright, and Packer, the magazine gained a reputation for delving into Iraq War issues more deeply than other publications. The plays offered through the Tricycle Theatre and the Culture Project benefit from the reputations of these organizations, which are known for their commitment to political commentary via theatre. While each is associated with a leftist viewpoint, each has found ways to extend its work to audiences other than those who might already agree with the theatres' politics. For example, Norton-Taylor and John McGrath's *Half the Picture*, a work about British arms sales to Iraq, was performed in the Houses of Parliament. Celebrity actors and public figures, from Vanessa Redgrave to South African archbishop Desmond Tutu, appear in Culture Project productions, and the theatre partners with numerous venues around New York City to attract diverse audiences. *Guantanamo: Honour Bound to Defend Freedom* has reached over five thousand outlets. Finally, most documentary plays make their source material available to audience members. The tribunal plays, for example, are redactions from public records of inquiries; the letters read in *Guantanamo* are the actual letters from detainees, and the evidence that Philip Ralph's *Deep Cut*, a presentation of the story of four soldiers who died at Deepcut barracks in Surrey, is based on is included in the appendices.

DOCUMENT/THEATRICALIZE

Placed next to each other, the two verbs, document and theatricalize, appear to be opposites: the first is associated with indexing facts; the second, with fabricating events. They also broach the three questions most associated with documentary theatre: why, given the excess of information available via other outlets, do we need theatre to be another? And, how is documentary theatre artistic? And, most significantly, how, given its hybrid, genre-crossing status, is it "true"? Part of the responses to these questions have scattered themselves throughout all of the discussions about the relevance of political theatre per se, but they are worth gathering and rehearsing here. First, political theatre, and especially documentary theatre, foregrounds its connection to real historical conditions. It stakes its very life on a contract of trust with the audience member: while it may invent scenarios to demonstrate its thesis, its aim is not *Wag the Dog*. Second, as a live, embodied event, it wants to produce not only discussion, but empathy, and even community and solidarity. These ambitions require the kind of hybridity at the heart of documentary theatre. Deep understanding may be created in the manner of collecting data and in the manner of enacting it—the works of Anna Devere Smith and Emily Mann are notable here, as are the works of Moises Kaufmann and the Tectonic Theatre Project, and those of Jessica Blank and Eric Jensen. Alternatively, it may arise from what Sergei Eisenstein calls the "pathos of fact" (quoted in Gaines 2007, 50). This dynamic underlies Packer's *Betrayed*, where the audience learns of the endangered lives of Iraqi translators working with US forces. The mundane task, for example, of eating in an Iraqi restaurant is fully rendered and reveals the gulf between the American presence and Iraqis' desire to stabilize their own country. As Gaines's observes, the depiction of the everyday is akin to Brechtian defamiliarization because it interrupts the mythology of war and reconstitutes our understanding of the effects of conflict (48). What we see is more than the events depicted on stage; in Brechtian fashion, the spect/actor/ship turns the lens to larger causes.

Along with this critical insight into both the ideological bases for our conduct, documentary theatre can produce empathy. Jessica Blank and Eric Jensen, the authors of *The Exonerated*, discuss how their play, which is about wrongful incarcerations, grew from a two-day event at Culture Project to six hundred off-Broadway performances, a television movie, and countless regional productions. It helped influence the Illinois governor to repeal his state's death penalty, brought healing to maligned, falsely accused men and women, and focused attention on the high incidence of wrongful conviction. Blank and Jensen contend:

> Narrative theater has at its heart the process *of empathy*... The very experience of watching a story unfold in the theater triggers identifications; these new identifications crack open our comfortable, sedimented everyday identities and generate reactions and questions—and when a culture grapples with these questions together, it begins to change (2005, 19).

Blank and Jensen go on to assert the capacity of documentary theatre to facilitate social change, arguing that the "theatre—where there is no screen between performer and audience, where we are not abstractions to each other but living, breathing beings—is the place to implicate ourselves in each other's stories" (20). The community-building ambition lies at the heart of the work being done at the Tricycle Theatre and Culture Project.

INEVITABLE WAR: *JUSTIFYING WAR, CALLED TO ACCOUNT, STUFF HAPPENS*

How did the Bush and Blair administrations decide, justify, and sell the invasion of Iraq as a necessary part of the War on Terror? Three documentary plays take up that question: Norton-Taylor's *Justifying War* and *Called to Account* and Hare's *Stuff Happens*. *Justifying War* is based on edited transcripts of the Hutton inquiry into the death of Dr. David Kelly, an expert on biological warfare and a former UN weapons expert in Iraq. Kelly was found dead in a wooded area, Harrowdown Hill, after he appeared at the Foreign Affairs Select Committee of the House of Commons, which was investigating whether or not he had provided information to a broadcaster, Andrew Gilligan. The center of this controversy revolved around the question of whether or not Blair and his advisors had "sexed up" the dossier about the extent to which Hussein had weapons of mass destruction and how quickly they could reach Britain. Sensationalized as the "45-minute" claim, the controversy focused on, in part, evidence that Iraq could launch a lethal weapon that could reach Britain in 45 minutes.

Unlike *Justifying War*, which reproduced already extant public testimony, the other two plays rely on a combination of public evidence and authorial invention. *Called to Account: The Indictment of Anthony Charles Lynton Blair for the Crime of Aggression Against Iraq* is a staged hearing about whether Tony Blair should be indicted as a war criminal. It uses the testimony of actual politicians, legal experts, and others who vary in their opinions about Blair's culpability. Additionally, there are two sets of lawyers—one leading the case against Blair, the other asserting the lack of legal foundation for the charge—that cross-examine 11 witnesses. Hence, while the frame and occasion are fictive, the opinions, and the facts they rely upon, are verbatim testimony from involved parties. Hare's play *Stuff Happens* represents the greatest mixture of public fact and authorial invention of the three works. It is not a hearing, but rather a series of scenes, drawn from public documents, in which the world's political leaders—from Bush and Blair to Rice, Cheney, Powell, and Rumsfeld—make the decision to invade Iraq seem inevitable. *Stuff Happens* is not a verbatim play; it is better described as a public evidence play, and even that description should be modulated to acknowledge the wholly fictional monologues Hare inserted into the play. Hare calls the work a history play, a designation that will be explored below.

First a word about the venues in which these plays appeared. The Tricycle Theatre, located in Kilburn, London, is a publicly subsidized theatre with a history of presenting plays on political themes, but it is most well-known for its tribunal plays. These works are verbatim plays drawn from the transcripts of public inquiries. They were written largely by Richard Norton-Taylor, a *Guardian* journalist who specialized in the activities of the intelligence services. With John McGrath, he co-wrote the first tribunal play, *Half the Picture* (1994), about the sales of arms to Iraq. At the behest of Nicolas Kent, the artistic director of the Tricycle Theatre, he went on to write such significant pieces as *Nuremburg*, *The Colour of Justice*, and *Bloody Sunday*. In all of his works, Norton-Taylor compresses pages of transcripts into a two-hour verbatim presentation in order to make the issues more accessible to audiences. Unlike press coverage, which is incremental, or the inquiry reports, which are long and unwieldy, the tribunal plays efficiently lay out the differing points of view and political agendas. Essentially, the audience hears the evidence in an abbreviated format. The Tricycle has mounted many politically engaged theatre pieces, but two others works present aspects of the Iraq War. *Guantanamo: Honour Bound to Defend Freedom*, a verbatim play discussed in the next chapter, takes on the question of extraterritorial detention, and *Deep Cuts*, a play that originated at the Cymru Theatre in Cardiff, examines suicides that occurred at a Surrey military base. David Hare's play, on the other hand, premiered at the larger, more prestigious National Theatre where is was directed by Nicholas Hytner. It was restaged in the United States, again at prominent venues: the Mark Taper Forum in Los Angeles and the Public Theater in New York City. It became, arguably, the best-know of the Iraq War plays.

In an article for the *New Statesman*, Norton-Taylor argues that the tribunal plays are ultimately less biased than other media. His comments bear repeating at length:

> Tribunal Plays have common themes—the evasion, buck-passing and dissembling of those in power. Real people unwittingly damn themselves, or emerge

as honest heroes, in their own words. This is how real people responded in the dock. But it is not how journalists normally report such inquiries as daily "news." We are tempted, often encouraged, to distort in an attempt to grab the attention of readers and news editors. Any editing is subjective, but far less so when it is for a two-hour script than for an article of a few hundred words, or a television clip of a few moments. A theatre audience thus gets a much better understanding of the issues. Judging by the response from audiences and critics alike, there is a growing thirst for theatre that is the antithesis of the whodunit. We know what happened and why this trial or that public inquiry was held, but often only the crudest and most superficial way. It is not only the exchanges between lawyer and witness which give the plays their drama. Telling details and moving anecdotes resonate more in a theatre than in the conventional news media—if, and it is unlikely, they are mentioned there at all (2004).

These qualities are evident in Norton-Taylor's work, especially *Justifying War*, the edited version of Lord Hutton's inquiry into the circumstances surrounding the death of Dr. David Kelly, the soft-spoken expert on biochemical weapons who provided intelligence assessments to the government and who participated in drafting and reviewing part of the dossier that argued for pre-emptive action against Iraq. The Hutton Inquiry sat for 25 days, and heard from 75 witnesses who gave some 110 hours of testimony. Hutton's report, delivered on January 28, 2004, ran over seven hundred pages.[6] Norton-Taylors's script for the Tricycle Theatre is based on the testimony of 12 of the witnesses, and with one exception, the testimony of Dr. Kelly's wife, Janice, it proceeds in the same order as the actual inquiry. The staging of *Justifying War* on October 20, 2003, occurred before Lord Hutton presented his report to the government (Norton-Taylor 2003, 7).

The relevant facts of the case are these: Tony Blair wanted a dossier that would publicly lay out the case that Hussein, in defiance of UN rulings, sanctions, and investigations, still possessed weapons of mass destruction that could quickly be deployed, and that therefore it was legal and necessary for the United Kingdom to join the United States in preemptive action. In preparing the dossier, the administration used information and conclusions provided by the intelligence community, a community that included Dr. Kelly. At some point, Kelly spoke with members of the press, including a radio correspondent, Andrew Gilligan, and a BBC reporter, Susan Watts. They reported, on air and in print, that an unnamed senior advisor believed that the evidence had been overstated. When the news broke on May 29, 2003, during a 6:00 a.m. newscast, Andrew Gilligan delivered a strongly worded allegation that the government knew that the claim that lethal weapons could reach Britain in 45 minutes was wrong. Tony Blair learned of the broadcast while he was in Iraq visiting British troops in Basra, and it undercut his goal of rallying the troops around a worthy cause. Immediately, the hunt for the identity of the senior official began. The Blair government decided to confirm Kelly's identity to any journalist who posed the question, and thus Kelly became the center of the firestorm. He was summoned to give evidence to the Foreign Affairs Committee of Parliament where MP Andrew MacKinlay, a zealous guardian of Parliament's right to scrutinize the government's decisions and procedures, suggested that Kelly was "chaff," a fall guy thrown up to divert probing. Kelly was caught in the crosshairs of investigation and speculation. Feeling himself hounded, he and his wife left their home and hid in Cornwall; a few days later, after they had returned home, he left for a walk and never returned. Police found his body the next day, July 18, 2003, and ruled the death a suicide. Amid the controversy of whether the BBC acted irresponsibly with unconfirmed allegations, or the government was hiding its own prevarications and manipulations, speculation about Kelly himself occurred, with one infamous allegation that he was a kind of Walter Mitty character.

In choosing these "scenes" from the Hutton Inquiry, Norton-Taylor selected witnesses whose testimony most demonstrated the interest of the various parties involved—members of the government, the BBC, the intelligence community, and the Kelly family. The technique that Norton-Taylor has developed over the years of writing the tribunal plays involves compressing the evidence into about a two-hour play while remaining absolutely faithful to the testimony as given. In this sense, the plays are "verbatim," but they are also affected by the author's editorial choices. Norton-Taylor aims to reproduce the broad outlines of the different points of view while retaining the speakers' words and vocal and gestural eccentricities. If Norton-Taylor decides to alter something such as the chronology of the witness testimony—as he does in *Justifying War*, where he puts the testimony of a civil servant before that of Kelly's wife, Janice—he discloses the change in the program notes. He also provides appendices with his sources, and he provides references to public documents. The transcripts of the Hutton Inquiry were posted online. The one choice that Norton-Taylor made that was left unexplained was his decision to omit the testimony of Tony Blair himself. Blair's testimony, available on the Hutton Inquiry website, is, of course, self-defensive, even as he frames his comments in his desire for the dossier to be a strong and accurate defense of his government's decision to invade Iraq. Norton-Taylor has not explained his reason for omitting Blair's testimony, but its inclusion would surely have changed the focus of the play from one about a man caught, indeed lethally caught, between the interests of government and media, to a play about the prime minister's veracity.

Justifying War exemplifies what Tom Englehardt described as the "urconglomerate" of media and government that affects the nature of war in the information age (1992, 630) and what James Der Derrian has termed the Military-Industrial-Media-Entertainment Network (2009b). As the play unfolds, the at-times co-operative but at other times competitive relationship of media and government materializes. Media coverage prompted the government's decisions, whether that decision involved taking the nation to war or exposing Kelly's identity—a decision, it should be noted, taken in the presence of the prime minister. Concurrently, media coverage, embedded within a constant flow of entertainment, considers rumors to be as newsworthy as hard facts. When Andrew Gilligan is questioned about his stark contention that the government knew the evidence about the 45-minute claim was "wrong," a word he modulated in later reports, he justifies himself by saying the word choice may not have been "perfect," but that the nature of the early morning show is more informal and hence his standard of accuracy need not be as high. The speculation that Kelly sought to aggrandize his role in high-level decision making—the Walter Mitty charge—reflects the further tabloidization of news stories where the so-called human element is the saleable commodity of sensationalization. The Hutton Inquiry ultimately exonerated the Blair administration on the basis that it did not know of the dissent within the senior intelligence community. The Inquiry then chastised the BBC; in its aftermath, Chairman Gavyn Davies, Director General Greg Dyke, and journalist Andrew Gilligan resigned within three days of each other. Nevertheless, the Inquiry (and its successor, the Butler Report) never fully laid the issue of government manipulation to rest, and the publication just a year later, in 2005, of the infamous Downing Street Memo reignited concerns about the Prime Minister's truthfulness.

What theatrical models emerge in the performance of *Justifying War*? For all of its verisimilitude in staging the Hutton Inquiry as close to the original hearing as possible, the result, oddly, is much less like a courtroom drama, such as *Inherit the Wind*, and more like a social drama by Henrik Ibsen or Arthur Miller, which clarifies the nature of opposing forces and focuses on the individual caught between them. But tagging it as a social drama does not quite fit either, since Kelly does not emerge as being as heroic as Dr. Stockman or John Proctor. Rather, like Chekhov, Norton-Taylor hears in the verbatim testimony the note of self-revelation or self-deception, and he sees in the witnesses' mannerisms the revealing detail. These details—whether in repeated deferrals, a self-incriminating pause, excessive self-justification, or a moment of naked grief—complicate the testimony. Too, like Chekhov, the characters press their own cause and underhear each other. While the format of the inquiry is a series of dialogues between attorney and witness, the speakers are addressing larger audiences than each other, correcting narratives already presented, and asserting the value of their particular viewpoint. Were one to assemble the figures together in a room, the scene might well resemble something from *Three Sisters* or *The Cherry Orchard*, where the characters speak past each other, voicing their own interests. Meanwhile, as beneath the surface action of a Chekhov play, some outcome is gathering force, one that may not be the complete truth but that will be consequential and include a tragic dimension: in Chekhov, the orchard will be lost, social class will change, and the servant will be forgotten; in Norton-Taylor, the government will be excused, Iraq will be invaded, and Kelly's death will be inconsequential.

Justifying War reveals both larger power dynamics and smaller, human foibles. Even as it conjectures that Kelly's motivation for speaking to journalists is a mixture of vanity and conscience, it displays the government's willingness to scapegoat a single person rather than take on fuller responsibility. In addition to asking audience members to think critically about the limited outcomes of an official inquiry, about governmental complicity, about media ratings-driven inaccuracies, and about the interdependence of media and politics, it also wants spectators to think through the larger questions of how power dynamics affect individual agency, whether that individual is David Kelly or a citizen wanting to know the truth about his or her government's decisions. In effect, *Justifying War* positions spectators to begin a kind of Foucauldian critique of power, knowledge, and discourse. Pathetically, at the play's end, Janice Kelly thanks Lord Hutton for the dignity of the proceedings—though the competition of self-vindication could hardly be described as "dignified."

Called to Account endeavors to address the very issue that official inquiries have skirted: whether Tony Blair is liable to be charged with a crime of aggression. The fundamental difference between *Called to Account* and *Justifying War* is that, as regards the former, no actual legal hearing took place. Instead, Nicolas Kent enlisted two lawyers, Phillipe Sands QC, for the prosecution, and Julian Knowles, for the defense, to conduct a "hearing" over two months in early 2007. The final script, a play comprising two acts of roughly even length, includes the testimony and cross-examination of 11 witnesses, beginning with that of an Iraqi Kurd and ending with that of a member of the ministry of defense. The opening and closing arguments set out a stark contestation: the prosecutor argues that Blair had committed Britain to join the plan for regime change in Iraq in 2002 even as he publicly maintained that no decision had been made, and that he may have manipulated the evidence on whether or not there were weapons of mass destruction. The defense argues simply that there is no proof that the prime minister "intentionally took the country into an illegal war knowing that it was illegal" (2007, 91). One of the witnesses, Richard Perle, who served in the Reagan and both Bush administrations, summarizes the difference between the two contentions when he concludes that the evidence at the time justifying war "was wrong, but it was adequate" (86). Though perhaps only two of the witnesses actually defend Blair, most of the others, however outraged, cannot prove absolute illegality. In the end, it appears that Perle's judgment is as unassailable as it is infuriating.

So if *Called to Account* does not make an ironclad case for Blair's intentional mendacity and illegality, what kind of judgments do emerge? *Called to Account* reminds audiences what regime change has meant for the Iraqi people and what the slipperiness of accountability has meant for the British. The play begins with the testimony of Dr. Shirwan Al-Mufti, an Iraqi Kurd. He describes the abuses under Hussein: random executions of anyone deemed suspect; the 5,500 victims of Halabja genocide in 1988; the widespread use of horrific, sadistic torture techniques. Al-Mufti testifies that the majority of Iraqi people were delighted to have Hussein removed from power, a feat they could not have managed without outside assistance. Al-Mufti admits that the basis for humanitarian intervention was, however, stronger in 1991 or 1988 than it was in 2003, but then goes on to query the emptiness of the word "humanitarian" for a people under prolonged and extreme distress, a distress that was diverted by discussion of weapons of mass destruction. "In my opinion, or the majority of the Iraqi people, the regime of Saddam Hussein was our weapons of mass destruction," Al-Mufti states (17). He ends his testimony by pointing out that the Bush administration erroneously predicted how democratization would occur in the Middle East, failing to predict how the neighboring countries would do their utmost to undermine a process that would next target their own regimes.

With this beginning, laying out the extreme oppression of the Iraqis under Hussein, the hearing moves on to other issues. Scott Ritter, a former marine who worked in intelligence and disarmament both for the US government and for the United Nations, minces no words: any claim that Iraq had not been disarmed was deliberately misleading. Michael Smith testifies as the journalist who broke the story of the infamous Downing Street Memo, the minutes of a secret meeting held on July 23, 2002, that came to light on May 1, 2005, when *The Sunday Times* published its contents. The memo contained comments from "C," the head of MI6:

> C reported on his recent talks in Washington. There was a perceptible shift in attitude. Military action was now seen as inevitable. Bush wanted to remove Saddam, through military action, justified by the conjunction of terrorism and WMD. But the intelligence and facts were being fixed around the policy (27).

When asked if Blair's public declaration to the British Parliament and public that no decision had been made in regard to Iraq, a stance he maintained until March 2003, was misleading, Smith simply answers, "Yes."

Other witnesses add to the case against Blair. Clare Short, who served as the secretary of state for international development but later resigned that post and her membership in the Labour Party, blasts Blair for reneging on his promise to work through the United Nations, and she condemns the behavior of Lord Goldsmith, Blair's attorney general, who, apparently under pressure, reversed his opinion that the war was illegal ten days after he issued it. From these internal and domestic disagreements, Kent and Norton-Taylor expand the discussion to include commentary from world figures, including Edward Mortimer, the director of communications for UN secretary general Kofi Annan, Juan Gabriel Valdes, Chile's ambassador to the United Nations, and Richard Perle, the American security advisor. Perle unapologetically lays out the neo-con thinking that had been brewing for decades, including his belief in preemptive war as a modern application of the right to self-defense. He skirts the issue of the US government's earlier relationship with Iraq—infamously captured in photos of Rumsfeld and Hussein together—as merely the lesser of evils. That Blair and Bush were planning for war, Perle maintains, may signify strategy but was not a complete commitment to wage war. After all, Perle says, "I have always regarded our two countries as the centre of the civilized democratic world" (82).

Called to Account makes no final judgment about whether Blair could be accused and convicted of a crime of aggression, and for all of the evidence it presents about manipulating information, Blair emerges as something of a greased pig, sliding through various legal nets and public outrage. Instead of accountability, the sad but inevitable conclusion of the play demonstrates how little the well-being of the Iraqis was considered; how grandiose the dream of reordering the Middle East was; and how inadequate the plans for the postwar period were. While some speculate about Blair's motivations, they remain unexplained: why would the once-popular Blair want to be Bush's lackey? That tantalizing question is not answered in *Called to Account*, but it is taken up in another documentary drama: David Hare's *Stuff Happens*.

In his author's note, Hare calls *Stuff Happens* a history play in which the staged events have been "authenticated from multiple sources, both private and public." He elaborates:

> What happened happened. Nothing in the narrative is knowingly untrue. Scenes of direct address quote people verbatim. When the doors close on the world's leaders and on their entourages, then I have used my imagination. This is surely a play, not a documentary, and driven, I hope by its themes as much as by its characters and story.[7]

Hare identifies his play, then, as a hybrid creation of public record, private sources, and imagined dialogues. To note, the key difference between *Stuff*

Happens and *Called to Account* is thematic. If *Called to Account* premises its charges of criminal aggression on Blair's willful mendacity—the prosecution's case—*Stuff Happens* claims to be a play about inevitability if we take its first line at face value: "The Inevitable is what will seem to happen to you purely by chance" (2004, 3). The play, however, exposes that the "inevitable" is more related to smooth political management than to chance.

Stuff Happens proceeds chronologically, a structure that itself seems to help charge the engines of inevitability. The common issues between *Called to Account* and *Stuff Happens* are addressed in the following questions, some of which have been settled through further evidence: (1) when did the Bush administration decide to pursue regime change in Iraq? When did Blair consent to ally his government with this policy? What were the motivations in pursuing regime change and a democratic Iraq? (2) To what extent did both administrations know the intelligence on Iraq's arsenal was flawed? And to what extent did that knowledge result in false presentations by Blair, Cheney, and Powell? (3) What was the degree of consensus within the two administrations about preparing for war? What was the consensus between the Bush and Blair governments? (4) How did preemptive war become a legitimate means of self-defense? What was the attitude toward UN consultation and resolutions? (5) What plans prevailed about postwar reconstruction and peace-keeping? In short, these issues revolve around global remapping, the security threat posed by WMDs, the US–UK alliance, just war and international law, and postwar reconstruction.

While the witnesses and attorneys in *Called to Account* debate policy and fact in their back-and-forth exchanges, the same issues arise in *Stuff Happens* in a linear narrative, albeit one that is interrupted by various introductions and inter-scenes and complicated by dramaturgical elements such as scene shifts and the multiple roles some members of the company assume. Hare breaks his play into two acts with a combined total of 24 scenes; 22 actors take on the roles of 44 nonfictional characters.[8] The play draws on recognizable scenes and information that are easy to substantiate. In the inter-scenes, characters who are not public figures—an Iraqi citizen, a New Labour politician—deliver monologues that break the continuity to give space to commentary. The scenes and players change quickly in the production as the actors reshuffle themselves into different characters and different locales. One minute, Colin Powell is hosting a lunch for members of the UN Security Council; with a turn of the circular playing space, he is in Condoleezza Rice's office, entreating her to help him get through to the president. The staging suggests simultaneous plotting and disconnection, with Bush as a kind of wily puppet master.

After premiering at the National Theatre in London in 2004, where it was directed by Nicholas Hytner, *Stuff Happens* made its US debut at the

Mark Taper Forum in Los Angeles in 2005 and then moved east to the Public Theatre in New York in 2006. Hare changed parts of the play as new evidence emerged. In combining what he imagined with what was recognizable from television and newspapers, Hare tapped into the media-driven appetite for the behind-the- scenes back-story or the personal story. For all the pleasures of the visual—the very recognizability of almost every figure in the play and the pleasure in seeing all of them impersonated—Hare really wanted his audiences to *listen* and to hear the rhetoric of exceptionalism in Rumsfeld's off-handedness, Cheney's brutal pragmatism, and Bush's maladroit speech. Neither Powell nor Blair speaks in these terms, and they are slow to recognize the discourse for what it is—the defiant speech of the Cold War winner who is opposed to internationalism, indifferent to international law, and protective of executive privilege. Perhaps the real achievement of *Stuff Happens* is, not only did it expose the run-up to war, but it also illuminated the logic behind Guantanamo, the Patriot Act, and Abu Ghraib.

The changes between the London production and the New York production involved deemphasizing Powell's heroism, and Hare admitted that while he saw Powell as a man "who knows what it's like to see people's lives destroyed by bombs," others told him he had taken "too benign a view of Powell" (quoted in Bumiller 2006, A14). Richard Norton-Taylor's tribunal plays allege manipulation, lies, and self-interest, but the plays depict points of possible intervention where even a single man—such as Alastair Campbell or Lord Goldsmith —could have exerted restraint or simply refused to act as they were bid. Tony Blair might have refused to include the 45-minute scenario in the dossier, or he might have insisted on protecting David Kelly's identity. These men are not, however, the tragic or romantic hero that Powell is.

Powell emerges as a modern-day Bussy D'Ambois, George Chapman's court reformer who eventually capitulates to corruption. The play follows the arc of Powell's reasoned arguments, to his frustration and anger, and finally to his submission, encapsulated in the low moment of his career, when he offered up his integrity at the United Nations in order to make the case that Iraq's arsenal was still a threat. The arc of Powell's downfall as well as the real chronology from 9/11 opportunism to the "Mission Accomplished" speech give structure to the play's events. Donna Soto-Morettini describes this structure as a "lucid and measured sequence of events, which imposes a kind of coherency and order onto what, for most of us, remains a strange mixture of heavily controlled media images, unlocated weapons of mass destruction, ideological tales of moral warfare and the outer reaches of weblog hysteria" (2005, 309). In her reading, the coherence of *Stuff Happens* imposes an undue order that makes Powell a tragic figure. For Soto-Morettini, following Hayden White's typology of historical emplotment, *Stuff Happens* does have elements of the tragic and the ironic, but it largely follows the mode of "romantic" emplotment.[9] This "romantic" notion suggests that the desires of a few powerful great men dictate history's direction. Indeed, much of the play seems interested in how and why a distinguished and ethical man, who is both popular and persuasive, becomes so ineffectual. That man is, of course, Colin Powell—not Tony Blair who might feel entitled to the same description—whom the play positions as a commanding but solitary man out-maneuvered by a fraternity of aging neo-cons, holdovers from the first Bush presidency.

The play's beginning underscores this premise. Each of the players is introduced with brief but revealing anecdotes: Vietnam shaped Powell's belief in "war as the politics of last resort"; Rumsfeld is a "towel-snapper" in the locker room; Cheney "never met a weapons system he didn't vote for"; Wolfowitz is more of a "velociraptor" than a hawk; Bush, who lost the popular vote, is a born-again alcoholic who believes "God wants" him in the Oval Office; Blair is an "original mix of theology and social duty." From the beginning, the play sets up how deep seated proclivities, even personality quirks, pressure history into shape. Further, more than a whiff of racism blows through the hallowed halls of White House privilege: Hare shows Powell reaching out primarily to Rice as a would-be ally, but she remains Bush's mouthpiece and general factotum. When the cabinet gathers together at Camp David after 9/11, a plantation atmosphere is hinted at: they dine on fried chicken and corn bread; George and Laura work on the white columns in a jigsaw puzzle of the White House; and Rice sings a hymn, "Amazing Grace." With these conspiring personalities and vestiges of race politics, the play hints that Powell never stood a chance. And neither did the Iraqis. In the final scene, an Iraqi exile speaks, shifting attention from what happened in the offices and corridors of power to what happened in the desert. He identifies Rumsfeld's dismissive statement, "stuff happens," as the "most racist remark I had ever heard" (120).

To limit *Stuff Happens* to an account of a marginalized dissenter ignores two of its other preoccupations: the imperial qualities of the Bush presidency and the abandonment of the Iraqi people. A thread woven throughout the play, largely at Powell's insistence, is the question: now that America is the only superpower, accountable to no one, are its founding values still intact? Powell reminds Bush, Cheney, and Rumsfeld that America is a republic not an empire. But Cheney and Rumsfeld in particular will have none of it. In a news conference, Rumsfeld assures listeners that America will go it alone if it must; it needs no allies, not even the loyal British. He categorizes France, England, and Germany as "old Europe" who envy American power and want to curtail it. Cheney despises Powell's internationalism and Blair's do-gooding ideals. When Powell protests that Blair's political life is on the line and that his loyalty merits American support, Cheney likens the British prime minister to a "preacher sitting on top of the tank" whom America doesn't need. When the "cat shit gets bigger than the cat," Cheney declares, "it's time to get rid of the cat" (104). The unilateralism that Bush's cabinet advocates, their desire to remap the world, and their belief that executive power can be expanded without check—these are imperial notions. Bush's fundamental belief that God put him in the presidency to smite Al-Qaeda and Hussein is an imperial mentality, even if its religiosity deflects self-glory. With so sure a sense of historical destiny in the president, and so arrogant a sense of historical exceptionalism among his deputies, the invasion of Iraq was indeed inevitable. The protocols of consultation, debate, evidence, policy, law—these Republican ideals for which Powell stands count for nothing in an empire.

Even more devastatingly, the lives that the Americans came to "save" count even less. In the final scene, an exiled Iraqi speaks, shifting attention from what happened in the offices and corridors of power to what happened in the desert. He goes on to observe, "They came to save us, but they had no plans. And now the American dead are counted, their numbers recorded, their coffins draped in flags. How many Iraqis have died? How many civilians? No figure is given. Our dead are uncounted." He adds, "Iraq has been crucified. By Saddam's sins, by ten years of sanctions, and then this. Basically it's a story of a nation that failed in only one thing. But it's a big sin. It failed to take charge of itself" (120).

This speech, which closes with the exiled Iraqi warning his compatriots never to expect help from America, contrasts directly with the play's first speech in which an angry British journalist rails against those who criticize the war and fail to recognize that Iraqis have been delivered from a tyrant. He concludes, "A people hitherto suffering now suffer less. This is the story. No other story obtains" (16). But other stories have obtained: a country that did not harbor Al-Qaeda does, and its reconstruction has not yet happened. Hare's play asks audiences to consider not only the tabloid story of how "stuff happened," but the harder, infinitely more complex political and ethical questions: when does one nation, for humanitarian reasons, violate another's sovereignty? How can the dis-interestedness of the intervention be demonstrated? And what ethical obligations persist after the tyrant has been deposed?

Culture Project: What Journalism Fails to Do

In its dozen years of operation, Culture Project has staged works that examine the issues that fray a workable democracy, including incidences of racial and gendered oppression and violations of human rights. Culture Project's most significant achievement, however, has been its vigilant response to the Iraq War. Since 2003, it has staged works about Iraq, making it possible to express and to hear views that were, for a time, automatically derided as unpatriotic. No other theatre in the United States or overseas has committed so much of its resources to responding to the conflict *as it was unfolding*, and in the process established itself as a voice of intervention, documentation, and analysis.

Of its Iraq War plays, all are in keeping with the Culture Project's emphasis on activism and intervention. A brief overview of these plays gives some sense of both the depth and breadth of commentary offered via performance and the way that Culture Project draws audiences in. For example, Culture Project was the first venue to stage *Guantanamo: Honor Bound to Defend Freedom*, the play written by Victoria Brittain and Gillian Slovo at the behest of Nicolas Kent, the director of London's Tricycle Theatre—notably, Nobel Laureate Archbishop Desmond Tutu joined the performance. This kind of celebrity staging is a common practice at Culture Project, and many of its works make use of the celebrity/activist model that has emerged as model of raising consciousness and funds in response to world crises. Additionally, as in the 2007 production of *Question of Impeachment*, a changing panel of commentators, from politicians and community activists to soldiers and psychologists, is brought to the stage. In its advertisement for *Question*, Culture Project asserted, "They took it off the table," so, "We put it on the stage"; this attitude well-describes Culture Project's vigilance over justice issues that have received either too little media coverage or coverage that was too biased. In terms of underrepresented issues, Culture Project staged *In Conflict*, a verbatim play created by students at Temple University, at the same time that it staged *The Treatment* by Eve Ensler, which starred Dylan McDermot and Portia, both well-known actors. Both plays examine the costs of the war as born by soldiers. Others, such as *Baghdad Burning: Girl Blog from Iraq*, offer room and time to underheard voices. Peter Morris's *The Guardians* takes the media to task by pairing coverage about Lynndie England and the Abu Ghraib scandal with a false report disseminated by the British paper *The Daily Mirror*.

Culture Project also takes chances on new works and new writers. The remainder of this essay will examine two of these. Both plays were written by journalists who had already published prominent investigative articles about the war in Iraq; the playwrights were therefore motivated by the perception that a live theatrical performance could provide a different kind of commentary than that offered in print. These plays, though quite different in form, stage already-published material, and in doing so provide compelling analysis of why we failed in Iraq and why we may be failing the War on Terror. In 2007, Lawrence Wright, author of *The Looming Tower: Al Qaeda and the Road to 9/11*, a book termed the "the bible" of information about Osama Bin Laden, decided to write and act in a one-man play that would, he hoped, would be part of a national conversation about who Al-Qaeda is and why the organization attacked America. The result, *My Trip to Al-Qaeda*, ran for six weeks before going on to the Kennedy Center. A year later, fellow *New Yorker* writer George Packer wrote *Betrayed*, a play based on a sixteen thousand–word article about the fate of Iraqi interpreters who had assisted American troops. It premiered at Culture Project in 2008.

Why stage already-published information? What motivated these writers to tell their story again, and what attracted the Culture Project to produce one play and commission the other? Both Packer and Wright have addressed why they felt it was important to recast their stories and, at first glance, their motivations seem very different: Packer wanted to write a work that allowed the Iraqis "to speak for themselves," while Wright wanted to tell his own story. But these different aims are attached to what each recognizes as the limits of journalism: *Betrayed* voices concern about omissions and erasure; Wright's work is about coverage that is ahistorical and superficial. Moreover, a palpable urgency underlies each composition and is felt in the performance: these plays not only seek to provide the crucial information and perspectives that have been omitted, but they also communicate a shared experience of shame, exasperation, and betrayal.

More than any other plays about global terrorism, these two works answer the most urgent, operational questions: Why did we fail to destroy Osama bin Laden and Al-Qaeda? Why did we fail to stabilize Iraq after Hussein's capture and death? What do these failures portend? Wright's play seeks to understand the circumstances, especially in Egypt and Saudi Arabia, that produced the Islamist mentality—a fundamentalism that bans music, segregates the sexes, and praises martyrdom—and make it attractive. In his analysis, the war in Afghanistan severely weakened Al-Qaeda but because of the Iraq War, terrorist cells have proliferated in Pakistan, North Africa, and Europe.[10] For Packer, the Iraqi interpreters who risked their lives to embrace the American project but now have no protectors in the world's most violent country are representative of the failures of American policy after the fall of Hussein (2008, viii). Both Wright and Packer demonstrate that the failures of the War on Terror and the War in Iraq are traceable to a single, deadly assumption: we do not need to know the culture of either our friends or our enemies.

Fire Under the Ashes: George Packer's Betrayed

George Packer's *Betrayed* dramatizes the fate of Iraqi interpreters whose belief in American values led them to put their lives at risk by working for the US Embassy after Saddam Hussein's capture. Despite good relationships with lower-level American staff members, the interpreters were largely dismissed or distrusted by the senior members of the embassy staff. The considerable help the interpreters could have provided, from contacts to cultural information, was not utilized because operationally no Iraqi, however pro-American, would ever be given full security clearance. While the death and displacement of the Iraqi interpreters is the work's most pressing topic, their stories represent the widespread suffering that resulted from the failure to quell violence and achieve civil order after the three months of American bombing. Though glibly dismissed by Donald Rumsfeld as the "messiness of freedom," the unplanned and poorly executed second phase of the war allowed the insurgency to take control of neighborhoods and establish their own reign of terror. *Betrayed* thus depicts how the small window of opportunity, when America could have helped to stabilize the country and acquire a durable ally in the Middle East, closed, perhaps permanently. If Packer's analysis is correct, America will leave Iraq in worse shape than it did Vietnam; it will have deserted its few remaining friends, damaged its moral reputation, given terrorists new home ground, and failed to provide the better life promised by removing a vicious dictator.

Arguably, despite the incessant media coverage, the mental pictures most Americans have of Iraq are from either the opening months of attack or from highly publicized scandals. *Betrayed* attempts to fill in this blank space by asking spectators to contemplate the substantially more complex political realities that ensued after George Bush declared victory. Structured in 23 short scenes, the play is set some three years into the Iraq war in order to demonstrate how the optimism around the 2003 "liberation" became its inverse: despair and distrust of an invasion and occupation.

While many other plays about the Iraq War have concentrated on how the Bush administration misled American citizens into war or on the abuses committed during it, Packer's play stands apart for its focus on how the war was executed. Such a perspective is relatively rare among the theatrical responses made to the Iraq War, with two notable exceptions: Wright's *My Trip to Al-Qaeda*, discussed below, and Iraqi American Heather Raffo's *Nine Parts of Desire*. While both Packer and Raffo describe Hussein's horrific abuses, each concludes that because Iraq's complex history and social makeup was either tragically misunderstood or strategically oversimplified, any hope brought about by Hussein's removal has been virtually extinguished. In *Betrayed*, the failure to stabilize Iraq is traced to two planning errors: the emphasis on military victory over political reconstruction and the consequential misjudgments of the Bremer Administration. The undervaluation of basic cultural and historical knowledge about Iraq and the bureaucratic structure that impeded collaboration produced the insular, "Green

Zone" mentality that failed to gauge the effect of lawlessness on daily life or deal with internal displacement. The human cost of this ignorance is made vivid in the play.

In the first scene, which takes place in a nearly abandoned Baghdad Hotel, two Iraqi interpreters, Adnan, a Sunni, and Laith, a Kurdish Sh'ia, meet clandestinely with an unseen reporter. Adnan describes how his perception of the American presence has shifted:

> I was totally against the word "invasion." Wherever I went I was defending the Americans and strongly saying America was here to make a change. But now I have my doubts (2008, 10).

From this point, *Betrayed* traces the lives of three Iraqi collaborators, two men and one woman, all of whom suffer because of their willingness to work with Americans: by the end of the play, the men must seek exile, and the woman is killed. Yet even while he is burning his possessions before taking up asylum in Sweden, Adnan's criticism of the military and political failures does not amount to a complete indictment of American values. He says:

> We know each other a little now, Americans and Iraqis, even if it is a terrible situation. Sometimes we are talking, sometimes we are fighting, but at least this is a relationship. It is not something to throw away or burn. But America does not want me...I can never blame the Americans alone. It's the Iraqis who destroyed their country, with the help of Americans, under the American eye. Until this moment I dream about America (108).

Adnan's opening and closing speeches frame an account of bureaucratic, tactical, and strategic mistakes so profound that even Ambassador Paul Bremer, the disastrous overseer of Iraq's disintegration into complete public disorder, admitted in an interview, "We paid a big price for not stopping [the looting] because it established an atmosphere of lawlessness" (2006). As the "Red Zone"—that is, all of Iraq except the secured American compound—was collapsing, the Green Zone, the bunker-like area of American presence reached by passing through the Assassins' Gate checkpoints, followed a transitional plan that was tethered to intractable and unrealistic policies produced in Washington and high-handedly administered in Baghdad. Packer concludes his book *The Assassins' Gate* with a scathing indictment of the Bush administration's failure to plan for postwar Iraq:

> I came to believe that those in positions of highest responsibility for Iraq showed a carelessness about human life that amounted to criminal negligence. Swaddled in abstract ideas, convinced of their righteousness, incapable of self-criticism, indifferent to accountability, they turned a difficult

undertaking into a needlessly deadly one. When things went wrong, they found other people to blame (2006, 448).

Packer decided that tactical explanations of American military and political procedures did not answer the deeper questions about how wary but workable alliances were formed between Iraqis and Americans—and why they collapsed. Motivated by "shame," Packer relistened to the countless interviews that had filled his tape recorder during six tours of Iraq and decided that dramatizing the "texture of life among Iraqi interpreters in wartime Baghdad," the group who represented the best chance for a mutual relationship, would honor their sacrifice and offer the American public another mode through which to understand the human costs of our policy decisions (2008, viii). Much like others who have written documentary dramas, Packer decided that while his characters would be composites and his scenes invented, much of the play's dialogue would be verbatim since the taped words had the "inadvertent bluntness and accidental poetry of a second language and the intensity of life caught in a reflective pause during an extreme time" (ix). In fact, without exception, Packer heard in "every individual version" of the interpreters' stories, an account of a "trajectory from suffering to hope—the kind of dazzling, outsize hope that comes when, as several Iraqis put it, your world is a prison and someone opens the door—through a slow, reluctant, increasingly brutal process of disillusionment to a sense of abandonment and betrayal" (viii). Distinct from strategic analyses, media spin, or propaganda, these stories spoke instead to "how the Americans and Iraqis saw one another, what kind of relationship was possible in violent circumstances, and the ability of inability of individuals to transcend their 'official' roles and maintain a human pulse" (x).

In the first scene, Adnan and Laith recall the cultural sea change that marked the American arrival: one could curse Saddam in the public square and mingle with Americans. In addition to reminding the audience of the promises made in 2003, the scene further disrupts the dominant media images of Iraqis as extremists or hyper-partisan. Adnan thinks of himself as a "non-belonger"; he is a careful and reflective intellectual who loved the English language so much that he read everything he could find, from existentialist tracts to pornography. When Bill Prescott, a State Department official who will later become both a friend and an advocate, asks him what he thinks of the Americans' arrival, Adnan replies that while it is a "chance for every Iraqi," he knows that living in the great "darkness" and "prison" of the Hussein years has produced a desperate mentality, one that Americans must understand if they are to be successful (2008, 27). He offers to help Prescott to gain such insight, an offer Prescott only belatedly understands and values. Despite the threats from both the American regional security officers who distrust him and the Iraqi insurgents who wish to punish him, Adnan remains committed to working with the Americans. Laith's reasons for joining the staff are more pragmatic: it is safer than going on raids with American soldiers, and he needs employment to support his family. Inistar, the female interpreter, has deeply resented the many restrictions placed on women under Hussein, and she refuses to wear a hijab after his execution. Her dream is that five years after the American liberation, she will be able to bring the banned English literature she loves so much to readers in the Middle East. By the end of the play, she is back to covering her head to avoid harassment from members of the insurgency. Like the times that George Bush defended his decision to invade Iraq and bomb Afghanistan as a way of liberating veiled women from oppression, Prescott, well-meaning but undiscerning, points to Inistar as an example of bravery and progress, failing to see her desperation.

All three characters are educated, informed, and willing to work not only with Americans but with each other—a receptivity toward peaceful coexistence that many argue characterized Iraq for centuries. It also signals a deep desire to turn away from the ethnic divisions that Hussein promoted, especially through his brutal, genocidal treatment of the Kurds, but also in his self-serving embrace of religious and tribal identities. Over the course of the play, however, as they become increasingly subject to threats of violence and their pleas for American protection go unheard, Adnan and Laith begin to attribute their disagreements more to ethnic differences than to the criminality of extremist groups. This shift represents what Ashraf Al-Akhalidi and Victor Tanner describe as the "hardening" that has occurred throughout Iraqi society, where daily violence forces ordinary citizens to choose sides in order to attain some sort of protection and avoid persecution. Once a relative has joined a radical group, they note, the entire family becomes trapped (2008, 6). For the interpreters, the inverse is also true: once someone is identified as working with the American government, their loved ones are imperiled.

About three-quarters of the way into the play, Adnan and Laith speak about the bombing of the Askariya shrine at Samarra on February 22, 2006.[11] The attack on the Golden Mosque is not well-known or well-understood in the United States, but for Iraqis it is a watershed event, marking the end of a restrained Shia response to escalated attacks against them. It can also be read as an event that manifests the problems Americans must deal with in Iraq currently and well into the future. In symbolic terms, if the toppling of the statue of Saddam Hussein represents how Americans envisioned a war in Iraq to be quickly completed, the bombing of the Golden Mosque represents the way the war has actually proceeded. Bringing down Hussein's statute encapsulated the preliminary assumptions that led most Americans to support Bush's arguments: that Hussein was a genocidal maniac and a supporter of terrorism, that taking him out would be easy and quick, and that once he was gone, America would establish a pro-Western government by helping Iraqis exiled in the United States to return to power. In retrospect, the plan seems so absurdly reductive as to be a caricature of a strategic plan, but when first publicized, its very simplicity and directness caught and fed the American desire for some quick fix to 9/11. It captures the combination of American exceptionalism, naïveté, and arrogance that the American characters—respectively, Prescott, the soldiers at Assassin's Gate, and the Regional Security Officer—in the play each exemplify.

The Askariya mosque bombing, on the other hand, signifies the political reality in Iraq after Hussein's execution, capturing the complex internal dynamics, the regional instability, and Iraq as the new front of terrorist activity. Arguably, all of these dynamics have worsened due to American missteps. Built in 944, the mosque is one of the Shias' holiest sites; three days of retaliatory violence followed the bombing, killing close to four hundred people. After the attack, talks between Shi'a and Sunni leaders about a coalition government were suspended, and both President Jalal Talabani and President George Bush issued public statements warning against civil war. Religious leaders also issued statements, using the occasion to further their own agendas. Grand Ayatollah Ali al-Sistani, considered one of Iraq's most influential clerics, encouraged peaceful rallies but suggested that expanded religious militias would assume security roles. Muqtada al-Sadr, the head of the Mahdi Army, repeated his demand for a US withdrawal. Predictably, Iranian president Mahmoud Ahmadinejad and Hezbollah leader Sayyed Hassan Nasrallah accused the United States and Israel of being behind the attacks. Some argued that the bombing was masterminded by Al-Qaeda in Iraq.[12] In sum, the image of the damaged golden domes signals a complexity completely opposite to the toppled statue. *Betrayed*, as an aesthetic, political cultural product, wants to function as the theatrical equivalent of the golden dome image. Through the accessibility of its portrait of the Iraqi interpreters, Packer's play wants to offer an analysis that can reject simplistic assessments and nevertheless do justice to the complexities of Iraqi society. Concurrently, it wishes to indicate how the failure to engage with these complexities has made Iraq more violent, the region more volatile, and Americans less safe. Integrating violence into daily life is the new normal for ordinary Iraqis. In fact, it has produced at least one new industry: for a fee, someone will search dumps and riverbanks for the bodies of loved ones (Al-Khalidi and Tanner 2009).

By the play's end, each interpreter has suffered the very fate they had warned the Americans would happen. Inistar tells Prescott that women who work at the embassy are regarded as prostitutes, and requiring her to wait an hour or more to pass through the approved checkpoint, wearing her embassy badge, makes her an open target. One night, she is abducted, her head is shaved, and she is shot and dumped into the back seat of taxi cab where she is driven around the city until she bleeds to death. The driver is suspected of working with Ansar-al Sunna, one of the Salafi jihadists who was part of the insurgency. When his younger brother is kidnapped and threatened with death, Adnan knows that unless he leaves Iraq, his family will be under constant surveillance. Laith comes under suspicion at the embassy because he has contacts in Sadr City, acting as a conduit between them and Prescott. To the regional security officer, a low-level by-the-manual functionary whose belief in polygraph tests is an apt metaphor for the many ways in which Americans have avoided complexity and direct engagement, the contact is evidence that Laith is an enemy agent. At the same time, he finds the severed head of a small dog in his yard and knows that he has been singled out by either Al-Qaeda or Jaish al-Mahdi. Prescott is also among those betrayed: sent back to the United States, overcome by guilt and inadequacy, he drives his car off the road. His efforts to convince the American embassy to provide protection for Iraqi interpreters yielded no results.

The Bomb at my Imagination: Lawrence Wright's My Trip to Al Qaeda

George Packer's *Betrayed* speaks to the consequences of failing to take the true measure of the challenges being faced. Lawrence Wright's *My Trip to Al Qaeda*, a monologue delivered by the author playing himself, offers a similar warning about the failure of American intelligence agencies and of the federal government to accurately assess the threat posed by Al-Qaeda. Wright goes further to argue against one of the most repeated assertions about terrorists: that we cannot understand them as human beings. If Hussein's statute can be taken as the image of dangerous reductiveness, and the golden dome of the complexities overlooked and dangers thereby produced, the depiction of Osama bin Laden as a seven-foot-tall cave dweller with failing kidneys who is apparently immortal is Wright's image for how America has helped to create the terrorist monster it could not seem to find. From numerous interviews, Wright concludes that bin Laden is likely less than six-feet, five-inches tall and does not need dialysis. But in the collective American imagination, bin Laden is the ghostly puppet master pulling the invisible strings of jihad. After the Navy seals raided his compound in Pakistan and killed him, his body was swiftly buried at sea. The disposal guarded against his body becoming fetishized but also bespeaks the almost magical hold he had on the world's imagination.

Appropriately, then, Wright stages his "lecture" on the roots of Islamic fundamentalism and his direct encounters with their leaders in front of a large screen with images, pictures, and videotapes that "demonstrate" the points he is making, though Wright does not turn around to look at it. Instead, the giant screen hovers over his shoulder much as the terrorist threat hovers over the post 9/11 world and much as global media technologies have eclipsed—or become—the real. The disproportion between screen and speaker actualizes the imbalance that Wright's play wished to address: telepresence dominating human presence, image overpowering word, myth governing analysis. The projected scenes also tacitly pose a number of questions: how do these images compare with those that have glutted our television and computer screens, and rooted themselves in our collective mind's eye? Which images are part of the terrorist arsenal, spreading fear as much in the portent as in the act, reminding us that the war is fought as much in the symbolic realm as in real places, be they subways, trains, buildings, boats, deserts, or mountains? And which are our own projections, formed in fear and ignorance or fostered by political manipulation? And while *My Trip to Al-Qaeda* is not multimedia theatre in any elaborate sense, the proxemics between live speaker and techno-image, and live speaker and live audience, effectively enact the David and Goliath struggle between the words of the witness and the power of the disembodied image. The audience members, all of whom have entered the theatre with already screened depictions of terrorism, are placed in a new scopic field, one that asks them to reorganize the projected images, the iconic images of terrorism, and Wright's commentary into a framework that acknowledges the power of symbolic exchange but does not dematerialize history.

For Wright, the questions above are not theoretical. A screenwriter and novelist as well as journalist, Wright wrote the script for a 1998 movie entitled *The Siege*, which imagines an Islamic terrorist attack on New York. Though a box-office failure, the film became the most-rented DVD after 9/11. It has another, even darker, prior history: a radical Islamist group bombed a Planet Hollywood restaurant in Cape Town, South Africa, claiming that the violence was a reaction to anti-Arab and anti-Muslim stereotypes in the film. Two British tourists were killed and a young girl lost her leg. Wright's distress over the episode was deepened further when he watched the twin towers fall, feeling as though he was witnessing a scene from the movie he had written. The next day, he informed his *New Yorker* editor that he was leaving for the Middle East to try to understand the terrorist group that had killed so many Americans—and seemed to have hijacked his imagination.

As he recounts these events to the audience, Wright wants his listeners to share his sense of urgency, and if his performance can be pared down to two essential warnings, they are that, first, in regard to Al-Qaeda, "We were absent-minded while we under assault," and second, our invasion of Iraq has "created the reality that we've imagined."[13] Our failures to protect ourselves are, Wright claims, institutional as well as political, but they also derive from our refusal to acknowledge that there are ways of explaining the attraction to the Islamist worldview that do not undermine its danger but do not deride it as wholly inexplicable or irrational. Further, the failure to understand the phenomena will continue to perpetrate not only inadequate and expensive responses to terrorism, but result in actions that invigorate it. The "War in Iraq breathed life back into Al-Qaeda," Wright warned, and gave the terrorists a home.

Since finishing his five years of research into the appearance and operation of Al-Qaeda—a project that took him to 12 countries to interview more than six hundred people—and writing a Pulitzer Prize–winning account about it, *The Looming Tower: Al-Qaeda and the Road to 9/11*, Wright sought other means to enact what he considered a journalistic obligation to provide a critical context for understanding the threat that the political leadership failed to supply. He began giving lectures in which he ruefully acknowledges that he knows more about terrorism than most people in the intelligence community. Some of these lectures are available on archived on websites, making it possible to see what, if anything, is the difference between Wright the guest lecturer and Wright the performer.[14] In some aspects, they are much the same: Wright speaks in the same measured Texas cadence, enlivens his observations with the same anecdotes, and draws the same conclusions. Yet, Wright himself sees one as a presentation, and the other as a performance, and he cites both David Hare's *Via Doloroso* and Anna Deavere Smith's plays as influences; Spalding Gray's *Swimming to Cambodia* is another.

The distinction between lecture and performance appears largely in the rhetorical stance of each work. Wright is clearly the invited expert in his lectures, whereas in his play, Wright offers himself as "more or less a representative of the community, going out to find out what is going on, and coming back to make a report." The common-man conceit expresses itself through some of Wright's down-home comparisons, like his story of the "hypnotized chicken" of his boyhood, but it's clearly a mixed presentation. On the one hand, Wright, like his spectators, seems to find many aspects of Arab life, particularly in Saudi Arabia, perplexing. He recounts, for example, how thousands of Saudis showed up for the opening of a new IKEA story as an index of the country's blend of boredom, repression, and consumerism. But on the other hand, Wright is clearly no common man: he had been a student in Cairo, speaks some Arabic, began this project the day after the 9/11 bombings, is a staff writer for *The New Yorker*, and obtained entry to Saudi Arabia by agreeing to mentor young reporters. Because he is so obviously more informed than any of his listeners, the "citizen Wright" persona often yields to that of the insider expert, but ultimately, the play's persuasiveness is linked primarily to its call for a kind of patriotic public action: to understand the threat, to analyze the US government's response, to honor our obligations to the Iraqi people whom we have promised to help, and to protest any degradation of American civil liberties in the name of security protection.

To understand the particular threat of Al-Qaeda, Wright contends that we must know about the culture and the personalities that shaped it. He begins, then, with the "man behind Osama bin Laden," an Egyptian doctor, Ayman al-Zawahiri, the leader of the Egyptian Islamic Jihad until it merged with Al-Qaeda in 1998. Pious and educated, like his Saudi partner, bin Laden, al-Zawahiri studied the writings of Sayyid Qutb, the most "prominent theoretician of the fundamentalist movements" (Wright 2007). Al-Zawahiri came to share Qutb's belief that Islam needed to be purged of all Western influences through jihad. In 1981, al-Zawahiri was imprisoned for his role in the assassination of Anwar Sadat. He was severely tortured, even having wild dogs set on him—an experience that added another level of connection to Qutb, who had also been imprisoned and tortured by dogs for his role in trying to kill Gamal Abdel Nasser in 1954. Wright observes that al-Zawahiri "entered a surgeon, but came out a butcher." He proposes that if Americans want to fully understand the tragedy of 9/11, they need to trace its origins back to the prison experiences shared by Qutb and al-Zawahiri. While the direct object of their anger was the secular government, they were also angry at the West for supporting the regime. Most importantly, Wright observes, they held the West responsible for corrupting and humiliating Islamic society. Indeed, the theme of humiliation, which is the essence of torture, is important to understanding the Islamists' rage against the West. Egypt's prisons became a factory for producing militants with a need for retribution. When Qutb was hanged in 1966, he thanked God for the death sentence: "I performed jihad for fifteen years before I earned this martyrdom." A videotape of al-Zawahiri, which is projected on the screen, shows a man in a white robe, obviously the leader, crying out that the only reason he and his fellow militants are imprisoned is because, "We are Muslims who believe in their religion, both in ideology and practice, and hence try our best to establish an Islamic state and an Islamic society."

From tracing the roots of Islamic fundamentalism, Wright moves to a description of Saudi Arabian society to which he gains access through temporary work training young reporters. There, in bin Laden's birthplace, he observes young men "incapacitated by longing," afflicted with hopelessness, and suffering from widespread depression. Women, "BMOs" or "black moving objects" as the local men call them, are so subject to strict religious law that they seldom share public spaces with men. Wright describes going to a mall with some of his male reporters who spy a completely veiled woman and with no apparent irony, exclaim, "Check 'em out." Wright himself is exasperated by his reporters' deep incuriosity—they are deeply reluctant to question official accounts of public events. He tells of charging his female reporters to write a piece about the education and treatment of girls on the one-year anniversary of a fire in girls' school. When a number of nearby people had rushed to help put out the blaze and rescue the girls trapped inside the locked building, they were turned away by a representative of the Commission for the Promotion of Virtue and the Prevention of Vice because the girls are not wearing abayas. For Wright, Saudi Arabia is marked most by boredom; civil society is virtually absent, and there is no "moderate, stabilizing ground between the government and the clerics."[15] With "nothing between the government and the mosque except shopping," the young especially feel a lack of agency or purpose.

In offering these "thick descriptions," Wright points out that the same economic polarities and extreme cultural repression that operate in both Egypt and Saudi Arabia produce a "fermented hatred." Because rebellion or dissent is nearly impossible, Wright suggests that joining a fundamentalist movement is one way of dealing with futility. The hopelessness is abetted by the fundamentalist rhetoric about the historical displacement and degradation of Muslims at the hands of the West. Though it is not clear why bin Laden, a member of an extraordinarily wealthy Saudi family, felt a personal sense of humiliation, it is the word he used most frequently to describe the plight of every Muslim. Wright comments that bin Laden chooses to live a humble life, casting off the advantages of his birth, because he believes deeply that humiliation has been the Muslim experience for centuries—perhaps back to another September 11 in 1683 when the king of Poland broke the Ottoman siege of Vienna, "definitively marking the moment when Islam began its long retreat into sullen isolation, watching helplessly as the Christian West regained its footing and once again became the custodian of learning and the captain of progress." Radicalized by the Soviet invasion of Afghanistan, bin Laden helped to raise millions of dollars for the mujahideen resistance, and he became convinced that if Al-Qaeda could inflict the Soviet Union with a "mortal wound," it could do the same to the United States. Before a picture of al-Zawahiri and bin Laden in smiling and close conversation, Wright describes how the partnership forged between Islamic Jihad and Al-Qaeda resulted in a global terrorist organization that has little political vision, but it has an intense dedication to a purification campaign and to the establishment of a separate Islamic state. The means to this end will be a protracted struggle with the West, carried out by the many who feel the profound humiliation that bin Laden and al-Zawahiri constantly describe. Because the "humiliated have a moral license to regain their dignity, they are entitled to hate," Wright asserts, and "hatred is delicious. It is the most narcotic emotion." Wright concludes that "perhaps Al Qaeda can be best understood as an engine that runs of the despair of the Muslim world, especially its young men, whose lives are so futile and unexpressed. Al Qaeda gives them an opportunity to make history. All they have to do is die."

The 9/11 attacks "struck all of humanity," Wright believes, in part because the "Trade Center dead formed a kind of universal parliament, representing sixty-two countries and nearly every ethnic group and religion on the world" (Wright 1997, 368). After Iraq, America stood alone. By failing to uphold American values, "our transparency, our system of justice, our freedoms," Wright tells his audience, we have fallen into bin Laden's trap. Shortly after 9/11, bin Laden told his followers to watch:

> I don't need to be on television to terrorize the American. All I need to do is to make a statement and carry out an attack once again, and the Americans will terrorize themselves. They will constrict their precious civil liberties. They will eventually bring their society to a state that is not recognizable before September 11th (Charles 2007).

Chillingly, bin Laden—and Wright and Packer—were right: America betrayed itself. We did not have, Wright concluded, the "fierce internal resistance" we should have had in order to denounce torture, to refuse the abrogation of civil liberties, and to protest the direction in which the country was being taken.

CHAPTER 7

BODIES COUNT: IN/VISIBLE SCANDAL AT GUANTANAMO AND ABU GHRAIB

> There isn't any other nation in the world that would treat people who were determined to kill Americans the way we're treating these people. They're living in the tropics. They're well fed. They've got everything they could possibly want.
>
> —Vice President Dick Cheney, 2005

DESPITE VICE PRESIDENT CHENEY'S ASSERTION, THE TRUTH is that the 774 prisoners ultimately detained at Guantanamo Bay did not get "everything they could possible want." When Shafiq Rasul, one of the "Tipton Three," a group of British friends who were seized in Afghanistan and then transferred to Guantanamo, was ultimately released and spoke about his experience, he offered a much different story:

> And it was really difficult for us, because for a start, we didn't know where we were. We didn't know what was going on. We were just taken, thrown on the back of a plane, had sacks put over our heads so we couldn't see anything. And being on the flight taking us there, being constantly beaten by the soldiers, then when the plane landed, dragged off the plane. And we were taken to a makeshift tent, which we were constantly beaten there again while we were waiting to be "processed," as they used to call it. And at that time, as we were being processed, we were being interrogated at the same time, so it was just a lot of things going on at the same time. Just having fear as well. You didn't know what was going on. We didn't know if they were going to kill us or what was going to happen. It was really, really, really scary for us (Rasul 2007).

Starting on January 11, 2002, when the first group arrived at a prison base that was erected in less than 96 hours by direct order of Secretary of Defense Donald Rumsfeld, shackled and blindfolded detainees were housed in small cages where they suffered intense heat, floodlights, and isolation.[1] These physical deprivations might have been endurable if any possibility of release could be grasped. Instead, various memos, executive mandates, and a persistent public rhetoric of extreme risk left the detainees at Guantanamo in a legal black hole. The detention policy at Guantanamo to which these bewildered, and possibly innocent, men were subjected was one of "potentially indefinite, virtually incommunicado incarceration, without charges, without recourse to courts or counsel, and without the benefits of the Geneva Conventions" (Margolis 2006, 25). The decision to deny habeas corpus and flout the Geneva conventions effectively precluded any chance for fair representation, even as it allowed the American government to keep the policies and practices secret and invisible.

Here again, we encounter a fundamental feature, however ironic it seems, of the mediated war we feel ourselves to be watching constantly: despite the relentless visibility, there is a capacity to hide the suffering body and substitute in its stead the terrorist figure. With both Guantanamo and Abu Ghraib, the proliferation of incremental news stories persisted alongside intense secrecy, control, and censorship. No matter that in the first months of detention at Guantanamo, two of those detained as "high-value" terrorists were over 90 years old, and several more were children—such cases were kept successfully out of the public's awareness.

The invisibility of those detained at Guantanamo and of the site itself permitted the eradication of fundamental legal rights and enabled policies of torture antithetical to American principles. Only when low-end technology, such as handheld cameras with phones and the spread of Internet access, became available across the globe did the military/political confidence in controlling information diminish. Interestingly, for this study, the manner in which the abuses at Guantanamo and Abu Ghraib came to be known correlates to the accelerated influence of citizen media on political events. As much as technology has enabled such information saturation that it is hard to sift through facts, it has also become the tool of exposure and a means of communication so quick that it can help fuel revolutions. At the time, however, the atrocities at Guantanamo unfolded slowly and somewhat invisibly. Although the first prisoners arrived at the extraterritorial base just four months after 9/11, it was not until the Associate Press filed a request under the Freedom of Information Act in 2006 that the names and stories of the prisoners were revealed (Worthington 2007, xiii). Conversely, the scandal at Abu Ghraib exploded into public awareness. Within just a few days, the infamous, atrocious images of prisoner humiliation were reproduced around the world. Anyone with access to television, newspaper, or the Internet has seen at least one photo, and the "Abu Ghraib man," the hooded prisoner, wired and posed atop a crate, became an emblem of American hypocrisy. From the period between 2002, when Guantanamo was designated as the place to hold uncharged "enemy combatants," to the first broadcast images from Abu Ghraib in 2004, the question of torture was not publicly debated; only when the photos from Abu Ghraib were made known did serious public discussion of America's lost moral compass begin. Phillip Carter, in his article "The Road to Abu Ghraib," writes:

> A generation from now, historians may look back to April 28, 2004, as the day the United States lost the war in Iraq. On that date, "CBS News" broadcast the first ugly photographs of abuses by American soldiers at Baghdad's Abu Ghraib prison. There were images of a man standing hooded on a box with wires attached to his hands; of guards leering as they forced naked men to simulate sexual acts; of a man led around on a leash by a female soldier; of a dead Iraqi detainee, packed in ice; and more. The pictures had been taken the previous fall by U.S. Army military police soldiers assigned to the prison, but had made it into the hands of Army criminal investigators only months later, when a soldier named Joseph Darby anonymously passed them a CD-ROM full of prison photos. The images aroused worldwide indignation, and illustrated in graphic detail both the lengths to which the United States would go to get intelligence, and the extent to which those efforts had been corrupted by the exigencies of the difficult war in Iraq (2004).

Carter may be right in identifying April 28 as the day when American righteousness was known worldwide to be as hollow as George Bush's statement a year earlier in observance of the United Nations International Day in Support of Victims of Torture. On that day, June 26, 2003, Bush declared that the "United States is committed to the worldwide elimination of torture, and we are leading this fight by example" (World Organization 2004, 1). What was less clear when the pornographic images of the humiliated detainees at Abu Ghraib became public was that the abuse was the logical expansion of the rhetoric, policies, and practices that redefined torture and made it acceptable. In this chapter, three plays address what happened when the American government decided, in Vice President Cheney's words, to "work" the "dark side" and "spend time in the shadows" (Mayer 2009, 10). More than just exposing governmental duplicity, the plays depict the political environment in which America (and its allies, particularly Great Britain) sacrificed its legal and ethical principles out of a fear that became obsessive, paranoiac, and, ultimately, self-defeating. These plays reenact the decisions of government leaders who countenanced any legal or ethical infraction if done in the name of "gathering intelligence." If there is a trope that fits this manic period of fear, it is that of an infinite circular chase: no amount of intelligence gathered would be enough, and what evidence was gathered was weak and therefore necessitated further interrogations and more captures. Since, as Secretary of Defense Donald Rumsfeld said, there would never be a signing ceremony signaling the end of the conflict, the cycle could never end, and the uncharged captives would never be released. With the canny bin Laden on the loose and invisible, the hunt was on, the stakes were raised, the cycle was unstoppable.

Yet, even the Bush administration, for all it did to create the cycle, knew it had a built-in element of self-destruction. Bush's claim to be "truly not concerned about" bin Laden in 2002, and Rumsfeld's dismissal of Iraqi insurgents in 2003 as "dead-enders" betray an awareness that they had talked themselves into a corner (2003). But slippery politicians, as all know, can slide around their own words, whereas men, shackled in cages, have no such flexibility. When the commander-in-chief has declared you a "killer," and has the executive authority to keep you locked up, the trope has performative power: it has become a detention cage. When the corporeal power of detention or interrogation failed to elicit useful information, the symbolic power of weaponized language took its place, with the detainees presented as persistent security threats and members of an invisible, active terrorist network. The War on Terror and the Iraq War has been about erasing the dead, mutilated body of the enemy and of the civilian casualty, and substituting in its stead, a textual body that evinces unparalleled fear.

To underline how significant a part language played in blurring legal boundaries, one particular anecdote is infamous. "Stress techniques" became the euphemism for torture, and the stress took many forms: being exposed to extreme heat and cold, being kept in a coffin-like metal locker, being chained in a bent-over position (known as "self-imposed stress," with its ludicrous insinuation of complicity), or being made to stand for hours. About this latter "technique," Donald Rumsfeld, who approved the legal memo asserting that these acts were not means of torture, observed that he stood writing at his desk for twice the amount of time detainees were made to stand. Other circumlocutions, like "enhanced" interrogation referred to water boarding, a process that had been designated as torture since 1901 but that Cheney, when asked about its use, called a "no-brainer for me" (Eggen 2006). As Jane Mayer has observed, the "Bush Administration's corruption of language had a curiously corrupting impact on the public debate, as well. It was all but impossible to have a national conversation about torture if top administration officials denied they were engaged in it." Rather than a debate within Congress, the administration adopted a "path of tricky legalisms adopted in classified memos" (2008, 151).

Guantanamo: Honour Bound to Defend Freedom by Victoria Brittain and Gillian Slovo is a significant play for many reasons but most of all for exposing the abuse taking place at the Cuban camp. Its timing is significant: it premiered three weeks after the Abu Ghraib photos became public, helping undermine the argument that the Abu Ghraib torture was an anomaly perpetrated by a few renegade soldiers. The excuse that torture occurs because of a few bad soldiers is further examined in Judith Thompson's *Palace at the End*. The second work discussed here, Thompson's triptych offers two versions of torture—one by a democracy; one by a dictatorship. Together, these two plays stand apart as key works that address an ethical turning-point in the American defense of itself as a global moral leader.

Thompson's *Palace of the End* also raises some of the issues considered in Eve Ensler's *The Treatment* and Frances Ya-Chu Cowhig's *Lidless*: the personal repercussions for American soldiers who administered torture, and by extension, the damage to the American value system. Thompson's monologues about Lynndie England, David Kelly, the British weapons expert who was the subject of *Justifying War*, and an Iraqi mother whose family was tortured by Saddam Hussein, give flesh to the cartoonish figures each became through media overexposure. Most of all, they examine how media has enabled a new high-tech form of scapegoating. Ensler's play, briefly considered here, moves the focus from those tortured to those ordered to implement the government policy. *Lidless* pursues the same theme, but with attention to the repercussions still felt years later.

The International Helsinki Federation for Human Rights has observed that "around the world, Guantanamo has become a symbol for the willingness of the US to sacrifice basic human rights principles and circumvent international standards on detention, due process, trials and torture in the 'war on terror.' Thus, it has become emblematic of how human rights can be trampled in the name of enhancing security" (Helsinki 2007, 2). Going further, the Helsinki Federation has described the "Guantanamo effect" as responsible for stifling the ability of the United States to criticize human rights problems in other nations and for emboldening governments with weak records on human rights to justify their policies by citing US practices. Similarly, an "Abu Ghraib" effect can be traced (Eisenman 2007). Together, these two prisons have become both the embodiment and the symbol of American hypocrisy and hubris.

HIDING THE BODY: GUANTANAMO AND THE PERILS OF EXECUTIVE PRIVILEGE

Brittain and Slovo's spoken evidence play is remarkable for the clarity with which it presents how the detention camp at Guantanamo Bay was established to be a site beyond the rule of law.[2] Brittain and Slovo edited dialogue from more than 26-hours of taped interviews in order to shape the play that Nicolas Kent, the artistic director of the Tricycle Theatre, had commissioned. It premiered in London on May 20, 2004. Its full title, *Guantanamo: Honour Bound to Defend Freedom*, is the motto of the Joint Task Force Guantanamo that hangs on a sign hung at the entrance of Camp Delta.

Michael F. Scheuer served as the chief of the Bin Laden Issue Station at the CIA's Counterterrorist Center until 2004, and he is the author of the anonymously published *Imperial Hubris*, the book bin Laden cited in a 2007 videotape (2004). Scheuer censured the growing number of renditions to the "black-site" prisons of US facilities in Afghanistan and Cuba, and he points out that these policies were contributing to the radicalization of the Muslim world. Once established, these off-shore prisons become a nightmare: there is no way to release the imprisoned since they are held outside of due process. Scheuer's comments accurately describe the mechanism of the exceptional state, as Giorgio Agamben describes it. In Agamben's analysis, a key feature of sovereign power is its very ability to hold someone beyond the reach of law—indefinitely. British Lord Justice Johan Steyn has a simpler term for what Scheuer and Agamben have observed: Guantanamo is a "legal black hole."

This assertion is the very first utterance of the play, *Guantanamo*: "The purpose of holding the prisoners at Guantanamo Bay," Steyn baldly states, "was and is to put them beyond the rule of law, beyond the protection of any courts, and at the mercy of the victors" (2004, 5). Consequently, those held at Guantanamo have "no access to the writ of habeas corpus to determine whether their detention is even arguable justified"; they are "in all respects subject to decisions of the President as Commander-in-Chief" who has "made public in advance his personal view of the prisoners as a group: he has described them all as 'killers'" (6). On this absolute condemnation of the camp's existence, the play unfolds.

The focus of *Guantanamo: Honour Bound to Defend Freedom* is on the British citizens who have been detained. In part, this emphasis sheds light on the situation of other foreign nationals who did not have the same access to counsel or families able to pressure government officials, but it also highlights the extent to which even British citizens—American's foremost ally—have been subjected to American military tribunals and placed outside the reach of any court. Much of the play's initial success in Britain was how it tapped into the public indignation around British political servility. The simmering anger was expressed by the British political left, but it also showed itself in media cartoons of the great empire reduced to being America's water boy and the articulate Tony Blair acting as George Bush's lap dog. Such sentiments appear in other plays such as David Hare's *Stuff Happens* and the National Theatre of Scotland's *Blackwatch*.

Slovo and Brittain constructed the spoken evidence they collected into a three-act play; each act takes up a larger theoretical question attached to the practice of extraterritorial detention while it depicts the specific kinds of suffering and degradation experienced at the camp. The first act looks at rendition and the random collection of prisoners; the second, at the tension between the evil of suicide bombing and the evil of detention without trial; and the third, at the domestic implications of expanded executive prerogatives. In its staging as well as its dialogue, the play highlights Guantanamo as an interstitial space, a legal nowhere specifically designed to be beyond the reach of the law and hence utterly within the purview of executive decision. Additionally, the play offers its own version of how language has been weaponized in the War on Terror, demonstrating how performative utterances, such as those made by Rumsfeld, have material effects, and how these utterances have migrated to shape the language and impact of other law and policies. (An obvious example is immigration policy.) In a war that has always been defined by linguistic assertions and equivalences made by the Bush and Blair administrations—the certainty of weapons of mass destruction; the Taliban and Al-Qaeda as equally culpable terrorist organizations; Hussein and bin Laden as categorically evil—Slovo and Brittain's play examines how the political vocabulary of the War on Terror undermines existing laws and treaties. In doing so, the play points most to the dangers of unchecked executive privilege—a topic hardly broached in the aftermath of 9/11 and the politically managed state of dread and threat. *Guantanamo: Honour Bound to Defend Freedom* exposes one of the fundamental dynamics of the war: the expansion of executive power that vitiates law and precedent and abrogates to itself the primary right to decide who has legal standing. Ultimately, it is a practice that decides which bodies count and which do not.

The first act attempts to lift the veil of secrecy around Guantanamo by showing the audience the stark conditions of the inmate's incarceration. The set never changes in the course of the play, nor does the bright, direct lighting. A large cage occupies the middle of the stage, replicating conditions at Camp Delta, where the open-air cages are about eight-by-six feet, with a toilet, sink, and cot and a few "comfort" items: a blanket, Koran, prayer cap, prayer mat, soap, and wash cloth. In the London production, the detainees stayed inside the cage for the entire play; all other characters delivered their lines from a playing area demarcated around the occupied center. The actors wore the orange prison uniforms required at Guantanamo.[3] They never left the stage, and the lights never dimmed, even during intermission or when the performance was over.

The set reenacts the material and symbolic apparatus of power. The orange uniforms and the cages enact an erasure of subjectivity: the detainees are coded the same and reidentified by a single word: terrorist. The erasure is further effected by a denial of personal voice: what we know of these men is second-hand—through their letters or through the commentaries of relatives. The cage, obviously a mode of brutalization, is also a synecdoche for the island, marking the American obsession with "homeland security." These prisoners must be doubly incarcerated, in the cage on an offshore location so that they never set foot on the soil they desecrated on 9/11. But, in case they have additional information—the bottomless possibility of their mendacity—they cannot be released or even executed. They must be available, since Guantanamo is a convenient "resource pool for American intelligence," as Gareth Pierce, a lawyer for Moazzam Begg, states in act two, and they must be watched. The constant surveillance is signaled through the bright lights and by the chain-links of the cages; these links also make a visual connection to the wrist and leg shackles that the prisoners wear when not in their cages. In act two, one of the British detainees describes the "four or five different types of chains" used in interrogation, depending on the type of pain that will be inflicted. These men—anonymous, voiceless, tethered, exposed, watched—are the real bodies that have nonetheless no rights or legal standings. When the audience files out at the end of the play, the prisoners remain on stage, left in their confinement.

The Joint Task Force Guantanamo describes its operation as "safe, humane, legal, and transparent." The meals it offers are "culturally appropriate," care is taken by guards to be respectful during prayer time, and an "Intellectual Stimulation Program" exists to provide library books, handheld electronic games, and satellite movies. Medical care is available and "all interrogations are voluntary."[4] There is a McDonald's and a Starbucks on the base, and Camp Echo is reserved for visitors.[5] Nothing of this humane, let alone considerate, treatment is apparent in the play—or in the witness given by those who have been released from the island.

In fact, the stories told by released prisoners are deeply horrifying: not only do they recount being kept shackled for hours, terrorized by dogs, blindfolded, water boarded, and sexually humiliated, they also describe being administered addictive levels of antidepressants and other drugs.[6] Given the fact that the Bush administration, over Secretary of State Colin Powell's objections, decided the Geneva Conventions were not applicable to those captured as part of the War on Terror, providing handheld games and satellite movies is a ludicrous gesture of "humane" treatment.

Lord Steyn's opening remarks force the audience to understand what the unfamiliar concept of "extraterritoriality" means in practice and why this US naval base, the oldest overseas, came to have a status different from that of one in Guam, for example, or another military base. The historical account is not fully given in the play since the political implications are more its focus. But it is worth knowing that the United States began leasing the location, located on the southeast corner of Cuba, in 1902, through an "agreement," known as the Platt Amendment, that has an imperial aspect: it was negotiated while the United States occupied the island. At the time, the lease specified that the 45-square-mile area be used for coal or as a naval station. Its transformation into a military prison has another interesting, neglected historical valance, one connected directly to the Bush family. George H. W. Bush decided that Haitian refugees working to overthrow the Astride dictatorship would be protected by being given tent shelters surrounded by barbed wire at Guantanamo, but when the refugees were forced to repatriate, the US government did nothing to intercede. George H. W. Bush's argument was that this extraterritorial site did not provide any constitutional protections to those living there. It is virtually the same argument used by his son to deny the war detainees their right to representation. When the Haitians left, those who were HIV positive were left behind, turning the camp into a medical gulag (Franklin 2005). Thus, as Amy Kaplan has argued, Guantanamo has always been a militarized, yet interstitial site; in its present iteration, it is the place where "contemporary empire building in the Middle East meets the history of imperialism in the Americas" (2004, 12).

Lord Steyn does allude to the longer history of what Kaplan calls a "global penal archipelago" (12). He tackles its most recent incarnation, arguing that Guantanamo came into being "because ill-conceived, rushed legislation" granted "excessive power to executive governments which compromise the rights and liberties of individuals beyond the exigencies of the situation" (Brittain and Slovo 2004, 5). Here, Giorgio Agamben's analysis in *State of Exception: Homo Sacer* is pertinent since it discusses the "suspension of the rule of law that was the condition of possibility for the establishment of camps" (quoted in De la Durantaye 2009, 336). Such suspension comes about, Agamben writes, at "the limit between politics and law," where there is a "point of imbalance between public law and political fact" (1995, 2). Lord Steyn contends that the point of imbalance was reached in the United States when it adopted "measures infringing human rights in ways that are wholly disproportionate to the crisis," using such means an "executive detention" (5). Steyn goes on to warn that often "the loss of liberty is permanent," a subject that the third act of the play takes up.

On October 26, 2001, the United States Senate passed the USA Patriot Act, the "rushed legislation" to which Lord Steyn refers. It allowed the attorney general to take into custody any alien suspected of activities that threatened national security. The act loosened restrictions on privacy laws: law enforcement agencies could more easily search telephone and email communications as well as medical, financial, and other records. It also eased restrictions on foreign intelligence gathering within the United States, broadened discretion in detaining and deporting immigrants, and expanded the definition of terrorism to include domestic terrorism.[7] On November 13, 2001, President Bush issued a "military order" that authorized the "indefinite detention" and "trial by military commissions" of noncitizens "suspected of involvement in terrorist activities" (Agamben 1995, 3). Agamben commented on the effect of Bush's order:

> What is new about President Bush's order is that it radically erases any legal status of the individual, thus producing a legally un-nameable and unclassifiable being. Not only do the Taliban captured in Afghanistan not enjoy the status of POWs as defined by the Geneva Convention, they do not even have the status of persons charged with a crime, according to American laws. Neither prisoners nor persons accused, but simply "detainees," they are the object of a pure de facto rule, of a detention that is indefinite not only in the temporal sense but in its very nature as well, since it is entirely removed from the law and from judicial oversight (4–5).

This situation, which Agamben terms a "state of exception," reinforces the sovereign power vested in the executive branch. Hence, the "state of exception" is not an anomaly but in fact a "paradigm of government," especially the democratic government that by law determines who exists outside the law but is de facto controlled by such exclusion. These are the regulated bodies that Agamben elsewhere has called the "homo sacer," drawing on its meaning in Ancient Rome as the man "set apart," who emblematizes state power. For Agamben, the War on Terror is an American declaration of a "global state of exception" that has the potential to transform the "juridico-political system [into] a machine which may at any moment turn lethal" (86). Lord Steyn ends his monologue with a description of such a juridical-political system at Guantanamo:

> The military will act as interrogators, prosecutors, defense counsel, judges, and when death sentences are imposed, as executioners. It is, however, in all respects subject to decisions of the President as Commander-in-Chief even in respect of guilt and innocence in individual cases as well as appropriate sentences (2004, 6).

In fact, Lord Steyn's worst-case scenario of the government handing down death sentences did not come true: in the first nine years the camp was open, only five convictions were obtained, three by plea deals and two by trials.[8] But the second-worst scenario did come true: years of lives were put on hold; detainees were repeatedly tortured and denied representation; suicides and suicide attempts at Guantanamo increased; and international and domestic disdain for America's observance of justice displaced sympathy for the 9/11 attacks.

After Lord Steyn's remarks, the play turns to how and why British nationals were detained at Guantanamo. At the time of the performance, 11 British nationals were known to be held at Guantanamo. Slovo and Brittain chose to tell the stories of four of them: Moazzam Begg, Bisher Al-Rawi, Jamal Al-Harith, and Ruhel Ahmed. What unfolds is a frightening account of how many roads there are to Guantanamo. To emphasize the silence imposed on the detainees, the relatives the playwrights interviewed tell how their family member ended up at Guantanamo. Moazzam Begg's father is the first to speak. Moazzam was born in Birmingham, England, to Muslim Pakistani parents who sent him to a Jewish grammar school, believing he would receive a superior education there. Mr. Begg describes his son as idealistic and anxious to improve society. Later, Moazzam, clearly his father's favorite, opened an Islamic clothing and bookstore and, unlike the rest of the family, became a more observant Muslim. He then decided to move to Kabul to open schools and dig wells; such humanitarian efforts necessitated dealing with the Taliban. In 2002, Moazzam was arrested by the Pakistani police who handed him over to the American military. He was held at Bagram Theatre Internment Facility for a year and then transferred to Guantanamo.

Mr. Begg's account of his son's travail is interrupted by that given by Wahab Al-Rawi, the brother of detainee Bisher Al-Rawi. In contrast to Moazzam's story, that of the Al-Rawi brothers is one of a business opportunity. The sons of a once-wealthy Iraqi businessman who fled to England after being arrested and abused by the Iraqi secret service, Wahab had enlisted Bisher's help in starting a peanut processing business in Gambia. Bisher had planned to stay only a month in Gambia. These accounts are interrupted by a third story, that offered by Jamal Al-Harith, who speaks on his own behalf. He tells of wanting to go to Pakistan on a "tableeg," a journey of religious discovery. While there, the truck he was travelling in was stolen by "gun-toting Afghanis" who then turned him over to the Taliban, believing he was a British spy. When he was released by the Taliban, he believed that the Red Cross would fly him home to Britain; instead he was detained by the American military who sent him to Cuba. The story of the fourth detainee, Ruhel Ahmed, does not get told until the second act. Ahmed was one of the "Tipton Three," a group of friends in their 20s from Tipton, England, who decided to travel to Pakistan, somewhat on a lark, but ended up in Guantanamo.

The specifics of each detainee's situation are told incrementally, but several threads emerge, pulling the stories together: prejudice toward Muslims, a deep lack of understanding of Islam and its religious duties, a superficial comprehension of Afghani society, the absence of due process, the pain of indefinite detention, and the mistreatment of the prisoners. At the time of the play's opening performance in 2004, two of the detainees had been released already, Ruhel Ahmed and Jamal al-Harith, while Moazzam Begg and Bisher Al-Rawi remained in Cuba. Ultimately, all were returned to England: Begg by special order of George Bush as a favor to Tony Blair in 2005, and Al-Rawi, in 2007.

Significantly, although act one examines the cases of the two men suspected of having firmer ties to terrorism, Begg and Al-Rawi, it does not reach a conclusion about complicity. Clearly, determinations about guilt were extremely difficult to make in the aftermath of 9/11, and *Guantanamo* does not offer any easy solutions; instead, it focuses on the absence of process in determining culpability. This focus on circumventing law and international conventions is one reason that the work has been performed in such venues as law schools and human rights organizations. "The Guantanamo Reading Project," cosponsored by the Center for Constitutional Rights and the Bill of Rights Defense Committee, not only made it possible to download the script in both English and Spanish, but it also provided instructions for how to stage local productions as well as school performances. The site lists over 25 community productions across the United States and 7 professional productions, including performances in New York, Chicago, Washington, DC, and San Francisco. *Guantanamo* not only toured significant venues in the United Kingdom and United States (it was staged at Culture Project), but it was also performed at Lahore Grammar School, an elite boy's school in Pakistan.

One of the speeches that stands out the most in the entire performance is that of Moazzam Begg's father, who states:

> If my son has done anything wrong, he should be brought back to this country... If he is [medically and physically] alright take him to court and let the Court decide whether he is guilty or not. If he is guilty, he should be punished. If he is not guilty he shouldn't be there for a second (53).

Later, Begg's father declares that he is not asking for mercy, but for justice; what emerges, however, from the accounts of why these men were arrested and sent to Guantanamo is the pervasive climate of suspicion under which Muslims lived. One review recounts hearing an American audience member observe that no American would understand why a Muslim would leave England for Pakistan or Afghanistan (Stoller 2004). But the stories that told of frequent police harassment and public suspicion in Britain go some way to answering that question. Frustrating the next terrorist act depended on levels of surveillance and tracking an individual's movements, but the focus of this play is the decision to use extralegal means to determine whether the suspect engaged in terrorist behavior. What emerges from Andy Worthington's *The Guantanamo Files*, an investigation into each of the stories behind the 774 prisoners kept at the camp, is a combination of ineffectiveness and brutality. While the Bush administration called the Guantanamo detainees the "worst of the worst," Worthington found that "very few of them had anything to do with 9/11 or al Qaeda, and the vast majority were either Taliban foot soldiers, recruited to fight an inter-Muslim civil war in Afghanistan that began long before 9/11 or al Qaeda, or they were humanitarian aid workers, religious teachers and economic migrants who were, for the most part, sold to the Americans by their allies in Afghanistan and Pakistan." Under duress, the prisoners confessed to anything. Ruhel Ahmed's confession is a case in point: he gave into the charge that he was at a terrorist training camp but eventually the MI5 discovered his original story was truthful—he had been in Birmingham, at work in a store.

Consequently, the major thrust of *Guantanamo* is the harm done to democratic ideals and to real, suffering bodies. That the play may be pleading the cause of those who have aided Osama bin Laden may be enough for some to dismiss it, and indeed suspicion lingers over at least one of the men, Moazzam Begg. Act two directly addresses the question of ethical equivalence: does the atrocity of 9/11 justify the atrocity of Guantanamo? Brittain and Slovo frame that discussion with comments by Tom Clark, an American whose sister was killed in the attack on New York. For Clark, his sister, who was concerned about issues of international justice, was "incinerated publicly, live on television, for an hour and forty minutes" (44). The suicide bombers, and those who abetted them, are "the most evil thing," and so he feels inclined to "let 'em rot" in Cuba (45). But by the end of the act, Clark is "furious" because "those who are innocent have lost three years of their life, much as I lost," and "if in truth they had done nothing wrong, I can't imagine a worse thing for any person: they deserve all our sympathies" (46). In between, Brittain and Slovo interweave excerpts from a press conference with Donald Rumsfeld with commentaries from solicitors, the detainees, and their relatives. When Rumsfeld speaks, the actor move to center stage, and, in contrast to the understated realism of the other actors, Rumsfeld inevitably appears as a caricature. Rumsfeld's own style—barbed geniality mixed with folksy defiance—is effectively self-satirizing. Asked about the status of prisoners, Rumsfeld equivocates so much that he sounds deluded:

> We said from the beginning that these are unlawful combatants, and we're detaining them. We call them detainees, not prisoners of war. We call them detainees. We have said that, being the kind of country we are, it's

our intention to recognize that there are certain standards that are generally appropriate for treating people who were—are prisoners of war, which these people are not, and—in our view—but there—and you know to the extent that its reasonable, we will end up using roughly that standard. And that's what we're doing, I don't—I wouldn't want to state that I know in any instance where we would deviate from that or where we might exceed it (32).

Rumsfeld's posturing and fulminating are countered by the bare facts and clear references to broken laws and international agreements that the solicitors offer and by the heartbroken testimony of relatives who know little about their loved ones' condition. Wahab Al-Rawi, the brother of Bisher, expresses his sense of betrayal most forcefully:

> I am angered by my Government and I don't see what difference is between Saddam Hussein and Bush and Blair. Saddam Hussein did exactly the same Thing to my country and that is why we came here and we end up with the same misery—ten times over—because this is supposed to be a land of freedom and laws (43).

In performative terms, Rumsfeld stands out as a parodic figure, surrounded by others that seem more "real." But the play, even as its primary desire is to illuminate the dark practices of detention and torture, performatively addresses the issue of real and constructed identities. The Rumsfeld character breaks the hard distinctions between the real and the fictional by calling attention to the mediated identity. In re-presenting what has already been seen, *Guantanamo* may wish to make the case that its skewering of politicians is no different than earlier political lampoons. However, more is at work performatively than the authors' apparent desire to present Rumsfeld as an outsized figure of political deceit. The incarcerated men and their families are representations never seen before; any representation of them, drawn from their letters and the interviews conducted, appears a reliable depiction of the truth of their personalities, motivations, and current situation. For the Rumsfeld character, a parodic presentation is desired—he is practically a mustachio-twirling melodramatic villain—but also unavoidable because of the media exposure that, in the aggregate, already produced such a constructed persona and, in part, because of Rumsfeld's own political buy-in, his own desire to be the tough guardian of American safety. By using the same technique for the prisoners, their families, and the politicians—replicating actual words—the play enacted the distinction between the unheard real words of the prisoners and the highly publicized words of the highly visible "Rumsfeld" persona. It insinuated that, in the case of the prisoners, words still provide access to truth. It is important to note, then, that since the play's release, Begg also has become a mediated figure, and his virtual presence and media celebrity may affect how the play is understood. Unlike the others, Begg still exacts suspicion: the FBI, CIA, and the Pentagon objected to his release, which George Bush authorized at Tony Blair's request, and even the head of Amnesty International's gender unit has denounced him. At the time of its performance, Begg was not yet "Begg"; given the mediatization that has occurred, the play may never again be performed and received as it was in London 2004 (Kerbaj 63).

FRAMES OF TORTURE

> To learn to see the frame that blinds us to what we see is no easy matter. And if there is a critical role for visual culture during times of war, it is precisely to thematize the forcible frame, the one that conducts the dehumanizing norm, that restricts what is perceivable and, indeed, what can be.
>
> —Judith Butler 2010, 100

Canadian playwright Judith Thompson's three-monologue play, *Palace of the End*, enacts the critique that detainee Wahab Al-Rawi's hoped might someday happen: people would see some connection between Hussein's dictatorship and Blair–Bush's democracy. Thompson's monologues belong to public figures, one of whom is notorious (Lynndie England), another mysterious (David Kelly), and third less well-known (Nehrjas Al Saffarh). Thompson uses their reputations as a starting point but then constructs an interior self for each person. In this decision, she goes further than the inventions made by Tony Kushner, for example, in his depiction of Ethel Rosenberg in *Angels in America*. Kushner reimagined a figure already historicized and textualized; Thompson works within the boundaries of biographical fact and historical event but also with the shape-shifting identity constructed through media presentation and Internet presence. She acknowledges the double-edged sword of greater public access to information and to disseminating opinion that the Internet allows. The advantages of electronic culture are offset by how technology further circulates constructed media figures—"Jessica Lynch," "Lynndie England," "David Kelly"—and then goes a step further to keep these presences alive on the web and interactively accessible through the blogosphere.

This point leads to a consideration of the Abu Ghraib photos. While there is a significant amount of poetry about Abu Ghraib, there is less drama, possibly because of the challenges of staging the deeply offensive images without rebrutalizing the victims. However, drama has paid much attention to the control of the visual field and the conceptual field as a means of waging war: my point throughout this book is that the intense mediation of images, the commercial conflation of news and entertainment, the increase in political spin and censorship, and the formative, interactive, and preservative qualities of the Internet make the control of images and knowledge qualitatively different in the War on Terror than it has been in previous conflicts. Because spectacularity and connectivity are deployed by more agents than governments and the press, they have become a means of waging war and spreading ideology as much as conveying it. As much as the posted photos of Abu Ghraib helped reveal the horrific abuses at the prison, they also acted as a screen for speculation. Susan Sontag controversially suggested that the Abu Ghraib photos were "us" because "the nature of the policies prosecuted by this administration and the hierarchies deployed to carry them out" made such acts of torture likely (Sontag 2004, 37). Judith Butler, not disagreeing, goes on to say that the role of art in time of war is "to thematize the forcible frame, the one that conducts the dehumanizing norm, that restricts what is perceivable, and indeed what can be" (2010, 100).

Judith Thompson's play takes up this responsibility. Her monologues are not platforms for public figures to make excuses or apologies; they are spoken and visual vehicles that frame the debate about the characters' actions and how they became politically instrumentalized or politically erased. The first monologue belongs to a "Soldier," one obviously based on Lynndie England, the young woman complicit in the tortures at Abu Ghraib. The third monologue is that of Nehrjas Al Saffarh, who recounts torture under Saddam Hussein. In between, Thompson imagines a monologue by David Kelly, the British scientist who committed suicide after accusing the government of overstating the evidence of weapons of mass destruction.

The monologues are arranged chronologically backward from the most recent to the earliest, and at the end, after Nehrjas has told the story of her young son's torture and death at the Palace of the End— an ancient castle turned torture-chamber by Saddam Hussein—the other two join her on stage. What seems at first to be three distinct monologs emerge as thematically connected by their reflection on three common questions: what truth is available to the public when the media creation supersedes the real person and the actual circumstances? What kind of witness can be obtained within a context of governmental censorship, media hype, and public information fatigue? And how can the coercive mechanisms used to achieve political ends, in democracies as well as in dictatorships, be recognized and countered?

While the monologs are separated in time and in geography, their combined effect is to offer a coherent presentation of the tragedy of the Iraqi people and a strong denunciation of Anglo-American political manipulation.

In opening with the Soldier's monologue, Thompson begins by depicting a corrupted and denigrating social culture tricked out in the high-flying rhetoric of American exceptionalism. Indeed, the pathetically deluded Soldier imagines herself as an American eagle of national righteousness. In ending with the articulate, muted, but horrific story that Nehrjas Al Saffarh tells about the unimaginable evil of Hussein's regime and her brief but ultimately vain hope that America would rescue Iraq, Thomson constructs a domestic and international sense of the magnitude of American failure, voiced with as much sorrow as condemnation. In between, Kelly's story of foiled dissent adds another layer to the erosion of democratic truth-telling. These stories are each delivered by characters who feel a great deal of personal guilt and, in adding this dimension, Thompson depicts the subjective state of those who feel intense failure and personal loss.

Palace of the End also enacts what happens when a media-created identity overtakes the living body. Clearly England is the most overexposed character of the three. With her cropped hair and tomboyish body, she offered an incongruous image: a petite, smiling girl doing unthinkably brutal acts. She became the face of Abu Ghraib. Everyone with access to television or a computer has seen the young woman holding a leashed Iraqi prisoner or smiling from behind a pyramid of naked men, or pointing, cigarette dangling, thumbs up, to a prisoner's exposed genitals. Why Thompson chose to call her only a "Soldier" has much to do with how the playwright worked with and against the portrayal of England in the media and blogosphere. Thompson's pregnant Soldier is and is not England *in the same way* that the media portrait is and is not England. And while almost everyone has seen England, few of us have ever heard her speak. At first it appears that Thompson is giving voice to this silent specter of shame, but the presentation is not an apologia by or on behalf of England; it is a complex Althusserian portrait of social interpolation. While the Soldier has a voice, her observations are little more than a ventriloquist dummy's. She mouths the jingoism and racism that rationalized the abuse even as she exhibits little understanding of how classism and misogyny played a role in making her the scandal's scapegoat. Some vestigial instincts of self-preservation operate—she has a fantasy of escaping to Quebec—but she is pathetically dedicated to the illusion that Charles Graner, her child's father and the leader of the abuse, loves her. A desperation lurks beneath this insipidness, and this Soldier, who Googles herself in the first two minutes of the play, knows that her virtual self has more meaning in the world than her real, pregnant body does. The Soldier, who tells us about her past—a poor girl working in the local Dairy Queen—will never speak louder than the virtual Soldier/England. This Soldier/England has received over six hundred thousand hits on the

Internet, and as the Soldier reads the posts, we witness a person confronting her own avatar, knowing this double has replaced her. "I ain't here no more," the Soldier says near the end of her monologue (15). The Soldier realizes that in contrast to that other girl from West Virginia, Jessica Lynch, who is "America's sweetheart"—though the story of Lynch's heroic rescue was embellished—she is "America's secret that got shouted out to the world. And they is not happy about that, not at all" (11).

Unlike the scandal at Guantanamo in which the United States defended the illegality of the prison and hid the identities of the detained, the scandal at Abu Ghraib exploded into visibility. This explosion—"America's secret"—was the revelation that the Bush–Cheney administration sanctioned torture. While initial outrage pinpointed Abu Ghraib, it subsequently became clear that the practice was widespread, that Bagram and Guantanamo enabled Abu Ghraib. In her monologues, we hear "the Soldier" reproduce the self-justifying rhetoric that was used to excuse the abuse of prisoners at Guantanamo: everything done was necessary to obtain intelligence. "They knew who was gonna blow up who and as far as I am concerned I was doin what had to be done, *to get to the intelligence*, and that is, according to their culture, me laughin at their willies was worse than a beatin way worse... I had a smile on my face but this was SERIOUS—INTELLIGENCE—WORK." For the Soldier, who "grew up singing God Bless America every single day of my life," the intelligence work is a sacred duty and a personal calling: "We was not entertaining ourselves. We was breaking down the terrorists." And therefore she is willing to "take the fall for my country any ole day." She is the yet-unrecognized "Joan of Arc" who would eventually get citations and medals (12–13).

That there might be limits in warfare or consequences for abusing an "enemy of freedom," who was merely a "Muslim monkey," is inconceivable for the Soldier and, in this respect, her functional name suggests an "every American" way of thinking about the War on Terror. At the same time, the monologue exposes the "coercive mechanisms" and subject-formation that have produced, on the one hand, an uncritical jingoism whose ugliest manifestation is Abu Ghraib and, on the other, the soldier's unconscious complicity with her own self-destruction. The Soldier has a dim but insufficient realization of the latter: "I done blew myself up," she observes (15). As she reads internet postings about herself, she simultaneously reveals but does not recognize an intense misogyny at work. Her major concern is about her looks: she is more wounded because she has been called ugly, a "dog," a "trailer whore," a "stupid girl willing to please" (9). Pathetically, she worries that her appearance is the reason the imprisoned Graner no longer contacts her. Like Naomi Wallace's *In the Heart of America*, Thompson's monologue connects Abu Ghraib not only to Guantanamo, but to a hideous slice of

American culture, heightened and actualized through cyber violence. The Soldier reads posted messages such as the following:

> Drown the slut in acid, she should be hogtied, damn she's ugly...show Her a fucking donkey, she's inbred poor white trash from West Virginia!...
> She's a trailer whore; even a dog wouldn't hump her. She needs her hole beat Oh so hard, I think she's HOT. Stupid pitiful excuse for a human being and worst of all a feminist!...I want to kill her by fucking her continuously, cut her buttocks into four parts, fuck each part, fuck to the mouth tear out her vagina (7).

The Soldier's response is to ventriloquize the Rush Lumbaugh view and associate the scabrous comments with "liberal pinheads" and "wussies." For Limbaugh, this "little outbreak of prisoner sadism" was "just boys and girls blowing off steam during a stressful situation." We should worry as much about hooding a prisoner as we should about the Ku Klux Klan—which for Limbaugh is not at all. The pictures are a distraction from the real purpose, according to Limbaugh:

> There's only one thing to do here, folks, and that's achieve *victory* over people who have targeted us for long, long time, well over 15, 20 years. It's the only way to deal with this, and that's why obsessing about a single incident or two of so-called abuse in a prison is nothing more than a giant distraction and could up being something that will really ties [sic] our hands and handcuffs us in what the *real* objective is here, which is the preservation of our way of life and our country (Meyer 2007).

Just as dismissing Abu Ghraib as the work of a few renegade soldiers denied how the behavior was tacitly sanctioned in every previous incarnation, dismissing Limbaugh's vitriol as a minority view is also dangerously inaccurate. Limbaugh had 20 million listeners in the United States, and many, like Lynndie England, were positioned in an "America first" mentality that countenanced atrocities and ignored domestic inequities.

The story of David Kelly, the second monologue in Thompson's *Palace of the End*, also takes up the subject of media scrutiny, but it is most interested in questions of denial and complicity. While the documentary drama about the Hutton Inquiry, *Justifying War*, discussed in the previous chapter, paralleled the questionable choices made by members of the press, who were driven by market demands for sensational stories, with the unethical decisions made by members of the government to achieve political priorities, Thompson's monologue also invokes these crushing dynamics and how Kelly's actions are interpolated within them. She goes further to raise broader questions of personal responsibility. David Kelly was a microbiologist who worked as a UN weapons inspector before joining the British Ministry of Defense as an expert on biological warfare. He vaulted into public view after he told a broadcaster, Andrew Gilligan, that the Blair cabinet had inflated the claims about the threat posed by Hussein's weapons of mass destruction. In particular, Kelly objected to the language that Iraq had the capability to launch a nuclear missile attack that would reach Great Britain within 45 minutes. In the popular press, Blair was accused of purposefully "sexing up" the dossier making the case for going to war against Iraq. Kelly's accusation forced the question of *causus belli*. He was made to appear before a parliament committee where he endured intense questioning. Two days later he was found dead in a wooded area by his home.

This monologue builds on a perennial theme—the principled dissenter who is pillaged—evident in drama from Sophocles to Miller. In Thompson's version, the enemy of the people is not only the forces of political manipulation and news spin, but also the uncontrollable afterlife of the virtual story. All of these pressures contribute to a pervasive culture of quiescence, exemplified by Kelly's despair. No small part of his agony was the realization, at least in Thompson's imagined reconstruction of his thinking, of how little he could do to counter the forces that quieted his dissent—until he solved the riddle.

David Kelly's monologue is shorter than the Soldier's: he has already ingested the pills that will kill him, and he has slashed his own wrists. It is the middle of the night, and he is dying in a hidden spot on Harrowdown Hill, a forest where he used to walk with his daughter. He hopes his child will not be the one to find him; he breaks the wall to thank the audience for being with him while he dies.

Unlike the Soldier, who is a traumatized part of the very atrocity she abetted and hence a compromised witness, David, more articulate and more self-conscious, has a highly developed sense of serving as history's witness. His suicide, however ambiguously interpreted, is his chosen form of witness, the only one available to him when telling the truth has failed. Kelly anticipates the reaction that the audience members know has already happened. He will be demonized as a spotlight seeker, a "Walter Mitty" who relished his 15 minutes of Warholian celebrity. His suicide will be read by conspiracy theorist as the work of MI5 or as the desperate act of a frightened man who could not take the pressure he was under. As if prescient, Kelly imagines what did in fact happen in popular culture:

There will be rock songs, art installations by angry Germans, television movies and the Internet will roil with talk of the murder of David Kelly by men in black, that's how I'll be remembered. The mousey scientist who set off a storm (23).

Kelly solved the riddle by realizing that in order to keep the story of the lie of weapons of mass destruction alive, he had to find a better, more saleable news story, and few are better than an unexplained death. He eluded the news hounds that would relentlessly pursue or consign him to oblivion for the wrong story by offering himself, sacrificially, as a different, more tantalizing story.

In imagining an alternative interpretation of his death, Thompson is not attempting to rescue Kelly from history's dustbin but rather to revalidate the very notions of witness, conscience, and agency. Because the audience knows that Kelly's motivations, even after the Hutton Inquiry, remain obscure and that his death has either been forgotten or recontextualized for political purposes, Thompson's decision to have Kelly predict these reactions in advance allows the audience to see how much cyber-commentary impacts the act of truth-telling. She does not recast Kelly as faultless. He admits to both vanity—liking the sound of his own voice too much as the world expert on biological weapons—and to denial. He told himself lies, Kelly tells the audience, "unforgiveable lie[s]" (26). When Kelly learned that American soldiers in Iraq, while searching for insurgents, murdered his close friend, a gentle, learned Iraqi bookseller, and raped his daughter, he could no longer refuse to see the truth. While he was willing to accept the rationale that a world without the monster Hussein was better than one with him, he saw that the invasion made things for the Iraqi people "far, far, far, far worse." His response, despite many opportunities to speak out, was to do nothing, until he learned about the fate of his friends. That day, Kelly says, "I blew myself up" by calling the BBC and telling the truth (26).

In popular culture versions of the Iraq War, the hero who tells the unpleasant truth, like the soldier in Paul Greengrass's 2010 film *The Green Zone*, is somehow rewarded if only by an on-screen validation of his integrity and, implicitly, an affirmation that this integrity belongs to real Americans, however flawed their political representatives are. No such comfort is given in Thompson's play. At the start of the monologue, Kelly says, mysteriously, that he has "solved the riddle." But the riddle remains until the end of his monologue, after he has admitted how naive he was to imagine that the parliamentarians would protect him. He felt himself "lashed, blasted," and crashing "through the looking glass" into an inversion of democracy. When he finally decided to kill himself, he saw it as a way to end the torment to which he would forever be subjected in the press, by the authorities, and by nattering neighbors. The riddle's solution would install him in the public imagination as an emblem of the cost of the Iraq War. By refusing to be "like what's his name, the character in Greek mythology, that is tied to a rock in the ocean and doomed to have his liver pulled out by ferocious vultures," Kelly has "defeated" them by disappearing (30). The them here are his countrymen; his enemies are the government he served and the press he sought. Kelly solves the riddle by turning the accusation that he was a fame-seeker into a real cause célèbre: death by the press; death by an indifferent government.

Nehrjas Al Saffarh speaks the third monologue, "Instruments of Yearning," the incongruous name for the Ba'ath secret police. Nehrjas was a member of the Iraqi Communist Party, and her husband was engaged in undermining Hussein and the Ba'athists. Unlike the Soldier and Kelly, Nehrjas's story is less likely to be known to an American audience, and Thompson strategically reveals it incrementally. When we first meet Nehrjas, she is a beautiful 40-year-old woman calmly drinking tea and speaking about her name (which means "daffodil") and the date trees outside. Her meditation is on the resilience of women, who are named for flowers, but who should more appropriately be compared to the trees, which endure. The audience does not know that Nehrjas is dead, that they are hearing a ghost. Tortured by Hussein's henchmen at the Palace of the End and made to watch her children tortured and they her, Nehrjas Al Saffarh was killed when her house was bombed by Americans during the 1991 Gulf War. That this beautiful woman has been tortured by Hussein and then killed by Americans encapsulates the sad history of the Iraqi people, oppressed by both rulers and saviors. In one sense, her monologue takes up where David Hare ended in *Stuff Happens*, and her story is similar to that of the artist in Heather Raffo's *Nine Parts of Desire*. At the end of Hare's play, an Iraqi character observes how unfortunate it is that the Iraqis did not save themselves. Nehrjas's monologue presents the near impossibility of breaking Hussein's brutal regime without outside help, and the tragedy of what form that help took.

Of all the plays about Iraq, Thompson's most directly engages the question of whether Hussein's treatment of the Iraqi people warranted intervention, and the play's answer is unambiguously yes. Nehrjas's describes the torture she endured, and her story is as nightmarish as any horror story ever told. She and her older son are taken to the Palace of the End, infamous for its three floors: the top of the castle is the interrogation room, where those who betray someone are released; the middle floor is reserved for "torture lite"; the basement is filled with discarded bodies, smelling of rotting flesh. When Nehrjas, then pregnant, and her older son are taken to the first floor, she is raped multiple times in front of him; he is beaten with hammers (41). When neither of them break down and reveal the whereabouts of Nehrjas's husband, they think for a moment they will be let go. Instead, Nehrjas's younger son, the eight-year-old Fahdid, is brought in, and he is tortured. When he too withstands the beatings, his small body is tied to a ceiling fan and he is spun to senselessness. Next, his body is dragged to the roof and his mother to the attic room beneath it where she can hear him dying. She never gives up her husband's name, holding vainly onto the hope they would not kill a pregnant woman and her child. For this error in judgment, Nehrjas's believes she has "committed the greatest sin of all" (44).

Nenrjas's harrowing tale leaves little doubt that without assistance, the Iraqi people could not halt the brutality. The age of Hussein, she says, was the age of darkness; the "liberation" of Iraq, a brief moment of hope that turned out to be "a flash, a lightening flash in the pitch dark" that cruelly vanished. Nehrjas compares the liberation of Iraq to a story of woman she knew who had been abducted during Hussein's regime and raped repeatedly by officials who left her by the side of the road. There, a kind family stopped, brought her to their home, and cleaned her up while they notified her family. As she lay in the bath, the husband entered the room and raped her again. Nehrjas bluntly spells out the analogy: "Those who say they have come to save us have come to destroy us" (37).

Read backward, the three monologues trace the failure in Iraq back to the American support of the Ba'ath coup, through the manufactured evidence justifying war and invasion, to the abuse at Abu Ghraib. The account of Hussein's megalomania and violence is not omitted, but it is framed within the context of the utter collapse of Western ideals. Abu Ghraib has succeeded the Palace of the End as a place for torture, and Hussein's thugs have been replaced by an ignorant young woman soldier.

THE AFTERLIFE OF ABUSE

Eve Ensler's *The Treatment* and Francis Ya-Chu Cowhig's *Lidless* examine a common question: what happens to the soldiers who torture? How do they live with their actions?

Ensler's play is unspecific in its location, but the references to sanctioned interrogation at an unnamed base obviously invoke Abu Ghraib and Guantanamo. The action revolves around a military psychiatrist's interviews with a sergeant suffering from extreme post-traumatic stress disorder which stem from his part in inflicting torture. The play, which debuted in September 2006 as part of the Culture Project's Impact Festival, starred well-know actors Dylan McDermott and Portia, which, along with Ensler's own reputation as the author of *The Vagina Monologues*, drew sold-out audiences. Were it not for all of these connections, the play would not likely have garnered much response since its political critique and its interest in the erotic aspects of torture get muddled. When the erotically charged reenactment of interrogation gets performed as some combination of therapy and desire, the audience may be voyeuristically engaged but not ethically or intellectually. When it turns out that the psychiatrist was persuading the sergeant to confess to her, she was not trying to help him; she was attempting to learn the truth about interrogation so that she could report it. Her intention is to uncover the abuse and demand accountability, but her methods of obtaining the information are cruel and unethical.

Frances Yu Chu Cowhig's play, on the other hand, compellingly presents the case that America has allowed torture into its own bloodstream. *Lidless* won the Yale Drama series competition for emerging playwrights, judged by David Hare who commented that he "admired the play because—although it was stylishly written, although the governing metaphor and basic realism were held in a fine balance—it also recalled the political urgency which had propelled a previous generation of writers into the theatre in the first place" (Cowhig 2010, xiii). The play splits the action between a day in 2004 at Guantanamo and a day some 15 years later. Alice, a Guantanamo interrogator authorized to break down prisoners through erotic and culturally offensive behavior, does as she has been instructed. She and her friend, Riva, an Iraqi American medic whose own father had been tortured at Abu Ghraib under Hussein, are anxious to serve out their time and return home. The time fast-forwards 15 years: Alice, now a florist, lives with her former-hippie husband, Lucas, and their teenage daughter, Rhiannon. One day, a dark stranger enters her shop: it is Bashir, the Pakistani prisoner she interrogated and sexually humiliated at Guantanamo. He is dying and needs a liver transplant. He believes Alice owes him that.

Cowhig has spoken of being influenced by Alfred Jarry's concept of "pataphysics," the "science of imaginary solutions,"[9] and in the play these solutions depend on a capacity to see the truth in its present guise, though this truth is always inflected with what has been suppressed from the past. The title of the play is explained after Rhiannon has died, and her mother finds her with her eyes wide open: Rhiannon's effort to understand Otherness through profound empathy, going so far as to bodily mimic the actions and experiences of the Other, strengthens her capacity to look unblinkingly at the truth. This is the play's ethical warrant.

This first scene establishes the play's opposing forces: the effort to uncover the truth and the effort to resist it. Here, Rhiannon's oral history assignment, which aims to discover a deep and personal understanding of another, is contrasted with various attempts to mute, control, or otherwise erase the past. Through temporal and spatial shifts within scenes and between scenes, however, Cowhig asserts that an unblinking understanding of the truth requires an acknowledgement of the persistence of the past in the present moment and an awareness that this point of space and time are but a sliver of the whole. At times, Cowhig's juxtaposed scenes demonstrate an eerie symmetry, such as in scene 13 when Rhiannon is mock-interrogating an imaginary prisoner, represented by an orange Guantanamo jumpsuit, while her parents are downstairs, interrogating each other. At other times, the spatial staging enacts something being resolved just as something else is spinning out. In the play's last scene, for example, Riva, who thought she had worked through the trauma of her time at Guantanamo and the death of her father at Hussein's hands, has been retraumatized just as the traumatized Alice is beginning to heal. This visual performance of both the enduring challenges of conflict resolution and of trauma's recidivism is one of the most complex and effective aspects of this—or any play—about Iraq.

When the play begins, Rhiannon enters wearing a black hoodie and retrieves her inhaler; she is having as asthmatic attack, and she tells herself to breathe. Riva, a medic, steps into the square of light, and her words echo Rhiannon's instructions to breathe, but the audience soon understands she is speaking aloud as she records a detainee's injuries; he has "severe abdominal pain and should be tested for liver disease," and he complains of respiratory problems, likely "stemming from a hood made of synthetic Material repeatedly place over the head and the neck" (5). The girl and the unseen prisoner are thus connected metaphorically by their hoods and breathing difficulties. That they will be bound to each other in actual, physical ways depends on the person who next enters the shaft of light. It is Alice. She has just learned about a newly sanctioned form of interrogation. Although Riva cautions Alice that she need not participate in the new "Invasion of Space by a Female" technique that Dick Cheney has just authorized, Alice, a Texas-born cowgirl, is gung ho like the president she serves. And like Lynndie England, she is immature and bedazzled by the role she has been asked to play. She attempts to titillate the prisoner, telling him they could be lovers as she strips.

The opening scene is purposefully opaque; it takes the audience some time to determine the relationship between past and future and between the Alice and Rhiannon, but as a performative technique for depicting the implications of unacknowledged trauma, it works extraordinarily well. So too does the equation of Bashir and Rhiannon, both of whom are literally and metaphorically choked and blinded by Alice. The split, but at times overlapping, time sequences tell audiences that justice always looks for injustice, and trauma communicates itself across generations.

Cowhig has spoken of her admiration for Naomi Wallace, and some of her structural choices invoke *In the Heart of America*. Wallace's use of the ghostly past in *Heart of America*—with its attendant caution about unsettled histories, such as that of Vietnam, or unacknowledged national ills, such as rural poverty and xenophobia—are mirrored in Cowhig's own apparitions and attention to sources of trauma. However, the apparition in *Lidless* turns out not to be the undead—though Rhiannon wants to keep the intrusive Bashir "buried" in order to save her family. Rather, like the layers of clothing that Rhiannon wears, trauma has come to characterize the family's relationships with each other. Lucas warns Rhiannon against asking her mother about her past, but Rhiannon's quest for knowledge is visualized by her layered identity. At one point, she wears the hoodie that associates her with Abu Ghraib over her mother's army jacket, and beneath that, the orange jumpsuit that belongs to Bashir. Judith Butler has written that the body is "where we encounter a range of perspectives that may or may not be our own." She continues:

> How I am encountered, how I am sustained, depends fundamentally on the social and political networks in which this body lives, how I am regarded and treated, and how that regard and treatment makes this life or fails to make it livable (2010, 53).

Rhiannon's layered clothing hides and ultimately reveals a body that is marked by the unacknowledged influences of her mother and Bashir's past. That she is willing to clothe herself in symbols of their identity and of history signals that her body will become the site of the reencounter that must inevitably occur.

Another means that Cowhig uses to blur time/space dimensions, and thereby explore her interest in connections that happen even across atrocity, is her minimal, nonrealistic staging. In the first scene, a shaft of orange light defines a rectangular interrogation space. Rhiannon's inhaler lies outside its perimeter, a visual equivalent of Bergsonian *duree*. Later, when Bashir enters the home of Alice and Lucas without knocking, Lucas explodes that the front door ought to separate "this family from the rest of the world"; the mess "on the other side of the door" should not come into his home (58). But walls and doors, like time and space, are permeable in Cowhig's play, in part to insist on the past's presence but also to explore the terrifying intimacy that can characterize conflict, violence, and trauma. When Alice was attempting to break Bashir down through sexual seduction, she thought of Lucas, and Bashir, trying to resist, imagined his own wife. The substitutions hold, installing a bodily, albeit confused, connection. Bashir tells Alice a confounding fact: when he thinks of his dead wife, who has committed suicide, he imagines Alice's face in place of his wife's. These shifts between being haunted and being hunted blur, so that the repugnance of the encounter at Guantanamo is somehow somatically stored as a physical connection.

Unsettlement can also be understood as a definition of trauma, and each of these characters have become, in Caruth's terms, the "symptom of history that they cannot entirely possess" (1995, 5). Setting the story 15 years after Alice's service in Guantanamo demonstrates the "endless impact on life" that trauma causes, however much that trauma remains to some extent opaque to the sufferer (7). In *Lidless*, Riva's father was murdered in Iraq; his severed hands delivered to her. After moving to the United States, she joined the army to finance a future medical career, but she found herself back in the castle of horrors. She is a symptom of the unresolved civil unrest in Iraq. Alice, who is haunted by work as an interrogator, takes anesthesizing medications to help erase the past which includes not only her military experiences but also the memories of her violent father, a haunted Vietnam veteran. Bashir, wrongly captured, detained, and abused at Guantanamo; ill with untreated hepatitis; and separated from his daughter, lost his wife to suicide when she despaired of his return. Lucas has a heroin addiction, though the reasons why are never explained. Rhiannon, who lives in a family of secrets, cannot breathe.

Like others who compulsively act out rather than work through the trauma, Alice chooses to erase Guantanamo rather than confront it. Here, like other victims of political atrocity discussed earlier, and like Judith Thompson's characters, she feels blame for a situation in which she was complicit but over which she had little control. Alice has become a specter in her own life. During much of the play, we see her on the edges of her family, watching Lucas and Rhiannon. Here, Dominick LaCapra's insights about historical trauma are relevant. LaCapra notes:

> A regime arising after acts of severe, violent perpetration may not recognize the importance of providing social contexts in which former perpetrators may acknowledge their past actions and attempt to work out a different relation to former victims and survivors—including the dead—in a manner that enables empathic response and the possibility of mourning, which require self-criticism and even depression but should not be conflated with melancholic or nostalgic forms of self-involvement (2001, 214).

The United States may not wish to classify itself as such a regime, but the number of suicides, drug addictions, and mental health problems that returning American soldiers suffer from argue otherwise.

Cowhig also has acknowledged her debt to Ariel Dorfman's *Death and the Maiden*, and while there is the obvious difference of the gender reversal of interrogator and prisoner, both plays explore the erotic aspects of torture. Harold Pinter, in plays such as *One for the Road* and *Ashes to Ashes*, also has examined the eros of torture; in *Lidless*, Cowhig makes her own contribution to this subject, a subject many would prefer to ignore. The explicitly erotic nature of the torture exposed through the Abu Ghraib photographs has forced recognition of America's own willingness to weaponize sexuality. Cowhig's treatment of sexual torture is different from the plays just mentioned in several important respects. First, Alice, though she engages willingly, is the low-level executioner, not the mastermind. Like the thugs in Pinter's *New World Order*, she implements a policy she associates with a larger national purpose, and she fails to understand how she will always remain at the bottom of national priorities. She is not, however, like Dorfman's villain, melding scientific research with sadism and dark sexual curiosity. In fact, both Alice and Bashir endure their roles by imaginatively invoking other situations, but within the space of an isolated interrogation cell, the imagination and the act become fused, and identities are transferred. Bashir's incredible losses, not only of his freedom but of his entire family, and his valiant efforts to endure an apparently limitless future of detention, cause him to substitute, or at least layer, Alice's identity onto his wife's. Alice, to do the deed she partly loathes but gets drawn into, initially imagines that Bashir is Lucas. Something of their emotional and psychic dispositions have been altered: Alice discovers her latent capacity for violence; Bashir has transferred identities, in something like the Stockholm syndrome. Bashir and Alice, then, are connected across time by dint of Alice's lingering guilt and responsibility. When it turns out that Bashir needs a liver transplant, he demands that Alice donate hers, knowing the liver regenerates, and that she is the direct cause of his illness. Bashir's search for justice is far more gentle than Dorfman's Paulina Salas or Pinter's Rebecca.

Lidless depicts the collective, social, and even generational effects of trauma more searchingly than Dorfman's play. *Death and the Maiden* shows Paulina's incapacity to live in the present and therefore to be in full relationship with her husband; Cowhig has expanded the ripple effects of trauma socially and generationally. Dominick LaCapra reminds us that "the after effects—the hauntingly possessive ghosts—of traumatic events are not fully owned by anyone and in various ways, affect everyone" (2001, xi). Moreover, LaCapra reminds us that "historical trauma is specific and not everyone is subject to it or entitled to the subject position associated with it" (58). While everyone "is subject to structural trauma but with respect to historical trauma and its representations, the distinctions between victim, perpetrators and bystanders is crucial. 'Victim' is not a psychological category. It is, in variable ways, a social, political and ethical category" (59). Cowhig wants to depict structural trauma. Riva, as suggested above, has not fully worked through her trauma because she has only addressed half of it: her work at Guantanamo. In refusing to speak Arabic, she refuses to reopen the wound of her father's murder and, consequently, of her role in a war that did not restore wholeness to the world that Hussein destroyed. When she purposefully treats Bashir in the future time sequence when he is taken to the hospital after Rhiannon has hit him, unaware of his compromised health, he bids her to pray for him in Arabic and thus brings back the issues she has compartmentalized. At the end of the play, the valiant Riva has fallen under the weight of suppressed memories and is taking the medication that Alice took to erase the past.

Rhiannon and Alice also connect to Bashir in profound and unexpected ways. Bashir visits Alice when she is working in her mother's shop, and she discovers in him the perfect subject for her school project. He answers her inventory of questions honestly, and she feels a connection to him. She even visits him in his hotel—which results in an unexplored instance of confused sexual/filial attraction—to learn more about him. But when Bashir comes to her home and Rhiannon senses the danger he poses to her family's wholeness, she assaults him. The emotional tension builds—Lucas has learned Alice raped Bashir, and he forces her to tell their daughter about her past—and Rhiannon, overcome and unable to breathe, dies in her room alone. When Alice discovers her, she donates her liver to save Bashir, realizing that she is spiritually, if not literally, his daughter.

Such an ending does indeed accord with Jarry's pataphysical solutions, but it is dismissible as merely metaphorical only if one does not believe that effective methods of reconciliation depend on psychological, emotional, spiritual, and, indeed, creative means of addressing mourning and loss.[10] A play in which an organ transplant takes place—a liver, thought by some to be the seat of the soul—is no less viable as a metaphor and even a literal model of reconciliation than the symbol and reality of conflict: bloodshed. In the end, Cowhig's play depicts trauma but also reparation and healing that may be the result of brave and intentional encounters. Cowhig's play, despite its many tragedies, underscores the recuperative effects and just consequences of such encounters.

CHAPTER 8

AFGHANISTAN AND "THE SPECTACLE OF OUR SUFFERING"

"YOU HAVE TO TAKE HOME WITH YOU NOTHING BUT the spectacle of our suffering." These words, spoken by a Tajik guide in Afghanistan as he helps a British woman, Priscilla, look for her missing mother, may have been among the lines most difficult for the audience to hear when Tony Kushner's play *Homebody/Kabul* premiered in New York on December 19, 2001, just three months after the 9/11 attacks. The spectacle of suffering had not ended; indeed, many more months would pass before the wreckage from the World Trade Center towers had been cleared away. But another line in the play was equally upsetting: spoken in angry warning by Mahala, an Afghani librarian who faults the West for aiding the Taliban, she tells Priscilla, "You love the Taliban so much, bring them to New York! Well, don't worry, they're coming to New York!" (85).

Lines such as these capture both the sorrow and terror caused by the attacks, but they also make it seem as though Kushner, like Shepard a decade ago, had rushed to his desk to pour out his reaction. In fact, Kushner had been working on the play for more than four years. Nevertheless, *Homebody/Kabul* spoke so directly to the feelings of insecurity, loss, and anxiety that the attacks provoked that Kushner's perspective seemed "uncanny," as if America's preeminent playwright possessed preternatural powers of prescience. To hail Kushner's prescience is to miss not only the nature of the work that the playwright has devoted himself to throughout his career, but also to miss one of the play's most important points: that the structures of history and power can be recognized, named, evaluated, decried, and even addressed. Kushner emphasizes that the signs of political change or crises are discernible to anyone willing to look for them:

> We ought to consider that the information required to foresee, long before 9/11, at least the broad outline of serious trouble ahead was so abundant and easy to access that even a playwright could avail himself of it; and we ought to wonder about the policy, so recently popular with the American right, that whole countries can be cordoned off and summarily tossed out of the international community's considerations, subjected to sanction, and refused assistance by the world's powers, a policy that helped blind the government of geopolitical reality, to say nothing of ethical accountability and moral responsibility (144–145).

I have chosen to place a discussion of the War in Afghanistan last in the book because the war all but ended with the death of Osama bin Laden. Americans no longer cared if Afghanistan was stable: too much domestic unemployment diverted attention away from anything but our own problems. Unlike the wars in Iraq, the War in Afghanistan, which lasted longer than the Vietnam War, shifted in and out of focus. Within three months of 9/11, American airpower had struck down every city held by the Taliban where bin Laden might have been given a haven. But bin Laden was never captured, the Taliban regrouped, and Al-Qaeda reconstituted itself. Despite the "never again" rhetoric that established the model of the short technowar in order to avoid a Vietnam-like quagmire, American troops remained in Afghanistan for more than a decade, and the question of how to counterterrorism remained an unknown. As Fatima Ayub and Sari Kouvo have observed, the plan to retaliate quickly and halt terrorism became embroiled in longer and larger questions about democratization and American security.[1] These questions were no longer the subject of much political discussion, and when economic problems surfaced, war-weary Americans were no longer interested in investigating any more time, money, or human life in the War on Terror.

In terms of theatrical productions about Afghanistan, relatively few works appeared. Only two are of note: *The Great Game* and *Homebody/Kabul*. The first is actually a 12-play cycle, arranged and presented by London's Tricycle Theatre. Nicholas Kent commissioned the plays, and the result was a day-long, nine-hour immersion into Afghani history via theatre. Kushner's *Homebody/Kabul* also offered historical and cultural insights, but its essential quality is its deep ethical meditation of loss and difference. Kent's production insists on reviewing the lessons of history and particularizing the conflict so that it becomes much more than a war between implacable forces, one of them demonized as irrational or insignificant. In a sense, Kushner's play works on these same premises—that suffering is particular, that all lives are grief-worthy, that history and culture have relevance for current political decisions—and in so doing affirms what Judith Butler has called the moral opportunity of vulnerability. In terms of the formative influences of mediatization I have been discussing throughout this book, these plays display both the markers of saturation and ideological pre-positioning as well as the drive toward censorship, ahistoricality, and invisibility. They demonstrate, again, the mixed semiotic environment that constitutes the way we know the world and act within it. I can think of no better pairing of theatrical productions with which to close this discussion of the value of political and ethical commentary through performance than these important works.

THE GREAT GAME

Kent introduces the collected volume of the plays he commissioned by commenting that:

> "The Great Game" was a term used for the strategic rivalry and conflict between the British Empire and the Russian Empire for supremacy in Central Asia. The classic Great Game period is generally regarded as running approximately from the Russo-Persian Treaty of 1813 to the Anglo-Russian Convention of 1907. Following the Bolshevik Revolution of 1917, a second less-intensive phase followed. The term "The Great Game" was introduced into mainstream consciousness by British novelist Rudyard Kipling in his novel *Kim* (1901) (2009, 9).

The production, which premiered in London and then toured the United States, first in Washington, DC, and then New York, is comprised of twelve short plays, grouped into three parts, covering the years 1842 to the present. The plays were written by such well-known dramatists as David Edgar, Lee Blessing, Stephen Jeffreys, and David Greig. Between each of the three parts, Richard Norton-Taylor produced verbatim interviews with current political and military leaders in the Afghan conflict, including Hillary Clinton, Ahmed Rashid, Masood Khalili, the current Afghan ambassador to Turkey, and General David Richards. In one noteworthy affirmation of the production, General Richards, the chief of the defense staff in Britain, went to see how he was impersonated on stage. Noting that he took members of his staff as well as senior treasury officials and several politicians, General Richards concluded that "nothing learned in the classroom will have the same subliminal effect as this. It is crucial that all of who work out there have a more nuanced view of the historical background that got us to this point" (2010, 43).

The plays are grouped into three parts—"Invasions and Independence 1842–1930"; "Communism, The Mujahideen and the Taliban 1976–1996";

and "Enduring Freedom 1996–2010"—and they invite both historical readings by group and thematic readings across the entire cycle. An example of the later is that the cycle is framed by two plays, *Bugles at the Gates of Jalalabad* by Stephen Jeffreys, which opens the day-long event and *Canopy of Stars* by Simon Stephens which closes it. Together they remind audiences of the simple fact that the British government—and hence, British soldiers—have been in Afghanistan for over 150 years.

Bugles begins with an observation pertinent to all of the works: "It is easy to argue on the wisdom or folly of conduct after the catastrophe has taken place" (17). The catastrophe referred to took place during the first Anglo-Afghan War in January 13, 1842. Some sixteen thousand British troops and camp followers died, some by the brutal weather, some by slaughter, as they tried to make their way from Kabul to Jalalabad, ninety miles away. *Canopy of the Stars*, the last play, tells of a different sense of catastrophe: a soldier, Jay, tells his wife that he wants to return to Afghanistan because he wants to finish the productive work of building an infrastructure and protecting Afghanis against the Taliban. He can simply no longer live at home, and he evidences the adrenaline rush of being in the front lines and the difficulty soldiers have returning to normal life. Thus, while one throughline in the production is the catastrophic decisions to intervene and occupy a sovereign nation, another is the ethical duty to address the horrors imposed by the Taliban as well as the damage the war has caused. *Bugles* foretells certain disaster: the British are outnumbered, unused to the terrain, and certain for slaughter. *Canopy* adds the level of psychological hold: even if nations can extricate themselves from losing political causes, the harm done to individuals lasts. In *Bugles*, the enemy is abstract; in *Canopy*, the Afghanis are sympathetic and caught in the crosshairs of larger geopolitical issues. Always, Afghanistan in a place of struggle.

Were these questions not complex enough, the cycle also considers the political realities of the past 150 years—realities in which both Britain and the United States used Afghanistan to protect their own interests. For Britain, this interest was a secure border to prevent Russian impingement on the British Empire. For the United States, Afghanistan was the battleground of Cold War antagonisms, but it also offered an opportunity to counter Iranian oil control and to respond to the 9/11 attacks. In sum, no audience member can leave *The Great Game* without a profound sense of Afghanistan's role as an imperial pawn in the rivalries between Great Britain, the United States, and Russia, and of its own internal struggles among tribal factions and even more crucially, the brutality of the Taliban. A few leaders emerge who might have made a difference in the lives of Afghani people, but they are felled by internal rivalries and external pressures.

The plays are remarkable for the degree of sheer historical information that they communicate but even more so for their flexible and inventive staging and vivid acting. The company numbers around fifteen actors who take on some ninety roles. All the plays are produced on the same open stage. In the Washington, DC, production at the Shakespeare Theatre Production, props were visible at the sides of the stages, adding a small note of Brechtian exposure. The props, however, were few: sand bags, rugs, boxes, tables. Occasionally, other backdrops are used: maps, poppy fields, and, in one inventive stage design, a mural of the history of Afghanistan is whitewashed over by the Taliban during the course of the play. While far from being twelve essays or dramatized position papers, each play still serves as a synecdoche for a larger political issue. Some common dramatic strategies emerge. Timing is set at the moment just before a decisive change or disaster: the buglers wait for the British survivors to arrive in Jalalabad, knowing they will not; Amanullah and his wife and father-in-law learn of the betrayal that will end their plans for modernization. Reproducing ideological and cultural differences in order to try to negotiate a political settlement is a plot structure shared by *Durand's Line*, about the 1893 remapping of Afghanistan, and *Honey*, in which a CIA operative tried to buy back American missiles in 1996 from Ahmad Shah Masoud. Other plays depict opportunities lost, because pivotal leaders, such as Amanullah in *Now is the Time* or Najibullah in *Miniskirts of Kabul* cannot succeed. There are the burdens born by ordinary soldiers and the tested idealism of relief workers; both are set against the incredible brutality of the Taliban. Thus, in some eight hours, spectators will have been exposed to the imperial game-playing that set the conditions for Afghanistan's perennial role as a strategically situated but largely abandoned bit player in contemporary politics. The story of Afghanistan that emerges from these performances is that there are few countries in the world more wretched and more used. It is not difficult to understand its despair or its anger.

Part one of *The Great Game* includes works by Stephen Jeffreys (*Bugles at the Gates of Jalalabad*), Ron Hutchinson (*Durand's Line*), Amit Gupta (*Campaign*), and Joy Wilkinson (*Now is the Time*) and covers the years from 1842 to 1930. A longer historical account of the British involvement with Afghanistan might encompass the figure of Shuja Shah Durrani, who signed an alliance with Great Britain in 1809 as a means of guarding against invasion by Russia, but who ultimately lost power to Dost Mohammed Khan. Khan, like every other major ruler, recognized and dealt with external manipulation, and the history of nineteenth-century Afghanistan is marked by alternating agreements with Britain and with Russia. Jeffrey's play focuses on a famous moment of British defeat, known as the Massacre of Elphinstone's Army. In Jeffrey's play, three British privates and a corporal wait in Jalalabad for signs of any surviving soldiers, knowing already that some sixteen thousand are dead. In the background, invisible to the soldiers, is Lady Florentia Sale, a general's wife. Her story, like that of the massacre is also mythic: with other officer's wives and children, she was held captive for nine months by the Afghanis and later published her diary account of this travail. In Jeffrey's play, the attitude of the desperate soldiers—that "this country is a death trap for foreign armies" (2009, 22)—is exacerbated by dealing with canny tribal leaders and with an unreliable imperial administration in London. The soldiers characterize the Afghanis as savage and irrational. The play iterates views that are still operative: Afghanistan is figured as a place where neither military power nor political maneuvering can succeed, and the Afghanis, to the extent that their culture is understood at all, are uncivilized, unreliable, and ungovernable. That Hamid Karzai felt the need to remind the American government that he was a "partner" not a "stooge," reflects this long mistrust. Lady Sale, in counterpoint, describes the British refusal to interact with Afghani culture as symptomatic of the imperial "habits": keeping to oneself, dethroning leaders to set up puppets, and denying self-government all in the name of protecting "civilization."

In the following play, *Durand's Line*, which depicts the efforts of Her Majesty's foreign secretary Sir Henry Mortimer Durand to come to an agreement on borders with the Amir of Afghanistan, Abdhul Rahman, in 1893, the word used instead of "civilization" is "order." Ron Hutchinson, the playwright, thus layers the audience's awareness of recent political doctrines about order, such as the Bush doctrine of the New World Order, with a kind of precedent. For like the New World Order's relationship to the end of the Cold War and desire for American global preeminence, coded as "rationality," and "order," Durand tries to convince Rahman to "birth a nation" by drawing borders that would protect India from Russian occupation. Durand also uses lofty rhetoric to convince Rahman of the benefits of his plan, first appealing to the advantages of national borders as the foundation for orderly self-government. "There is no government without a map," he tells Rahman, and "that which has no shape has no meaning" (2009, 46). Durand believes the map is the "way forward to the modern age," and Rahman counters that it is the way toward "endless conflicts" and "endless war" (46). The spectators see that both propositions have come to be: that the modern age of nation-states has been the site of endless conflicts especially in those places—Iraq, Afghanistan, Rwanda—where cultural and tribal affiliations have had contested political status. Hutchinson's play also speaks to the hubris and overreaching in the Anglo-American desire to remap the world. Rahman insultingly brings up the embarrassing moment when Durand's father, also a member of the British government, attempted to enter the city to receive honors and decided to do so riding the back of an elephant, though he was warned against it. He did in fact fall, "landed at the feet of the very people he meant to overawe" and was carried away with a broken back and died (43). Durand's insistent triumphalism and his subsequent humiliation has played itself out in many moments since Americans bombed Afghanistan and Iraq in 2003: the bravado about capturing Osama bin Laden and failing to do so; expecting to be hailed like World war II liberators in Baghdad; the farcical Mission Accomplished episode.

The final two plays continue to make the case for history repeating itself. Joy Wilkinson's *Now is the Time*, like *The Bugles of Jalalabad* freezes a historical incident. It is 1929 and Amanullah Khan, the King of Afghanistan from 1919 to 1929 is fleeing by car through the snows north of Kabul with his wife, Soroya Tarzi, and her father, Mahmud Tarzi, an important Afghan nationalist and intellectual. Their car gets stuck, and while they wait for the driver to bring help, they discuss Amanullah's record—one regarded skeptically even by his wife who insinuates that her husband can be arrogant and impulsive. Amanullah attempted to modernize Afghanistan by providing better schooling, improved rights for women, and a modern constitution. Despite this record of reforms, Amanullah's program was never wholly or sufficiently supported by Britain, Russian, or other monied nations, and internally, some objected to the rapid rate of change. When the Mullahs began to work more strenuously against hum, Amanullah fled into exile, expecting to return. This is the moment of Wilkinson's play. The hope for the very progress toward a modern state that Durand attempted to bring into being through a map, went unsupported. Even Tarzi and his daughter betray their own ideals—signified when Soraya veils herself—and abandon Amanullah. To emphasize how little this part of Afghani history is understood, Amit Gupta's *Campaign*, depicts American and British political lackeys trying to cajole an Islamic scholar to rewrite Afghani history. They want, as part of an exit strategy, to promote the establishment of a secular liberal democracy as a specifically Afghani idea—the idea of Mahmud Tarzi. With the coerced assistance of the professor, they will recast the deeply anti-British, anti-imperialist Tarzi as the original proponent of Westernized government. They will exhume his memory and even his newspaper (though it criticized the British at every turn) to begin a propaganda campaign.

The second and third parts of the play cycle also excise critical historical moments to showcase lasting political mistakes. Part two opens with *Black Tulips*, by David Edgar, which recounts the Russian occupation. Lee Blessings's *Wood for the Fire*, addresses American complicity in arming the mujahideen against the Russians follows. Both plays portray a smug, utilitarian view of Afghani politics that comes back as foolish and hubristic—again a theme that hangs over the entire production. The Russians and Americans have little idea of what will defeat them: they believe that a well-armed military and experienced military strategists will conquer any insurgents. Edgar's play depicts the five years it took for the Russians to finally understand that they are being "sent into an alien and hostile land to do battle with a resolute enemy in dangerous and inhospitable terràin" (2009, 90). The next two plays, David Grieg's *Miniskirts of Kabul* and Colin Teevan's *The Lion of Kabul*, trace the growing repression under the Taliban. The themes of these plays spill over into the work that opens the final installment. Ben Oakrent, in *Honey*, imagines a CIA operative trying to convince Ahmad Masood and Masood Khalili to help him retrieve some American missiles since it has become apparent that the United States is arming all sides. Taken together, the plays trace the difficulty of making any political headway with either the mujahideen or the Taliban. *Honey* in particular suggests that, had the United States been able to forge a more reliable relationship with Ahmad Masood, the 2001 attacks might have been prevented. But the play ends with Masood opening the door to his would-be assassins and the lights darkening, until suddenly they are lit again to reveal a projection of airplanes flying into the World Trade Center.

The final three plays, Abi Morgan's *The Night is Darkest Before the Dawn*, Richard Bean's *On the Side of Angels*, and Simon Stephens's *Canopy of Stars*, each raise a different, but related, moral question about withdrawing Western support from Afghanistan. Morgan decided to focus her play on the fact that schooling is a luxury in Afghanistan and being a woman teacher means courting death (2009). In the world she conjures, it is 2001 and the Taliban have been defeated, but Afghanis, particularly girls and women, are leery of the Taliban's return. The patriarchal culture is also at work, and a girl in the poppy fields is worth more than a girl at school. Richard Bean's play, about NGOs in Afghanistan, is cynical and acerbic. In his work, NGO workers are willing to make terrible compromises—such as marrying off a young girl to an old man—and they will countenance propaganda, if its "for the good." This play, the most intentionally irritating of the cycle, tries to raise a discussion about cultural imperialism, but the basic needs of the Afghani people—just depicted in the preceding plays—are so great that Bean's concerns seem to trivialize the real labor of relief workers. What follows—Stephens's *Canopy of the Stars*—makes a particularly strong case for ordinary decency. Hearkening back to Morgan's play, Stephens imagines a soldier who wants to return to Afghanistan instead of remaining in England with his wife and child. Admittedly, his life is far duller at home, but Jay also feels a commitment to what he was involved in there: the safeguarding of children as roads and schools were built.

Unlike the plays about Iraq, then, the cycle of works about Afghanistan are far more inconclusive about whether American and British presence is productive or helpful. Certainly the plays expose all manner of self-interest and political obtuseness, but they also suggest that something valuable may be at work. Nicholas Kent noted that he was a pacifist before he went to Afghanistan and he returned convinced that Britain should remain involved. Spectators may leave the theatre equally convinced that there is merit in remaining there, but also chastened by the unambiguous message that every foreign army has failed in Afghanistan.

ATONEMENT AND RECOGNITION: THE RADICAL ETHICS OF HOMEBODY/KABUL

The first act of *Homebody/Kabul* is a long monologue by a middle-aged woman, the "Homebody." Disappointed in marriage and motherhood, she is as desperately loquacious as Beckett's Winnie from *Happy Days*. Where Winnie holds onto a large bag of objects to ground herself, the Homebody has her own bag, containing hats she has purchased from an Afghani refugee, and a book, an outdated tourist guide to Afghanistan. With these slight objects, the play connects an unhappy marriage to a wrecked and neglected country.

Because *Homebody/Kabul* premiered on December 19, 2001, just three months after the attacks, much commentary focused on how impossible it was to separate the two events and on Kushner's remarkable prescience. Kushner was hailed as prophetic—a point that his own play rebukes in its firm assertions that the outlines of history can be grasped if one is willing to read them. Nevertheless, *Homebody/Kabul*, for its timing and its wide production, as well as for its intelligence and strong ethical mandate, is among the most important plays written about global politics and ethical responsibility. As Peter Dickinson notes, *Homebody/Kabul* was produced when the West was "suddenly clamoring for information about Afghanistan its complicated history," one result of which was the play was produced in major theatrical venues around the world as well as in smaller houses (2005, 437). More than a decade later, it merits asking, had *Homebody/Kabul* not coincided with the attacks, would it be so famous? Or put another way, would this play be read differently?

There is some irony, perhaps, that the most famous play in this discussion is one that was *not* written after the attacks. This aligns Kushner's works with those written by Caryl Churchill and Harold Pinter, but those plays describe the dynamics of terrorism, not an actual event. Kushner stands alone in producing a work of such historical and political specificity that was not written in direct response to 9/11. It contained so much information about Afghanistan—its long history in the first act, and its current status in the second—that it met the immediate need for information and context. But the essence of Kushner's dramaturgy is to focus in on geopolitical pressures that, however unobserved, affect individual subjectivity. *Homebody/Kabul* may be regarded as an extension of the critique Kushner has offered through his earlier plays. Like *Angels in America*, *Homebody/Kabul* presents the forces of history bearing down on men and women who, if they are able to read its painful symptoms in their own lives, are not able or willing to trace the arc of historical change. M. Scott Philips argues that *Homebody* is "Kushner's latest exploration of a theme recurring throughout his work, that of cultural and political apocalypse, of the millennial anxiety afflicting a world at the brink of spiritual and moral negation" (2004, 1). In the Gramscian sense of "at the brink," both of these plays are interregnum plays, where the past has not receded enough to allow the future to be met, but where characters, at least sensitive ones, have a palpable sense of impending change. Kushner would argue that such historical analysis is available to any who would undertake the labor.

Philips and others have written of these plays as being apocalyptic, but it is worth noting that the rhetoric of terrorism is always apocalyptic. Terrorism wants the end to an order, not to a policy, and nothing short of the complete eradication of the enemy's ideology will suffice. A terrorized world—which was the state of the globe years before 9/11—feels like a world about to unravel, and the apocalyptic mindset shows itself in the language of irreconcilability, annihilation, and cultural superiority. The apocalyptic feel, however, is one that may be attached to a moment when the tipping point of social change has been reached (as in *Angels in America*) and the anxiety about change shows itself as an anxiety about endings. Kushner's ability to depict the terror that accompanies desirable or even less desirable but inevitable change, is one of his great achievements: he depicts the emotional stranglehold of fear that precedes liberation (Prior's angel in *Angels in America*) or resistance (Louis's behavior in *Angels*). In addition to an individual's deeply felt anxiety, the apocalyptic mode inhibits a long-lensed historical and political analysis that could counter the discourse of irreconcilability and the politics of brutal endings. With this longer lens, terrorism in *Homebody/Kabul* is connected to the growth of "internationalized capitalism." For some political scientists, terrorism is the enemy that the "new empires" of globalization have created (Cirhinlioglu 2008, 56).

To return to Kushner's "prescience," it is true that he gives the Homebody a kind of intelligence that relies on intuitive grasp, but she also actively searches for connections and insight. She pays attention. Because of her obsessive reading, the Homebody can reproduce the long history of Afghanistan and recognize it as a place that had endured multiple occupations and displacements. Her reading does not arise from a self-schooling in political awareness—her book is out of date and Orientalist—but acts as a form of escape from her husband, who cannot bear to hear the sound her voice, from her futile antidepressants, and from her daughter's unhappiness. When she goes, on a whim to buy some colorful hats imported from Afghanistan as favors for a diverting party she will host, she is prepared, because of her reading, for the encounter she has with the store owner. He sells cultural objects stripped of their history and meaning and commodified as entertainment trinkets for Western consumers, objects that the Homebody recognizes as having been "doodahs of a culture once aswarm with spirit matter and are now "Third World junk" (2002, 17).[2] She imagines a

> many-cameled caravan, having roamed across the entire postcolonial not-yet-developed world, crossing the borders of the rainforested kingdoms of Kwashiorkor and Rickets and Untreated Gum disease and High Infant Mortality rates, gathering with desperate indiscriminateness—is that the word?—on the mudpitted unpaved trade route its bits and boodle, had finally breached its great heavy no longer portable self in a narrow coal-scuttle of a shop on _____ (gesture) *here*, here caravanserai here in the developed and overdeveloped and over-overdeveloped paved wasted now deliquescent post-First World postmodern city of London: all the camels having flopped and toppled over and fallen here and died of exhaustion, of shock, of the heartache of refugees, the goods simply piled high upon their dromedary bones, just where they came to rest, and set up shop atop the carcasses, and so on (20).

Amidst all this speculation of the origins of things, she sees the hat seller's mutilated hand, the fingers sliced evenly off as a brutal punishment. And this sight registers: "Here, in London, that poor mutilated hand. Imagine" (21). This is the Homebody's Damascene conversion: the moment she could suddenly understand Pashtu, hear the refugee's pain, imagine the mutilated hand inside of her vagina as she makes love to the Afghani, and recognize that what is known about Afghanistan, a fist-shaped map of misery, is only a partial truth. Afghanistan, ranked 168th out of 174 on the Human Misery Index, has been swallowed whole by a blind, voracious cannibal and spat out as a product. Its history and is future is a shop for fun atop a carcass.

In this moment of conversion, the Homebody realizes that she must change. It is "dreadful, really unpardonable to remain dry," she concludes, to pretend she is protected in her privileged enclave of a kitchen, "on her culpable shore, suffering uselessly watching others perishing in the sea" and "never joining the drowning" (28). Her conversion is not messianic; it is not even humanitarian. She desires human solidarity, and she seeks repentance.

The Homebody intuits that her leaving will be an act of personal atonement, and perhaps—we do not hear her thoughts after act one—of familial regeneration. She knows that privacy is gone, and that the time is one of division. The Homebody is not a theorist; she does not speculate about technological intrusion, economic domination, or political power disguised as religious piety. She simply recognizes the falsity of shores and boundaries. All is connected, she believes, and therefore all is "touched" and "touch corrupts." "All must be corrupted," she declares (11). The word-mad Homebody knowingly chooses the dangerous word, "corrupt," invoking the fear that cultural and tribal superiority will be contaminated by outsiders. But she inverts the loathing associated with the taint of the other: if all is corrupted by touch, all will be mixed and bridged. The Homebody probably knows, too, that "corrupt" shares the stem of the word "rupture," and that the break from isolation, luxurious comfort, and her own family will involve violence.

The Homebody begins her remarks with the admission that these are "awful times" (11). Initially, the audience thinks she is describing *only* the present historical moment, but this turns out not to be the case. The present, the Homebody reminds us, as the "scene of our crime" and the "place of our shame," is always an "awful place to be" (11). She poses the difficult question, how much, given that wisdom comes only with retrospective illumination of the past, are we expected to know and to do about the "awful present"? This question also lingers over the mutilated hand and reveals the Homebody's double sense of guilt. That someone has been butchered in our times appalls her, and she feels implicated. There is another guilt closer to home: her daughter, Priscilla, is also damaged. Like the seller, she is a reproach. The Homebody understands that her daughter is "starving," but "I...withhold my touch" (28). The culpability deepens: "The touch that does not understand is the touch which corrupts...and which corrupts itself" (28). The Homebody compares a child to a country: "What, after all is a child but the history of all that has befallen her, a succession of displacements, bloody, beautiful?" (27). Such a history needs to be seen, for "what else is love but recognition" (28). The second act will reveal that the Homebody is wracked by her own culpability for what her daughter has experienced: suicide, abortion, electroshock therapy. The ruined hand seems to be parting a curtain and beckoning the Homebody to a place where she "might seek in submission the unanswered need" (28). And so she leaves for Kabul.

In his afterward, Kushner quotes from the Talmud: "Repentance preceded the world" (2002, 149). Viewing repentance as the grounds for life, rather than the consequence of choices about life, may initially perplex readers, but it goes further to explain why all touch corrupts, and why Kushner regards his play as hopeful. The corrupting touch derives from privileging the self and the denigration, if not complete erasure, of the other. No scale or degree (or exculpatory evidence or argument) operates in the purity of this logic. The assertion that a "touch which does not understand that which it touches is the touch which corrupts what it touches, and which corrupts itself" (28) defines human interaction. Until we can live according to ethics that do not begin with the self, but begin with the relational in the purest form, human interaction will endlessly recycle misunderstanding, injury, and conflict. The Homebody herself believes that "most of us will be adjudged guilty when we are summoned before the judgment seat" (24). Though she tries to slough off the idea of personal guilt as somehow narcissistic or simply outmoded, she wrings her hands as she speaks: she cannot embrace denial. That Kabul is the burial place of Cain also fascinates the Homebody; perhaps she feels some identification, as well as pity, for this dislocated and rootless man who has been punished with a sentence of homelessness.

For Emmanuel Levinas, "Only repentance can cause salvation, but objective events of a political character produce this repentance which is both a manifestation of human freedom and a product of an external cause" (1997, 72). Here Levinas speaks to the freedom—which by definition allows for human immorality—that manifests itself in political violence and in political quiescence. The Homebody, aware of the concentric circles of culpability, feels ringed by her own disengagement and the political violence committed with her tacit consent by government and marketplace. The desire to recede, she recognizes, to stay on the shore, occurs because one is both agent and object of misunderstanding. The withdrawal cannot be other than a withdrawal of love, which affects self, family, and community. In this doom loop of blame and guilt, the Homebody learns that the recognition that happened when she allowed the mutilated hand to "touch" her has set her on a path of radical re-cognition. In taking this leap into a place of need and atonement, she beckons her family to follow. She achieves this "at-onement" through an act of exchange, one that might be regarded as a kind of substitutionary atonement.

In the Christian, Jewish, and Muslim traditions, the word repentance is connected to the word for "return." In Hebrew, it is also linked to sorrow, and in the New Testament, repentance is associated with metanoia—to think differently. Anya Topolski has explained how much of Levinas's ethics derived from his understanding of *teshuvah*, commonly understood as forgiveness though also meaning "return," as a "double-movement" that mandates a turn to the good (*yetzer-tov*). Topolski notes that Levinas's interpretation of teshuvah involved "a turn away from the violence of singularity towards the *tikkum olam* of alterity (2008, 1).

This double-movement is enacted in the second part of *Homebody-Kabul*. Uncompromising in its depiction of Afghani suffering, poverty, political and religious oppression, act two takes up the search for the missing mother.[3] The medical doctor (also possibly the man the Homebody marries) clinically recites the particulars of her dismemberment—an attack that left her body parts possible strewn through the city, though she was never "dishonored" through rape (2002, 21). Milton, her husband, accepts the news as absolute fact and spends most of the rest of his time in his hotel room with the ridiculously named Quango Twistleton. The dead-end of British imperialism, Twistleton is a drunk and a junkie whose only value is that he possesses exit papers. Milton drinks and drugs away the hours while his daughter ventures forth to find her mother.

The search takes Priscilla on her own journey toward recognition: not a small feat for someone who has barely left the house in some years. This search for her mother's face leads her through cemeteries, to the burial place of the brother-hating Cain, through septic hospital wards and morgues, and finally to meet Mahala, another cast-off wife. She is asked to take Mahala, a librarian and hence, like her mother, a great reader, back to London. Along the way, Priscilla must come to grips with her mother's disappearance which she reads as abandonment.

The play suggests more "rational" motives than the radical altruism the Homebody has come to embody. Because Afghanistan is a country "so at the heart of the world the world has forgotten it" (28), perhaps the Homebody feels in her own "essential surfeit of inconsequence" (12) a kinship with its invisibility. Her empathy leads her to make the kind of choice that is read by family members as desperate and selfish, but that incarnates her impatience with the "Rhetorical Colloidal forever" of inaction. More than politics or idealism are at work here; the Homebody's action resonates with what is called holy: she is willing to give up her place and to take another's.

Mahala is most markedly the Other, but perhaps she can be seen as the Homebody's twin: a fellow reader, unloved by her husband, discounted by the world. Mahala is more violent-tempered than melancholic. She is driven to uncontrollable rage by the treatment of women and the eradication of learning. Her library not only housed knowledge, but it also distributed bread to the poor: both have been outlawed. She will be killed because she defies the Taliban. She needs to be saved, and in honoring what appears to be her mother's wishes, Priscilla has sex with the pathetic Quango in order to get the exit papers. Given that her last sexual act led to suicide and abortion, she, too, has exchanged something in order to ransom Mahala. The Homebody has also saved her daughter and, in a small way, Afghanistan. She has, in Levinas's terms, struggled personally with the calls of justice and of responsibility. She has defined "her relation to alterity, in the form of substitution" as central to her "responsibility to the other, or to the justice for all others" (Topolski 2008, 4). The identity of the Other is not important, a point Kushner underlines by the difficult Mahala. Summarizing Levinas, Topolski writes that "what defines the self as ethical is the choice to respond to the call or face of the other, a response that requires taking responsibility for that other" (4). This responsibility is done by means of substitution. Taking responsibility means to apologize for prioritizing my being over that of the stranger. Reversing this ontological prioritization means to recognize how the other transforms "me" into an "I." In this sense, the other constitutes the self (4).

In his afterward, Kushner writes that "tragedy is the annihilation from whence new life springs" (148), and it is surely the case that Priscilla, the suicidal daughter, would never have come back to life were it not for her mother's extraordinary disappearance. Plausibility is not at issue here, and there is little hope that any explanation or final truth about the mother's disappearance will ever be found. But the Homebody knew already how elusive fact and truth could be in Afghanistan. She imagined the Afghani hat seller back in London trying out every kind of explanation for what happened in Kabul:

> There is no life here only fear, we do not live in buildings now, we live in terror in the cellars in the caves in the mountains, only God can save us now... only terror can save us from ruin only never ending war, save us from terror and never ending war, save my wife they are stoning my wife... save us from God, for war, from exile, from oil exploration, from no oil exploration, from the West, from children with rifles (24).

When she fails to find out if her mother is dead or alive, Priscilla decides to accept the poetic truth of her mother's life. In this empathetic act, she has become her mother's daughter, and when she decides to take Mahala back to London and install her in her mother's place, she completes the circle of her own atonement. Kushner has called his final scene the "periplum," a word he tells us that Ezra Pound invented to describe a "tour which takes you round then back again and produces knowledge (8).[4] The periplum, then, is also a return or a reversal. Unlike her father, who does not appear in the last scene, Priscilla recognizes the relational as foundational to her own living. The words she exchanges with Mahala, who tends her mother's unweeded garden and reads her mother's books, are ones of mutuality and dependence. Priscilla has learned that "each individual... is called to leave in his turn, or without awaiting his turn, the concept of the ego... to respond with responsibility: *me,* that is, *here I am for the others*" (Levinas 1998, 185, emphasis in original). They have, through the Homebody's agency, saved each other. The paradigm the play establishes is more radical: it is not enough to try to help another; one must exchange places; one must be touched.

As the play ages, its status as the play that "predicted" 9/11 will fade, all to the good. History, Kushner would agree, is there for the reading, for guarding against the disposal of inconvenient facts. Afghanistan, like Iraq, has suffered under American friendship, under American neglect, and under American attack. This record attests to the sad truth of The Great Game metaphor: Afghani lives have been treated as so many insignificant pawns.

Judith Butler suggests that however much one affirms the sanctity of life or opposes violence, one still reaches a dead end if "certain lives are not perceivable as lives" (2010, 51). She goes on to say that the "critique of violence must begin with the question of the representability of life itself: what allows a life to become invisible in its precariousness?" (51). This discussion in its entirety, has attempted to disrupt the many ways that visibility—through media, through performative politics, through censorship—has made the precarious life invisible and how we have been complicit in this self-blinding.

"What else is love but recognition" (Kushner 2002, 28)?

Notes

INTRODUCTION: SPECTATOR OF CALAMITIES

1. Sontag is quoted in David Carr, 2003.
2. For the entire text, see Karlheinz Stockhausen, 2002. While it is deeply reductive to characterize Stockhausen's contributions to art by this single event, it should be noted that as a composer who explored the sublime in his own creations, Stockhausen expertly recognized the attacks as partaking in aspects of the sublime in both aesthetic and religious dimensions. Also, the effect of media coverage is itself reductive: it is seldom interested in the long context of a comment made; hence Stockhausen, like Sontag, is criticized for his defensible insights. See also a discussion of Stockhausen's comments in Lentricchia and McAuliffe, 2003, 6–11.
3. Tom Englehardt coined the term "total television" in his article "The Gulf War as Total Television" (1992, 630). And James Der Derrian defines "virtuous war" as "technology in the service of virtue that has given rise to a global form of virtual violence" (2009, xxvii).
4. Thomas Irmer's discussion "A Search for New Realities: Documentary Theatre in Germany" is part of *TDR*, fall, 2006. This entire issue, guest-edited by Carol Martin, is essential reading for anyone interested in this form.

1 FIVE POLITICAL CRISES: THE NEW SEMIOTIC ENVIRONMENT

1. Philip Taylor (1992b) describes the interruption of the nightly news with the first accounts of the 1991 war, and the news that both President George Bush and Prime Minister John Major were watching the war they declared on television (32). In "Military Censorship and the Body Count," Margot Norris writes about the effects of censorship and concludes that the Persian Gulf War "inaugurated the creation of something like an originary silence—a partially blank space of discourse and representation whose absence can only be inferred, rather than an effacement whose occlusions may be lifted or an erasure whose traces may be restored" (1991, 225). The practice of allowing approved reporters to travel with troops ("embedded

reporting") was a strategy devised in the 2003 Persian Gulf War to replace the much-criticized pool system used in the 1991 war; it, too, essentially created a "controlled information environment" (Taylor, 1992b, 31). (For a description of the pooled information system, see Taylor,1992b, 51–59.) In addition to the account of the media given by Taylor, two other books were particularly useful: *The Media and the Persian Gulf War*, edited by Robert E. Denton Jr., and *The Media and the Gulf War*, edited by Hedrick Smith.

2. In examining these theatre pieces about the Gulf War against media reportage of the same historical incident, I am in agreement with Douglas Kellner's insistence that "theories of media and culture are...best developed through specific instances of concrete phenomena contextualized within the vicissitudes of contemporary society and history. Thus to interrogate contemporary media culture critically involves carrying out studies of how the culture industries produce specific artifacts that reproduce the social discourses which are embedded in the key conflicts and struggles of the day" (1995, 4).

2 Turning History into Happening: The First Iraq War

1. Pre-lot text to sale of Paik's "Petroglyph Hawk" at Christie's. See: http://www.christies.com/LotFinder/lot_details.aspx?intObjectID=5055497.
2. George Bush declared a ceasefire and made the statement on February 28, 1991.
3. See Henry Jenkins, *Convergence Culture*.
4. Reported in the *New York Times*, September, 23, 1990.
5. The UNICEF's estimate is 500,000.
6. David DeRose discusses the genesis of *States of Shock* in his book *Sam Shepherd*. He recounts how Shepherd was working with his old colleague Joseph Chaikin on *The War in Heaven (Angel's Monologue)*, which Chaikin was preparing to perform. This piece, about the "loss of personal order" and a "state of crisis" or "shock" took on political overtones when the 1991 Persian Gulf War began (133–140).
7. Claudia Orenstein discusses the importance of "political clowning" in the Mime Troupe's work (1998, 3). Her study of the Mime Troupe as a type of festive-revolutionary theatre makes the important point that this kind of popular, political theatre is largely excluded from Max Horkheimer and Theodor Adorno's critique of the "culture industry," a critique that "proposes a dialectic between mass culture and the Kantian concept of a work of art" but fails to address "nontechnological forms of popular theater that are instances neither of mass culture not of elite art" (10–11). She also notes that part of the Mime Troupe's strategy in its political clowning is to dissemble its own serious purpose, but their playfulness offers trenchant social critique even as it generates the forms of subjectivity and activism it "only pretends to display" (9).

8. Alessandra Stanley writes that the network anchors in the 2003 war came across "as the omniscient narrators of a daily novel" (2003, B14). An illustrative incident that exemplifies the higher degree of patriotism required in the 2003 war is the story of the reporter Peter Arnett. Arnett was praised during the 1991 war for his decision to remain in Baghdad to report on the war. In 2003, Arnett was fired from MSNBC and *National Geographic* when he appeared on Al Jazeera television in an interview with Iraqi reporters.
9. Wallace explained her role as a coproducer of *Playwrights Against the Embargo*, with Tony Kushner, Eve Ensler, Reggie Gaines, and others, as a protest against the embargo of drugs, such as penicillin and aspirin, against Iraq, which has contributed to the death of close to a million children in a ten-year period (2010, 3).
10. Here, I am in disagreement with critics such as Timothy Bottoms who observes that Stubbs seems more like a Vietnam veteran than a Gulf War soldier (Bottoms 1998, 246).
11. Department of Defense Directive 1332.14.

3 THE PERSIANS

1. For further commentary on the baby incubator episode, see Douglas Kellner, 1992, 67–72.
2. Stanton Garner, in "Politics Over the Gulf: Trevor Griffiths in the Nineties," writes that the result of the referential layering in Griffiths's play acts as denotation of a complex geopolitical event and depiction of fragmentation and mutual estrangement (1996, 385). He goes on to describe how the play "decenters the Western point of view of the Gulf War and the Middle East in general, making the British characters the play's foreigners and intensifying the play's focus on cultural difference" (385). I agree with Garner and would add that in addition to being cast as foreigners, the British characters are also clearly opportunists. Also, the referential layering adds to the confusion of the play's opening minutes and stands in contrast to the false lucidity of media reports. Jonathan Bignell discusses the challenges posed by the structures of Griffiths's play in "Trevor Griffith's Political Theatre" (1994).
3. I spoke with members of the Mark Taper Forum who described the audiences leaving midway through the play. Some critics applauded Sellars's ambitious undertaking: Sandra Kreiswirth, writing for *The Daily Breeze*, called the production "adventuresome theatre" and hailed the portrayal of Xerxes as an "explosive, humanizing performance, one that makes ancient messages modern and enemies easier to understand" (1993, B6). John Lahr, in his review, "Inventing the Enemy," in *The New Yorker* writes that "Aeschylus' boldness in imagining the other is matched by Sellars' bravery in linking the play's theme to the Gulf War and to a contemporary multicultural agenda. From the Indian Wars to the Cold War, fear of the other has been a dominant American theme" (1993, 103).

4. Sellars, 2006, 8. Steven Leigh Morris voices an objection to this psychologizing. In his review he writes, "but Xerxes is just a wild-child who had problems with his daddy. Oh please!" (1993). Craig Lucas, however, also connects the dysfunctional family to militarism in his Iraq play *Prayer for My Enemy* (2009).
5. Clare Bayley writes that, in the opening moments of *The Persians*, "our political senses are awakened as well as our intimate responses. The human and the technological meld in a new synthesis of understanding" (1993, 10).
6. Judith Thompson writes about Saddam Hussein's torture palace in *Palace of the End* (2009).
7. An important discussion of America's tolerance for human rights abuses is Samantha Power's *A Problem from Hell: America and the Age of Genocide* (2002).
8. The notion of "white men saving brown women from brown men" as one the reinforces a cultural politics of dependency was first articulated by Gayatri Spivak in "Can the Subaltern Speak?" (1985). Miriam Cooke invokes Spivak's phrase in her essay "Saving Brown Women" (2002).
9. Raffo notes that in the West, the abaya has become the symbol of all Iraqi women, though many do not wear it. This comment is from Raffo's notes to her play (2006).
10. According to a 2003 Human Rights Watch Briefing Paper, "The Background on Background on Women's Status in Iraq Prior to the Fall of the Saddam Hussein Government," after seizing power in 1968, the secular Ba'ath party embarked on a program to consolidate its authority and to achieve rapid economic growth despite labor shortages. Women's participation was integral to the attainment of both of these goals, and the government promulgated laws specifically aimed at improving the status of women in the public and—to a more limited extent—the private spheres. The Iraqi government also passed labor and employment laws to ensure that women were granted equal opportunities in the civil service sector, maternity benefits, and freedom from harassment in the workplace. The fact that the government (as opposed to the private sector) was hiring women contributed to the breakdown of the traditional reluctance to allow women to work outside the home. The Iraqi Bureau of Statistics reported that in 1976, women constituted approximately 38.5 percent of those in the education profession, 31 percent of the medical profession, 25 percent of lab technicians, 15 percent of accountants, and 15 percent of civil servants. During the Iran-Iraq War (1980–88), women assumed greater roles in the workforce in general and the civil service in particular, reflecting the shortage of working-age men. Until the 1990s, the number of women working outside the home continued to grow. While most advances in women's status occurred in the political and economic spheres, the government also made modest changes to the personal status laws in 1978. See http://www.hrw.org/backgrounder/wrd/iraq-women.htm.
11. "Shaking Hands with Saddam Hussein: The US Tilt toward Iraq, 1980–1984," *The National Security Archive*. http://www.gwu.edu/-nsarchive/NSAEEBB/NSAEBB82. Accessed February 2003.

12. Huda's analysis, articulated from an Iraqi viewpoint, is complemented by the oral history provided by Brent Scowcroft, who served as the national security advisor to President George H. W. Bush. Scowcroft concedes that neither political advisors nor field commanders shared Bush's hope that an Iraqi rebellion would finish off Hussein; that the decision to allow helicopters through no-fly zones provided a loophole that the Iraqi military exploited; and that the United States had "underestimated" Hussein's ability to survive. See www.pbs.org./wgbh/pages/frontline/gulf/oral/scowcroft/5.html. Accessed January 24, 2011.
13. The facility had been used as a civil-defense shelter during the Iran-Iraq War, and, according the Human Rights Watch, remained a clearly marked site for civilian use. US intelligence sources maintained that it was used as a military command center. At the time of the bombing, on February 13, 1991, at 4:30 a.m., the shelter was occupied by mostly women and children. More than four hundred people were killed. Raffo's character is based on a woman, Umm Greyda, who lost eight children there and has lived on site to act as a guide to the bombed shelter.
14. Lila Abu Lughod addressed the problematic notion of saving Muslim women in an interview with Asia Source: "When you save someone, you are saving them from something. You are also saving them to something. What violence are entailed in this transformation?" See http://www.asiasource.org/news/specials_reports/lila.cfm. Accessed September 25, 2010.

4 FROM THE RUINS OF 9/11: GRIEF AND TERROR

1. Joan Didion's remarks are included in Linda Kauffman's excellent survey article "World Trauma Center" (2003).
2. "The Portraits of Grief" series began three days after the attacks. The *Times* describes it thusly: "The portraits were never meant to be obituaries in any traditional sense. They were brief, informal and impressionistic, often centered on a single story or idiosyncratic detail. They were not intended to recount a person's résumé, but rather to give a snapshot of each victim's personality, of a life lived. And they were democratic; executive vice presidents and battalion chiefs appeared alongside food handlers and janitors. Each profile was roughly 200 words. In the weeks that followed the attacks, amid nonstop news coverage of the disaster and the war, reading 'Portraits of Grief' became a ritual for people nationwide." The portraits have been collected in *Portraits 9/11/01*, Times Books, 2002.

5 FACING TERROR

1. Antonin Artaud, 1972.
2. See Anthony Tommasini, 2001.
3. Durkheim contrasted altruistic suicide, motivated by the beliefs of a group into which one has become integrated, with egotistical suicide. *Suicide: A Study in Sociology* (1979) New York: The Free Press.

4. See interview with Mohamed Mokhtar, a fellow student. (October, 2001).
5. Jenny Hughes raises similar questions in "Theatre, Performance and the 'War on Terror,' 2007.
6. IRA is the Irish Republican Army; the UVF is the Ulster Volunteer Force; the PKK is the Kurdish Workers Party; the NRA is the National Resistance Army; and the AAB is the Al-Aqsa Martyrs Brigade.
7. See Jerrold Post, 2007.
8. The essays are by Alecky Blythe, artistic director of Recorded Delivery; Peter Cheesman of the Old and New Victoria Theatre, North Staffordshire; Elyse Dodgson of the Royal Court; and playwright David Hare.
9. The same phenomena was true of Tony Kushner's *Homebody/Kabul*, which was being staged as the 9/11 attacks occurred. I will discuss Kushner's important play in the final chapter. For further discussion of *Talking to Terrorists* and verbatim drama, see Christopher Innes, 2007.
10. See Mitchell, 2004 and 2005.
11. Elin Diamond has written that "the mystifications of the body in representation has come to serve as a metaphor for the concealments of human, and especially female experience, under patriarchy and capitalism." To this important insight about Churchill's attention to the "ideological nature of the seeable" (1988, 191), I would add that capitalism, operating in and through its globalized, technologized frames, produces the robotic, reproducible body that Churchill places center stage in *Far Away* and *A Number*.
12. Remarks made at a lecture given at Case Western Reserve University on November 30, 2006, based on author's notes.

6 War Documents

1. http://downingstreetmemo.com/memotext.html
2. It is important not to underestimate the global protest against the War in Afghanistan: some thirty-seven thousand people protested across the United States on October 2, 2001, and over ten thousand protesters marched in NYC. Protests were also held in Spain, India, the Netherlands, Greece, Scotland, Germany, Sweden, Australia, England, and India. See: http://en.wikipedia.org/wiki/Protests_against_the_War_in_Afghanistan _(2001%E2%80%93present). Accessed June 4, 2009.
3. See Carol Martin, 2006.
4. See especially, Douglas Kellner, 2005.
5. This formulation is a version of filmmaker Jean-Luc Comoli's definition of documentary film, cited in Gaines, 2007, 46.
6. Transcript of the Hutton Inquiry maybe accessed at www.the-hutton -inquiry.org.uk.
7. David Hare, 2004. Stephen Bottoms argues that Hare's refusal to identify his sources and the way that his places his imagined scenes on par with those documented are ethically problematic, given that the play takes as its subject the "fine details of the language used in the run-up to the war" (2006, 60).

8. For a discussion of the coherence of the play, see Donna Soto-Morettini, 2005, 309–319.
9. Soto-Morettini references Hayden White's *Metahistory* in which White offers a method for understanding historical events according to their modes of emplotment, argument, and ideological implication. See White, 1973, 3.
10. Wright made this comment in a post-production talk with *New Yorker* editor David Remnick, which I attended, June 6, 2008.
11. The shrine, one of the most important Shia mosques, was built in 1991 and bombed in both 2006 and 2007. The first attack damaged the mosques' famous golden dome. Knight, S. (2006) "Al-Askariya Shrine: 'Not just a Major Cathedral.'" *TimesOnline.co.uk*. http://www.timesonline.co.uk/article/0,,7374-2053168,00.html.
12. For accounts of the bombing see Robert Worth, 2006.
13. Because *My Trip to Al Qaeda* is unpublished, quotations are taken from notes I took while seeing the play on June 6, 2008.
14. See "Authors@Google" Lawrence Wright by Lawrence Wright. http://www.vodpod.com/watch1420612-authorsgoogle-lawrence-wright-by-lawrence-wright-on-online-video-free-audio.
15. Personal notes.

7 Bodies Count: In/Visible Scandal at Guantanamo and Abu Ghraib

1. For a fuller description of the conditions at Guantanamo, see Joseph Margolis 2006.
2. Other Guantanamo plays have appeared: *In God We Trust* by Peshkar Productions; *Rendition Monolgues*, a verbatim play about Bisher al Rawi; *Waiting for Mamdouh*, about Mamdouh Habib, who played himself.
3. For new arrivals, the color orange is associated with execution and hence alarms them.
4. See the official website of the Joint Task Force Guantanamo: http://www.jtfgtmo.southcom.mil/index/sept%202010%20pdfs/PG4%20Detainee%20Programs.pdf. Accessed August, 29, 2008.
5. More information is available at http://www.globalsecurity.org/military/facility/guantanamo-bay_delta.htm. Accessed August 29, 2008.
6. One example is the account given by Mohammad Saad Iqbal, who spent six years in American custody, five at Guantanamo; he was never charged or convicted of a crime and was released without explanation. When he returned to Pakistan, he needed to be weaned from "a cocktail of antidepressants and antibiotics" (Perlez et al. 2009).
7. For a summary of the Patriot Act, seehttp://en.wikipedia.org/wiki/USA_PATRIOT_Act. The text of the bill is Accessed
8. http://www.deseretnews.com/mobile/article/700084691/Civilian-courts-work.html. "Civilian Court Works," editorial in *Miami Herald*, Nov. 23, 2010.

9. See the Austinist Interviews: *Lidless* Playwright Frances Yu-Chi Cowhig, 2009, http://austinist.com/2009/02/11/austinist_interviews_lidless_playwr.php#. Accessed Feb. 15, 2010.
10. See LaCapra: "Any truly viable reconciliation on a collective level depends not only on such processes as empathy and mourning but also on concrete economic, social and political reforms in a larger context in which mourning itself has a broader, indeed a political meaning" (2001, 215).

8 Afghanistan and "The Spectacle of Our Suffering"

1. See Fatima Ayub and Sari Kouvo, 2008.
2. For a particularly rich discussion of act one, the Homebody's monologue, see Framji Minwalla, 2003.
3. Catherine Stevenson examines motherhood in "Seek for Something New," 2005.
4. Judith Miller entertains and rejects any charges of "exoticism" in Kushner's play that would be associated with a tour abroad (2006, 216).

Works Cited

Adams, L. (2008) "Beyond the Burka." *New York Times Book Review*, January 6, p. 12.
Auletta, R. and Aeschylus. (1993) *The Persians*. Los Angeles: Sun and Moon Press.
———. (1996) Program Notes for the Los Angeles Festival Production, Mark Taper Forum.
Agamben, G. (1995) *Homo Sacer: Sovereign Power and Bare Life*. Stanford: Stanford University Press.
———. (2005) *State of Exception*. Chicago: University of Chicago Press.
Als, H. (2008) "Friends and Lovers." *The New Yorker*, March 31, pp. 132–133.
Al-Khalidi, A. and Tanner, V. (2009) "More than Shiites and Sunnis: Post-Sectarian Strategy in Iraq," *United States Institute of Peace*. http://www.usip.org/events/2009/0303_shites_sunnis.html. Accessed Feb. 1, 2010.
Amich, C. (2007) "Bringing the Global Home: The Commitment of Caryl Churchill's *The Striker*." *Modern Drama* 50, pp. 394–419.
Anderson, R. (2006) *A Century of Media, A Century of War*. New York: Peter Lang.
Angus, I. and Jhally, S. (eds.) (1988) *Cultural Politics in Contemporary America*. London: Routledge.
Appadurai, A. (2004). "Disjuncture and Difference in the Global Cultural Economy." In Lechner, F. and Boli, J. (eds.) *The Globalization Reader*. Oxford: Blackwell, pp. 101–108.
Arac, J. (1986) *Postmodernism and Politics*. Minneapolis: University of Minnesota Press, 1986.
Artaud, A. (2001) "To Have Done with the Judgment of God." In Hirschman, J. (ed.) *Artaud Anthology*, 2nd ed. San Francisco: City Lights Books.
Ayub, F. and Kouvo, S. (2008) "Righting the Course? Humanitarian Intervention, The War on Terror and the Future of Afghanistan." *International Affairs* 84.4, pp. 641–657.
Bapat, N. et al. (2007) "Perfect Allies? The Case Of Iraq and Al Qaeda." *International Studies Perspective* 8.3, pp. 272–286.
Barthes, R. (2000). *Camera Lucida*. London: Vintage.
Baudrillard, Jean. (1983) "The Ecstasy of Communication." In Foster, H. (ed.) *The Anti-Aesthetic: Essays on Postmodern Culture*. Seattle: Bay Press.
———. (1983) *Simulations*. New York: Semiotexte.

———. (1995) *The Gulf War Did Not Take Place*. (Paul Patton, trans.). Bloomington: Indiana University Press.
———. (2002) *The Spirit of Terrorism*. (Chris Turner, trans.). London: Verso.
Bayley, C. (1993) "The Persians: Things We Never Saw or Heard." *American Theatre*, December, pp. 10–11.
Benjamin, W. (2002) *The Arcades Project*. Cambridge, MA: Harvard University Press.
———. (1936) *The Work of Art in the Age of Mechanical Reproduction*. London: NLB.
Berkoff, S. (2002) *Requiem for Ground Zero*. Oxford: Amber Lane.
Bhabha, H. (1990) "The Third Space." In Rutherford, J. (ed.) *Identity, Community, Culture and Difference*. London: Lawrence and Wishart, pp. 207–221.
Bignell, J. (1994) "Trevor Griffith's Political Theatre: from '*Oi for England*' to '*The Gulf Between Us*.'" *New Theatre Quarterly* 10.37, pp. 49–56.
Bigsby, C.W.E. (2008) *Neil LaBute: Stage and Cinema*. Cambridge: Cambridge University Press.
Billington, M. (1992) Review of *The Gulf Between Us*. *Theatre Record*, 1, pp. 15–28.
Birchall, P. (1993) "The Persians." *Los Angeles Reader* 8, n.p.
Blanche, E. (2004) "Rumor, Conspiracy and Gobbledygook." *Middle East* 342(February), pp. 14–17.
Blanchot, M. and Derrida, J. (2000) *The Instant of My Death/ Demeure: Fiction and Testimony*. Stanford: Stanford University Press.
Blank, J. and Jensen, E. (2005) "The Uses of Empathy: Theatre and the Real World." *Theatre History Studies* 25, pp. 15–22.
Blumenthal, S. (2007) "Bush Knew Saddam Had No Weapons of Mass Destruction," *Salon.com*. http://www.salon.com/opinion/blumenthal/2007/09/06/bush_wmd/. Accessed Jan. 25, 2009.
Bond, E. (1993) *Tuesday*. London: Methuen.
Borradori, G. (2003) *Philosophy in a Time of Terror: Dialogue with Jurgen Habermas and Jacques Derrida*. Chicago: University of Chicago Press.
Bottoms, S. (1998) *The Theatre of Sam Shepard*. Cambridge: Cambridge University Press.
———. (2006) "Putting the Document into Documentary: an Unwelcome Corrective?" *The Drama Review* 50.3, pp. 56–68.
Bourdieu, P. (1998) *Acts of Resistance: Against the Tyranny of the Market*. New York: New Press.
Bowden, M. (2003) "The Dark Art of Interrogation." *The Atlantic Monthly*, October, pp. 51–76.
Bremer, P. (2006) Interview with David Gregory. *Meet the Press*, NBC, January 15.
Brittain, V. and Slovo, G. (2004) *Guantanamo: Honour Bound to Defend Freedom*. London: Oberon Books.
Brown, L. and Romano, D. (2006) "Women in Post-Saddam Iraq: One Step Forward or Two Steps Back?" *NWSA* 18.3, pp. 51–70.
Bumiller, E. (2006) "Iraq War Faces Some New Critics (the Theatre Kind)." *New York Times*, April 3, p. A14.

Bush, G. W. (2001) "Address to Joint Session of Congress," September 20. http://archives.cnn.com/2001/US/09/20/gen.bush.transcript.
———. (2003) "Mission Accomplished Speech, May 2, 3003." http://www.cnn.com/2003/ALLPOLIITICS/05/01/bush.carrier.landing. Accessed August 18, 2007.
———. (2009) "Bush Defends Record, Acknowledges Mistakes," MSNBC. http://www.msnbc.com/id/28617979/. Accessed Jan. 15, 2009.
Bush, G.H.W. (1990) "Address to Joint Session of Congress," Weekly Compilation Of Presidential Documents, 26(September 11). http://www.sweetliberty.org/issues/war/bushsr.htm
———. (1991) January 17 speech. http://www.historyplace.com/speeches/bush-war.htm.
Bush, G.H.W. and Scowcroft, B. (1998) *A World Transformed*. New York: Knopf.
Butler, J. (2004) *Precarious Life: The Powers of Mourning and Violence*. London: Verso.
———. (2010) *Frames of War*. London: Verso.
Calame, Byron (2006) "Preventing a Second Jason Blair," *New York Times*, June 18. http://www.nytimes.com/2006/06/18/opinion/18public.html.
Callens, J. (1997) "Published and Unpublished Wars: Contextualizing Sam Shepard's States Of Shock." In Giorcelli, C. and Kroes, R. (eds.) *Living with America: 1946–1996*. Amsterdam: VU University Press, pp. 223-234.
———. (2003) "Staging the Televised (Nation)." *Theatre Research International* 28.1, pp: 61–78.
Carr, D., Rutenberg, J., and Steinberg, J. (2003) "Telling War's Deadly Story at Just Enough Distance." *New York Times*, April 7, p. B13.
Carter, P. (2004) "The Road to Abu Ghraib." *Washington Monthly*, April 11. http://www.washingtonmonthly.com/features/2004/0411.carter.html#byline.
Caruth, C. (1995) *Trauma: Explorations in Memory*. Baltimore: John Hopkins University Press.
Chaney, D. (1993) *Fictions of a Collective Life: Public Drama in Late Modern Culture*. London: Routledge.
Charles, S. (2007) "Lawrence Wright's Trip to Al- Qaeda." *The American Prospect*, June 8. www.prospect.org/cs/articles?article+lawernce_wrights_trp_to_alqaeda.
Cheney, R. (2005a) "Cheney Calls War Critics Opportunists," MSNBC. http://www.msnbc.msn.com/id/10078197/.
———. (2005b.) "Cheney: Iraq will be an enormous success." CNN.com, June 24. http://www.cnn.com/2005/POLITICS/06/23/cheney.interview.
———. (2009). "Cheney Defends Dark Side Interrogations." http://articles.cnn.com/2009-04-24/politics/pm.dark.side_1_cia-interrogators-secret-cia-memos-dick-cheney?_s=PM:POLITICS.
Chomsky, N. (2001) *9/11*. New York: Seven Stories Press.
Churchill, C. (1993) *Mad Forest: A Play from Romania*. London: Nick Hern Books.
———. (2000) *Far Away*. New York: Theatre Communications Group.
———. (2002) *A Number*. London: Nick Hern Books.
Cirhinlioglu, Z. (2008) "Globalization, Modernity and Terror." In Kaya, C. and Erdemir, A. (eds.) *Social Dynamics of Global Terrorism and Prevention Policies*. Amsterdam: IOS Press, pp. 53–64.

Cohn, C. and Enloe, C. (2003) "A Conversation with Cynthia Enloe: Feminists Look at Masculinity and the Men Who wage War." *Signs* 28.4, pp. 1187–1207.
Colleran, J. (2003) "Disposable Wars, Disappearing Acts: Theatrical Responses to the Gulf War." *Theater Journal* 55, pp. 613–632.
Connor, S. (1989) *Postmodernist Culture: An Introduction to Theories of the Contemporary*. London: Blackwell.
Conrad, J. (1973) *Heart of Darkness*. In Kermode, F. and Hollander, J. (eds.) *Modern British Literature*. London: Oxford University Press, pp. 105–171.
Cooke, M. (1995) "Arab Women, Arab Wars." *Cultural Critique* winter, pp. 5–28.
———. (1997) "Listen to the Image Speak." *Cultural Values* 1.1, pp. 101–117.
———. (2000) "Multiple Critique: Islamic Feminist Rhetorical Strategies." *Nepantia: Views from the South* 1.1, p. 91–109.
———. (2000) "Women, Religion and the Postcolonial Arab World." *Cultural Critique* 45.Spring, pp. 150–184.
———. (2002) "Saving Brown Women." *Signs* 28.1, pp. 468–469.
Cornell, Drucilla. (2005) "The New Political Infamy and the Sacrilege of Feminism." In Rockmore, T., Margolis, J. and Marsoobian, A. (eds.) *The Philosophical Challenge of September 11*. London: Blackwell, pp. 108–124.
Cowhig, F. (2010) *Lidless*. New Haven: Yale Drama Series.
———. (2009) "Austinist Interviews: *Lidless* Playwright Frances Yu-Chi Cowhig." http://austinist.com/2009/02/11/austinist_interviews_lidless_playwr.php#.
Crewdson, J. (2004) "In Prague, a Tale of 2 Attas: Mistaken Identity Muddied 9/11 Probe." *Chicago Tribune*, 19 (August), p. 29.
Danner, M. (2004a) "Abu Ghraib: the Hidden Story." *The New York Review of Books* 15, p. 51.
———. (2004b) *Torture and Truth: America, Abu Ghraib and the War on Terror*. New York: NYRB Collections.
Danto, A. (2005) *The Art of 9/11*, exhibition at Apex, New York, September–October. http://www.apexart.org/exhibitions/danto.php.
Debord, G. (1987) *Society of the Spectacle*. Great Britain: Reble Press.
De la Durantaye, L. (2009) *Giorgio Agamben: A Critical Introduction*. Stanford: Stanford University.
Delgado, M. and Heritage, P. (eds.) (1996) *In Contact with the Gods? Directors Talk Theatre*. Manchester: Manchester University Press.
DeLillo, D. (2001) "In the Ruins of the Future." *Harpers*, December, pp. 33–40.
Denton, R. Jr. (ed.) (1993) *The Media and the Persian Gulf War*. Westport, CT: Praeger.
DeRose, D. (1992a) *Sam Shepard*. Toronto: Twayne.
———. (1992b) "States of Shock." *Vietnam Generation Journal* 4, 3–4. http// lists.village.virginia.edu/sixties/HTML_docs/Texts/Reviews?DeRose. StatesShock.
De Saint-Exupery, A. (1982) *Pilote de Guerre*. Paris: Gallimard.
Der Derrian, J. (2009a) . *Critical Practices in International Theory: Selected Essays*. New York: Routledge.
———. (2009b) *Virtuous War: Mapping the Military-Industrial-Media-Entertainment-Network*. New York: Routledge.

Diamond, E. (1988) "(In)Visible Bodies in Churchill's Theatre." *Theatre Journal* 40.2, pp.188–204.
Dickinson, P. (2005) "Travels with Tony Kushner and David Beckhan, 2002–2004." *Theatre Journal* 57, pp. 429–450.
Dorfman, A. (1991) *Death and the Maiden*. New York: Penguin.
———. (2004) *Other Septembers, Other Americas: Selected Provocations*. New York: Seven Stories.
Dunnigan, J. and Bay, A. (1992) *From Shield to Storm: High-Tech Weapons, Military Strategy and Coalition Warfare in the Persian Gulf*. New York: William and Morrow.
Eagleton, T. (2005) *Holy Terror*. Oxford: Oxford University Press.
Eggen, Dan. (2006) "Cheney's Remarks Fuel Torture Debate." *The Washington Post*, October 26. http://www.washingtonpost.com/wp-dyn/content/article/2006/10/26/AR2006102601521.html.
Eisenman, S. (2007) *The Abu Ghraib Effect*. London: Reaktion Books.
Elia, N. (2006) "Islamaphobia and the 'Privileging' of Arab American Women," *NWSA* 18.3, pp. 155–161.
Engle, J. (2010) "A Better World... But Don't Get Carried Away." *Diplomatic History* 34.1 (January), pp. 25–26.
Englehardt, T. (1992) "The Gulf War as Total Television." *The Nation*, May 11, pp. 630–632.
Ensler, Eve. (2007) *The Treatment*. New York: Dramatist's Play Service.
Falkoff, M. (ed.) (2007) *Poems from Guantanamo: The Detainees Speak*. Iowa City: University of Iowa Press.
Fireston, D. and Shank, T. (2003) "Huge Iraq Costs Anger Democrats." *The Plain Dealer*, July 11, p. 1.
Fischer-Lichte, E. (1997) *The Show and the Gaze of Theatre*. Iowa: University of Iowa Press.
Foreman, R. (2004) "American Theatre Reflects on the Events of 9/11." *American Theatre*, pp. 6–7.
Foster, H. (1983) *The Anti-Aesthetic: Essays on Postmodern Culture*. Seattle: Bay Press.
———. (1996) *The Return of the Real*. Cambridge, MA: MIT Press.
Franklin, J. (2005) "How Did Guantanamo Become a Prison?" History News Network. http://hnn.us/articles/11000.html.
Galbraith. P. (2006) "The True Iraq Appeasers." *Boston Globe*, August 31.
Gaines, J. (2007) "The Production of Outrage: The Iraq War and the Radical Documentary Tradition." *Framework: The Journal of Cinema and Media* 48.2, pp. 36–55.
Garner, S. (1996) "Politics Over the Gulf: Trevor Griffiths in the Nineties." *Modern Drama* 39, pp. 381–391.
Gerbner, G. (1992) "Persian Gulf War, the Movie." In Mowlana, H., Gerbner, G. and Schiller, H. I. (eds.) *Triumph of the Image: the Media's War in the Persian Gulf- A Global Perspective*. Boulder: Westview Press.
Gitlin, T. (1980) *The Whole World is Watching*. Los Angeles: University of California Press.
Griffiths, T. (1992) *The Gulf Between Us*. London: Faber and Faber.

Haberman, C. (2010) "For Many, Wars are Out of Sight, Out of Mind and Out of Debate." *New York Times*, October 25. http://www.nytimes.com/2010/10/26/nyregion/26nyc.html?_r=1.

Hall, L. (1997) "CNN in Baghdad, January 16, 1991." *Electronic Media* 16.30.

Hammond, W. and Steward, D. (eds.) (2008) *Verbatim/verbatim: Contemporary Documentary Theatre*. London: Oberon Books.

Hare, David. (2004) *Stuff Happens*. London: Faber and Faber.

Hauerwas, S. and Lentricchia, F. (eds.) (2003) *Dissent from the Homeland*. Durham: Duke University Press.

Havis, A. (2001) (ed.) *American Political Plays: An Anthology*. Urbana: University of Illinois Press.

———. (2010) (ed.) *American Political Plays After 9/11*. Carbondale: Southern University Press.

Hedges, C. (2009) *Empire of Illusion: The End of Literacy and the Triumph of the Spectacle*. Toronto: Knopf Canada.

Herbert, B. (2005). "Stories from the Inside." *New York Times*, February 21, pp. A27.

Hersford, Wendy. (2006) "Staging Terror." *TDR* 50.3, pp. 29–41.

Hersh, Seymour. (2004) "Torture at Abu Gharib." *The New Yorker*, May 10, pp. 42–47.

———. (2003) "Selective Intelligence." *The New Yorker*, May 12, pp. 52–57. http://www.newyorker.com/archive/2003/05/12/030512.

Hoyt, M. et al. (2007) *Reporting Iraq: An Oral History of the War by the Journalists who Covered It*. Hoboken: Melville Publishing House.

Hrycyszyn, D. "Nothing's Shocking: Mainstream Media Manipulation and the Gulf War." http://flag.blackened.net/revolt/issues/war/gulf_media.html- link doesn't work. Accessed March 9, 2006.

Hughes, J. (2007) "Theatre, Performance and the 'War on Terror': Ethical and Political Questions Arising from British Theatrical Responses to War and Terrorism." *Contemporary Theatre Review* 17, pp. 140–164.

Hutcheon, L. (1998) *A Poetics of Postmodernism: History, Theory, Fiction*. New York: Routledge.

Iannuci, A. (2003) "Shoot Now, Think Later." *The Guardian*, April 29, p. G2, 16.

Innes, C. (2007) "Towards a Post-Millennial Mainstream? Documents of the Times." *Modern Drama* 50, pp. 435–452.

International Helsinki Federation for Human Rights. (2007) "US Human Rights Advocacy: The Guantanamo Effect," pp. 1–10. http://www.icj.org/IMG/IHF.pdf.

Irmer, T. (2006) "A Search for New Realities: Documentary Theatre in Germany." *TDR* 50.3 (Fall), pp. 16–29.

Jamieson, K. H. (2007) "Justifying the War in Iraq: What the Bush Administration's Uses of Evidence Reveal." *Rhetoric and Public Affairs* 10.2. pp. 249–273.

Jenkins, H. (2008) *Convergence Culture: Where Old and New Media Collide* New York: NYU Press.

Jhally, S. et al. (1991) "TV: The More You Watch, the Less you Know." *FAIR*. http://www.fair.org/index.php?page=1517.
Jonas, L. (1993), Review of *The Persians*. *Drama-logue*, October 7–13, n.p.
Kaplan, A. (2004) "Violent Belongings and the Question of Empire Today." *American Quarterly* 56:1 pp. 1–18.
Kaplan, E. A. (2005) *Trauma Culture*. Brunswick: Rutgers University Press.
Kardori, A. (2007) "Stage Wright: His Trip to Al Qaeda and Why Lawrence Wright Is Still Very, Very Scared." *Huffington Post*, March 9. http://www.thehuffingtonpost.com/eat-the-/2007/03/09/stage-wright.
Kauffman, L. (2003) "World Trauma Center." *American Literary History Advance Access Publication* 2, p. 647. http://0-journals.ohiolink.edu.library.jcu.edu/ejc/pdf.cgi/Kauffman_Linda_S.pdf?issn=08967148&issue=v21i0003&article=647_wtc.
Keen, S. (1991) *Faces of the Enemy*. New York: HarperCollins.
Kellaway, K. (2004) "Theatre of War." *The Observer*, August 29, p. 5.
Kellner, D. (1992) *The Persian Gulf TV War*. Boulder: Westview Press.
———. (1995) *Media Culture: Cultural Studies, Identity and Politics between the Modern and the Postmodern*. London: Routledge
———. (1998) "Marcuse." In Critchley, S. and Schroeder, W. (eds.) *A Companion to Continental Philosophy*. Malden, MA: Blackwell Publishers, pp. 389–396.
———. (2003). *Media Spectacle*. London: Routledge.
———. (2005) *Media Spectacle and the Crisis of Democracy: Terrorism, War, and Election Battles*. Boulder: Paradigm Publishers.
Kendrick, M. (1994) "The Never Again Narratives: Representations of First and Third World Countries in the Persian Gulf War." *Cultural Critique* 28, pp. 129–147.
Kent, N. et al. (2009) *The Great Game*. London: Oberon Books.
Kerbaj, R. (2010) "Amnesty International is Damaged by Taliban Link." *The Sunday Times*, February 2, p. 63. http://www.timesonline.co.uk/tol/news/world/afghanistan/article7017810.ece.
Kershaw, Baz. (1992) *The Politics of Performance: Radical Theatre as Cultural Intervention*. New York: Routledge.
Khan, S. (1998) "Muslim Women: Negotiations in the Third Space." *Signs* 23.2, pp. 463–494.
Krauss, R. (1977) "Notes on the Index: Seventies Art in America." *October* (Spring), pp. 68–81.
Kreiswirth, S. (1993) "Persians: Explosive Insight into Gulf War." *The Daily Breeze*, October 2, B6.
Kuhn, A. (1985) *The Power of the Image*. London: Routledge.
Kushner, T. (2002) *Homebody/Kabul*. London: Nick Hern Books.
LaBute, N. (2003) *The Mercy Seat*. New York: Faber and Faber.
LaCapra, D. (2001) *Writing History, Writing Trauma*. Baltimore: Johns Hopkins University Press.
Lahr, J. (2006) "A Touch of Bad." In Wood, G. *Neil LaBute: A Casebook* London: Routledge, pp. 11–22.
———. (1993) "Inventing the Enemy." *The New Yorker*, October 18, pp. 103–106.
———. (1993) "The Forest and the Trees." *New Yorker*, April 12, pp. 105–107.

Leiss, W. (1989) "The Myth of the Information Society." In Angus, I. and Jhally, S. (eds.) *Cultural Politics in Contemporary America*. New York: Routledge, pp. 282–298.

Lentricchia, F. and McAuliffe, J. (2003a) *Crimes of Art and Terror*. Chicago: University of Chicago Press.

———. (2003b) "Groundzeroland." In Hauerwas, S. and Lentricchia, F. (eds.) *Dissent from the Homeland*. Durham: Duke University Press, pp. 95–106.

Lester, G. (2002) "The Balm of Ancient Words," interview with Peter Sellars. *American Repertory Theatre Articles Online* 1(1). http://www.americanrepertory theater.org/node/1640.

Leung, R. (2004) "Bush Sought 'Way' to Invade Iraq?" *60 Minutes*, January 11. http;//www.cbsnews.com/stories/2004/01/09/60minutes/main592330.html.

Levantine Center. "Heather Raffo." http://www.levantinecenter.org/pages/heather raffo.html. Accessed August 18, 2007.

Levinas, E. (1969) *Totality and Infinity: An Essay on Exteriority*. Pittsburgh: Duquesne University Press.

———. (1997) *Difficult Freedom: Essays on Judaism* Baltimore: The Johns Hopkins University Press.

———. (1998) *Otherwise Than Being: Or Beyond Essence*. Pittsburgh: Duquesne University Press.

Lucas, C. (2009) *Prayer for my Enemy*. New York: Theatre Communications Group.

Luckhurst, M. (2008) "Verbatim Theatre, Media Relations and Ethics." In Holdsworth, N. and Luckhurst, M. (eds.) *A Concise Companion to Contemporary British and Irish Drama*. London: Blackwell, pp. 200–222.

Lyotard, J. F. (1985) *Just Gaming*. Minneapolis: University of Minnesota Press.

MacArthur, J. (1992) *Second Front: Censorship and Propaganda in the Gulf War*. New York: Hill and Wang.

MacDonald, H. (1991) "On Peter Sellars." *Partisan Review* 58.4, pp. 707–712.

Margolis, J. (2006) *Guantanamo and the Abuse of Presidential Power*. New York: Simon and Schuster.

Martin, C. (2006) "Bodies of Evidence." *TDR* 50.3, pp. 8–15.

Mason, S. (ed.) (2005) *The San Francisco Mime Troupe Reader*. Ann Arbor: University of Michigan Press.

Mayer, J. (2005) "Outsourcing Torture." *The New Yorker*, February 14, pp. 106–109. http://www.newyorker.com/archive/2005/02/14/050214.fa_fact6

———. (2008) *The Dark Side*. New York: Doubleday.

Meyer, D. (2004) "Rush: MPS Just Blowing Off Steam." May 6. http://www .cbsnews.com/stories/2004/05/06/opinion/meyer/main616021.shtml.

McGrath, J. (2002) *Hyperlynx*. London: Oberon.

Miller, D. (1993) "Self-Consciously Avant-Garde, 'Persians' Sends Viewers Fleeing." *L.A. Life*, October 2, p. 6.

Miller, E. and Yetic, S. (2001) "The New World Order in Theory and Practice: The Bush Administration's Worldview in Transition." *Presidential Studies Quarterly* 31.1, pp. 56–68.

Miller, J. (2006) "New Forms for New Conflicts: Thinking about Tony Kushner's *Homebody/Kabul* and the Theatre du Soleil's *Le Dernier Caravanserail*." *Contemporary Theatre Review* 16.2, pp. 212–219.

Milne, K. (1992) Review of *The Gulf Between Us*. *Sunday Telegraph* 26. Reprinted in *Theatre Record* 15–28, p. 105.

Minwalla, F. (2003) "Tony Kushner's *Homebody/Kabul*: Staging History in a Postcolonial World." *Theatre* 32.3, pp. 29–43.

Mitchell, W.J.T. (2005a) "Picturing Terror: Derrida's Autoimmunity." *Cardoza Law Review* 25.2, pp. 913–925.

———. (2005b) *What do Pictures Want? The Lives and Loves of Images*. Chicago: University of Chicago Press.

———. (2006) "Cloning Terror: The War of Images, 9–11 to Abu Ghraib." Talk given at Baker-Nord Center, Case Western Reserve University, November 30. http://artsci.case.edu/bakernord/events/archive/w_j_t_mitchell.php.

———. (2011a) Interview. http://www.metropolism.org/features/interview-with-w.j.t.mitchell/.

———. (2011b) *Cloning Terror: The War of Images 9/11 to the Present*. Chicago: University of Chicago Press.

——— and Ranciere, J. (2008) Panel discussion at Columbia University, April 23. http://www.page291.com/blog/archives/73.

Modleski, T. (ed.) (1986) *Studies in Entertainment: Critical Approaches to Mass Culture*. Bloomington: Indiana University Press.

Mokhtar El Rafei, M. (2001). "Interview:A Mission to Die For." November 12. http://www.abc.net.au/4corners/atta/interviews/mukhtar.htm.Morgan, A. (2009) "How I Put the Taliban on Stage." *The Guardian*, April 8, p. 24.

Morris, S. (1993) Review of *The Persians*. *L.A. Weekly*, October 8–14, n.p.

Mowlana, H. et al. (1992) *Triumph of the Image: the Media's War in The Persian Gulf, A Global Perspective, 244–247*. Boulder: Westview Press.

Nelson, A. (2003) *The Guys*. New York: Dramatists Play Service.

New York Times Editors. (2004) "The Times and Iraq," *New York Times*, May 26. http://www.nytimes.com/2004/05/06/international/middleast/26/FTE_NOTE?ex=140099.

Nightingale, B. (1992) Review of *The Gulf Between Us*. *The Guardian*, January 23. Reprinted in *Theatre Record* 15–28 (January), 106.

Nordman, A. and Wickert, H. (1998) "Shamanism vilified and Redeemed: Sam Shepard's *States of Shock*." *Contemporary Theatre Review* 8.4, pp. 41–54.

Norris, C. (1992) *Uncritical Theory*. Amherst: University of Mass. Press.

Norris, M. (1991) "Military Censorship and the Body Count in the Persian Gulf War." *Cultural Critique*, 19.0, pp. 223–245.

Norton-Taylor, R. (2004) "Spirit of Inquiry." *New Statesman*, June 7. http://www.newstatesman.com/node/148148.

———. (2003) *Justifying War: Scenes from the Hutton Inquiry*. London: Oberon Books.

Norton-Taylor, R. and Kent, N. (2007). *Called to Account*. London: Oberon Books.

Orenstein, C. (1999) *Festive Revolutions: The Politics of Popular Theatre and the San Francisco Mime Troupe*. Jackson: University of Mississippi Press.

O Tuathail, G. and Luke, T. (1994). "Present at the (Dis)integration; Territorialization and Reterritorialization in the New Wor(l)d Order." *Annals of the Association of American Geographers* 84.3, pp. 381–398.

Packer, G. (2006) *Assassin's Gate*. New York: Farrar, Straus and Giroux.

———. (2008) *Betrayed*. New York: Faber and Faber.

———. (2011) "Coming Apart." *The New Yorker*, September 12, pp. 62–71.

Paget, D. (2004) "Jeremy Sandford: A Docu-Retrospect." *New Theatre Quarterly* 20.1, pp. 45–58

Patton, P. (1995) "Introduction." In Baudrillard, J. *The Gulf War Did Not Take Place*. Bloomington: Indiana University Press, pp. 1–21.

Pavis, P., Shantz, C. and Carlson, M. (1998) *Dictionary of the Theater*. Toronto: University of Toronto Press.

Perle, R. (2003) "War critics Astonished as US hawk Admits Invasion was Illegal." *The Guardian*, November 20. http://www.guardian.co.uk/Iraq/Story/0,2763,1089158,00.html.

Perlez, J. et al. (2009) "Ex-detainee of U.S. Describes a 6-year Ordeal." *New York Times*, January 6, pp. A1, A10.

Philips, M. S. (2004) "The Failure of History: Kushner's *Homebody/Kabul* and the Apocalyptic Context." *Modern Drama* 47.1, pp. 1–20.

Pinter, H. (1989) *Mountain Language*. New York: Grove.

———. (1991) "New World Order." *American Theater* November, pp. 28–30.

———. (1996) *Ashes to Ashes*. New York: Grove Press.

———. (2005) "Art, Truth and Politics." Lecture given at Nobel Prize award ceremonies, December 7. http://nobelprize.org/nobel_prizes/literature/laureates/2005/pinter-lecture-e.html.

Polan, D. (1986) "Above All Else to Make You See." In Arac, J. (ed.) *Postmodernism and Politics*. Minneapolis: University Of Minnesota Press, pp. 55–69.

Portrait of Grief Series. (2002) *Portraits 9/11/01*. New York: Times Books.

Post, J. (2008) *The Mind of the Terrorist: the Psychology of Terrorism from the IRA to Al Qaeda*. New York: Palgrave- Macmillan.

———. Ali, F. et al. (2009) "The Psychology of Suicide Terrorism." *Psychiatry: Interpersonal and Biological Processes* 72.1, pp. 13–31.

Power, S. (2007) *A Problem from Hell: America and the Age of Genocide*. New York: Harper Perennial.

Prados, J. (2004) *Hoodwinked*. New York: The New Press.

Ralph, P. (2008) *Deep Cut*. London: Oberon.

Raffo, H. (2006) *Nine Parts of Desire*. New York: Dramatist's Play Service.

Rasul, S. (2007) *Torturing Democracy: The Project*. http://www.gwu.edu/~nsarchiv/torturingdemocracy/interviews/shafiq_rasul.html.

Rayner, A. (1994) *To Act, To Do, to Perform: Drama and the Phenomenology of Action*. Ann Arbor: University of Michigan Press.

Reagan, R. (1980) "Peace: Restoring the Margin of Safety." Speech given at VFW Convention, Chicago, Illinois, August 18.

Rebeck, T. and Gersten-Vassilaros, A. (2003) *Omnium Gatherum*. New York: Samuel French.

Rich, F. (2004) "Watching Operation Iraqi Infoganda." *New York Times Magazine*, March 28, p. 21.
Richards, D. (2010) "Revealing the Truth Behind the Art of War." *The Times* 8.3, p. 43.
Rockmore, T. et al. (2005) *The Philosophical Challenges of 9/11*. London: Blackwell.
Rosen, C. (1992) "Silent Tongues: Sam Shepard's Explorations of Emotional Territory." *Village Voice*, August 4, pp. 34–42.
Rumsfeld, D. (2003a) Department of Defense News Briefing-Secretary Rumsfeld and Gen. Myers, April 11. http://www.defense.gov/Transcripts/Transcript.aspx?TranscriptID=.
———. (2003b) "Rumsfeld Blames Iraq Problems on Pockets of Dead Enders." http://www.usatoday.com/news/world/iraq/2003-06-18-rumsfeld_x.htm.
Sachs, S. (2003) "As Iraq's Artists Strive for Freedom, a Gunman Silences a Pro-Hussein Singer." *The New York Times*, May 20.
Sageman, M. (2004) "Understanding Terror Networks." *Foreign Policy Research Institute*. http://www.fpri.org/enotes/20041101.middleeast.sageman.understandingterrornetworks.
Salamon, J. (2003) "New Tools for Reporters Make War Images Instant but Coverage No Simpler." *The New York Times*, April 6, p. B13.
Schechter, D. (1998) "War... and Peace." *The Nation*, March 19, p. 10.
Schjeldahl, P. (2000) "Pragmatic Hedonism." *The New Yorker*, April 3, pp. 94–95.
Schulte-Sasse, J. and Schulte-Sasse, L. (1991) "War, Otherness, and Illusory Identifications with the State." *Cultural Critique*, 129.0, pp. 67–95.
Scheuer, Michael. (2004). *Imperial Hubris* Dulles, VA: Brassey's.
Sellars, P. (1993) "Program Notes." Presented at Mark Taper Forum, Los Angeles. pp. 4–5.
Seymour-Ure, C. K. (1974) *The Political Impact of Mass Media*. Constable: London.
Shepard, S. (1993) *States of Shock, Far North, Silent Tongue*. New York: Vintage.
Shewey, D. (1997) *Sam Shepard*. New York: DaCapo Press.
Simpson, D. (2006) *9/11: The Culture of Commemoration*. Chicago: University of Chicago Press.
Skloot, R. (2004) "Where Does it Hurt?: Genocide, the Theatre and the Human Body." *Theatre Research International* 23.1, pp. 51–58.
Smith, H. (ed.) (1992) *The Media and the Gulf War*. Washington, DC: Seven Locks Press.
Soans, R. (2005) *Talking to Terrorists*. London: Oberon Books.
———. (2008) In Hammond, W. and Steward, D. (eds.) *Verbatim/verbatim: Contemporary Documentary Theatre*. London: Oberon Books, pp. 17–44.
Solomon, A. (ed.) (2001) "Theater and Social Change." *Theatre* 31.3, pp. 47–51.
Sontag, S. (1973) *On Photography*. New York: Picador.
———. (2001) "Talk of the Town." *The New Yorker*, September 24, pp. 28–29.
———. (2003) *Regarding the Pain of Others*. New York: Picador.
———. (2004) "Regarding the Torture of Others." *New York Times Magazine*, May 23, pp. 24–29.
Soto-Morettini, D. (2005) "Trouble in the House: David Hare's *Stuff Happens*." *Contemporary Theatre Review* 15.3, pp. 309–319.

Spivak, G. (1985) "Can the Subaltern Speak?" *Wedge* 7/8(Winter-Spring), pp. 120–130.

Spring, S. and Packer, J. C. (2009) "George W. Bush: An Address to the Joint Sessions of Congress and the American People September 20, 2001," *Voices of Democracy* 4, p. 127.

Stanley, A. (2003) "Lengthy Hours Magnify Strengths and Foibles." *The New York Times*, March 26, p. B14.

Stauber, J. and Rampton, S. (2005) *How PR Sold the War in the Persian Gulf.* Boulder: Ethica Publishing. http://www.prwatch.org/books/tsigfy10.html.

Stevenson, C. (2005) "'Seek for Something New' Mothers, Change and Creativity in Tony Kushner's *Angels in America*, *Homebody/Kabul* and *Caroline or Change*." *Modern Drama* 48.4, pp. 758–776.

Stockhausen, K. (2002) "Huuuh! Das Pressegesprach." *MusikTexte* 91, pp. 69–77.

Stoller, T. (2004) "Injustice is Served." http://www.hotreview.org/articles/injusticeis.htm. Accessed September 15, 2004.

Taylor, P. (1992a) Review of *The Gulf Between Us*. *The Independent*, January 23. Reprinted in *Theatre Record* 15–28 (January), p. 107.

———. (1992b) *War and the Media: Propaganda and Persuasion in the Gulf War*. Manchester: Manchester University Press.

Tekinay, A. (1996) "Sam Shepard's *States of Shock*: Nihilism in Political Drama." *Journal of American Studies in Turkey* 3, pp. 69–74.

Thompson, J. (2007) *Palace of the End*. Toronto: Playwrights Canada Press.

Tommasini, A. (2001) "Music, The Devil Made Him Do It." *New York Times*, September 30, p. 10. http://www.nytimes.com/2001/09/30/arts/music-the-devil-made-him-do-it.html.

Topolski, A. (2008) "The Ethics and Politics of Teshuvah: Lessons from Emmanuel Levinas and Hannah Arendt." *Journal for Jewish Thought* 2, pp. 1–10.

Tucker, M. (1992) *Sam Shepard*. New York: Frederick Ungar Books.

Virilio, P. (1977) *Speed and Politics: An Essay on Dromology*. New York: Semiotext(e).

———. (2003) *Art and Fear*. London: Continuum.

———. (2005) *Desert Screen: War at the Speed of Light*. London: Contimuum.

———. (2008) *Pure War*. Cambridge, MA: Semiotext(e).

Wallace, N. (2001) "In the Heart of the Country." In Havis, A. (ed.) *American Political Plays: An Anthology*. Urbana: University of Chicago Press, pp. 97–147.

———. (2003) "Strange Times." *The Guardian*, March 29, p. A1.

———. (2010) "Politics, Poetry and Playwriting." *TDR* 55.3, pp. 9–17.

White, Hayden. (1975) *Metahistory*. Baltimore: John Hopkins's Press.

Willadt, S. (1993) "States of War in Sam Shepard's *States of Shock*." *Modern Drama* 36, pp. 147–165.

Wood, G. (2006) *Neil LaBute: A Casebook*. London: Routledge.

World Organization for Human Rights USA (2004) "Leading By Example" pp. 1–23. http://www.unponteper.it/liberatelapace/dossier/0604_Wordorg_HR_USA_Report.pdf.

Worth, R. (2006). "Blast Destroys Shrine in Iraq, Setting Off Sectarian Fury." *New York Times*, February 23. http://www.nytimes.com/2006/06/22/international/middleast/22cnd-iraq.html.

Worthington, A. (2007) *The Guantanamo Files: The Stories of the 774 Detainees in America's Illegal Prison.* London: Pluto Press.

Wright, L. (2007) *My Trip to Al-Qaeda* (unpublished). Notes based on performance.

———. (2002) "The Man Behind bin Laden." *The New Yorker*, September 16.

———. (2007) Interview with David Martin. *Sunday Morning*, CBS, September 9.

———. (2007) *The Looming Tower.* New York: Knopf, 2007.

Young, I. (2003) "The Logic of Masculinity Protection: Reflections on the Current Security State." *Signs: A Journal of Women in Culture and Society* 29.1, pp: 1–25.

Zizek, . (2002) *Welcome to the Desert of the Real.* London: Verso.

———. (2008) *Violence.* New York: Picador.

Index

9/11 Commission 98

Abu Ghraib 5, 14, 25, 26, 54, 80, 88, 122, 135, 141, 152, 155, 169–173, 183–187, 191, 192, 194, 195, 221
Aeschylus 51, 58, 59, 66–69, 71, 217
Afghanistan 2, 6, 10, 13, 19, 27, 72, 73, 85, 87, 95, 105, 118, 131, 132, 156, 160, 166, 169, 174, 180, 181, 199–213, 220n, 222n
Aftermath 136
Agamben, Giorgio 54, 55, 174, 177, 178, 223n
Al Saffarh, Nehrjas 183–185, 190, 191
Albee, Edward 99–100
al-Zawahiri, A. 113, 165, 166
Amiriyah Shelter 61, 75, 79
Anthems: Culture Clash in the District 91
Appadurai, Arjun 7, 20–22, 24
Artaud, Antonin 44, 106, 219n
Ashes to Ashes 122, 195
Askariya mosque bombing 160, 161
Assassin's Gate, The 161
Atta, Mohammad. 9, 104, 108–114, 132
Auletta, Robert., 58, 59, 66–69, 71

Ba'ath Party 58, 76, 77, 112, 190, 191, 218
Back to Normal 30, 39–46, 84, 85
"Bare Life," 54, 55, 127
Barthes, Roland. 88, 223
Baudrillard, J. 20, 38, 43, 63, 66, 70, 96, 100, 105–107, 118, 127, 139
Bean, Richard. 206

Beckett, Samuel. 33, 49, 207
Benjamin, Walter 84, 88, 89, 129
Bergson, Henri. 106
Berkoff, Steven 91, 93
Betrayed 136, 137, 141, 142, 156–158, 161, 162
Bhabha, Horni. 83
Bin Laden, O. 4, 14–19, 22, 25, 58, 59, 87, 88, 90, 95, 104, 105, 109, 111–114, 126, 132, 156, 162, 165–167, 172, 174, 175, 181, 200, 205, 235n
Black Tulips 205
Blackwatch 8, 136, 141, 175
Blair, J. 134
Blair, T. 32, 59, 87, 93, 131, 132, 140, 143–153, 174, 175, 180, 182, 183, 188
Blanchot, M. 79
Blank, J. 136, 142, 143
Blessing, L. 201, 205
Blueprint for Accountability 136
Bond, E. 106
Bourdieu, P. 20
Brecht, B. 44, 138, 142
Brittain, V. 26, 120, 136, 155, 173–181
Buchman, A. 6, 136
Bugles at the Gates of Jalalabad 202–205
Burke, G. 136, 141
Bush, George W. 1, 3, 4, 8, 14, 15, 16–19, 22–23, 31, 34, 46, 59–60, 72–73, 80, 83, 87, 90, 92–93, 101, 110, 127, 131–135, 140, 143–144, 148–154, 157–158, 160, 161, 171–172, 174–178. 180–183, 186

Bush George W. H. 3, 16, 29–32, 34, 36–37, 40–42, 44, 47, 51, 57–60, 64, 77, 204, 215n, 216n, 219n
Bush Doctrine 30, 37, 204
Bush, Laura 9, 135, 153
Butler, Judith 3, 11, 26, 27, 51, 55, 81, 91–94, 102, 183, 184, 194, 201, 214

Called to Account 59, 131, 136, 143, 148–151
Calley, Lt. William 30, 46, 48, 50, 52
Campaign 203, 205
Canopy of the Stars 202, 206
Caruth, Cathy 194
Chekhov, Anton 147, 148
Cheney, Dick 26, 32, 77, 87, 97, 111, 112, 134, 140, 144, 151–154, 169, 171, 172, 186, 193
Chomsky, Noam 96
Churchill, Caryl 6, 9, 15, 16, 50, 59, 108, 118–129, 207, 220n
Cloning 118, 119, 121, 126–129
CNN 3, 29, 34, 38, 40–42, 71, 84
Cooke, Miriam 74, 80, 218n
Cowhig, Frances Ya Chu 27, 60, 173, 191–197, 222n
Culture Clash 91
Culture Project 6, 136, 141–143, 154–156, 180, 191
Cyberblitz, 5

Debord, Guy 40, 45, 46
Deep Cut 136, 142, 144
Defuse spectacle 45
Delillo, Don 88
Der Derrian, James 106, 107, 121, 147, 215n
Derrida, Jacques 79, 80, 119
Didion, Joan 94, 219n
Documentary theatre 8, 115, 120, 133, 135, 137, 140, 150, 159, 187
Don't Ask, Don't Tell 53
Dorfman, Ariel 94, 195, 196
Downing Street Memo 131, 147, 149
Drunk Enough to Say I Love You 119, 129

Durand's Line 203, 204
Durkheim, Emile 111, 219n

Eagleton, Terry 106–110
Edgar, David 201, 205, 206
Embedded reporters 16, 24, 84, 215n, 216n
England, Lynndie 14, 25, 43, 46, 88, 137, 155, 173, 183–187, 193
Ensler, Eve 9, 155, 173, 191, 217n
Exonerated, The 142

Far Away 108, 118–128, 220n
Foreman, Richard 89
Foucault, Michel 54, 55

Gerstem-Vassilaros, Alexandra 87
Governmentality 54, 55
Gray, Spalding 164
Great Game 10, 200–203, 214
Grieg, David 206
Griffiths, Trevor 6, 9, 58, 60–69, 73, 85, 217n
Ground Zero 3, 14, 87, 88, 100–102, 126
Guantanamo Effect 173
Guantanamo 169–196, 221n
Guantanamo: Honor Bound to Defend Freedom 155
Guardians, The 155
Gulf Between Us 9, 58–69
Gulf War, 1991 (also Persian Gulf War) 3, 6, 9, 15, 16, 19, 20, 25, 29, 30, 34–53, 57, 58, 61, 65–68, 71, 78, 84–86, 99, 121, 132, 134, 190, 215n, 216n, 217n
Gulf War, 2003 7, 16, 20, 30, 85, 216n
Gupta, Amit, 203, 205
The Guys 91, 93, 94, 98, 100–103, 117,

Halabja Genocide 57, 149
Half the Picture 136, 141, 144
Hare, David 6, 8, 59, 97, 115, 120, 131, 134, 136, 139–144, 150–154, 163, 175, 190, 192, 220n

Havis, Allan 6, 9, 107–115, 118, 128
Homebody/Kabul 10, 91, 199, 200, 207–213, 220n, 222n
Homo sacer 54, 55, 177, 178
Honey 203, 206
Hussein, Saddam 47, 57–60, 67–78, 81–83, 87, 88, 90, 111, 112, 132–134, 145, 149, 150, 154, 156–162, 173, 175, 182–185, 188–193, 196, 218n, 219n
Hutchinson, Ron 203, 204
Hutton Inquiry 143, 145–148, 187, 189, 220n
Hyperlynx 91, 93, 95

Ibsen, Henrik 147
In Conflict 8, 136, 141, 155
In the Heart of America 46–54, 65, 186, 193
Indefinite detention 7, 91, 178, 180

Jeffreys, Stephen 201–203
Jensen, Eric 136, 142, 143
Justifying War 136, 143–149, 173, 187

Kaufmann, Moises 142
Kellner, Douglas 6, 16, 19, 20, 36, 58, 124, 132, 139, 216n, 217n, 220n
Kelly, David 137, 143–152, 173, 183–190
Kent, Nicholas 6, 131, 136, 144, 148, 150, 155, 174, 200, 201, 207
von Kleist, Heinrich 108, 109
Kurds 36, 57, 77, 160
Kushner, Tony 6, 9–11, 50, 59, 101, 135, 183, 199–214, 217n, 220n, 222n
Kuwait 29, 31, 36, 37, 57, 60, 112, 132

LaBute, Neil 6, 9, 91–100
LaCapra, Dominick 195, 196, 222n
Lentricchia, Frank and Jody McAuliffe 9, 101, 106–109, 118, 128, 215n
Levinas, Emmanuel 51, 56, 211–213

Lidless 173, 191–196, 222n
Lindh, John Walker 24, 87, 90
Lion of Kabul, The 206
The Looming Tower 113, 155, 164
Lynch, Jessica 25, 43, 46, 88, 112, 135, 183, 186
Lyotard, Francois 17, 18

Mad Forest, a Play from Romania 15, 16
Major, John 16, 215n
Mamet, David 97
Mann, Emily 142
McGrath, John 87, 91, 93–96, 141, 144
Media events 16, 22, 34, 35, 42, 139
Mediatization 3
Megaspectacle 16, 17, 30, 34–37, 42
Mercy Seat 91, 93, 96–99
Miller, Arthur 147
Miniskirts of Kabul 203, 206
Mission Accomplished Speech 3, 16–18, 35, 88, 135, 152
Mitchell, W. J. T. 4, 5, 25, 126–129, 220n
Morgan, Abi 206
Morris, Peter 69, 155
My Lai Massacre 30, 50
My Pyramids 8
My Trip to Al Qaeda 8, 113, 136, 137, 141, 156, 157, 162, 163, 221n
Mythoterrorism 106, 111, 116

National Theatre of Scotland 8, 131, 136, 144, 175
Nelson, Anne 6, 9, 87, 91–102, 117
New World Order 6, 30–38, 47, 49, 51, 62, 63, 68, 86, 204
New World Order (play) 31, 33, 34, 122, 196
New York Times 27, 98, 134, 216n
Night is Darkest Just Before the Dawn, The 206
Nine Parts of Desire 9, 10, 23, 58, 59, 72–86, 157, 190

Norton-Taylor, Richard 6, 59, 131, 136–152, 201
Now is the Time 203, 205
A Number 108, 119, 121, 125, 127, 128, 220n

Oakrent, Ben 206
Omnium Gatherum 91, 103, 104
On the Side of Angels 206
Only We Who Guard the Mystery Shall be Unhappy 9, 101, 135
Operation Desert Shield 50
Operation Desert Storm 42, 50
Operation Enduring Freedom 90, 132

Packer 2, 6, 8, 136, 137, 141, 142, 156–162, 167
Palace of the End 173, 183–191, 218n
Patriot Act 59, 132, 152, 177, 221n
Patton, Paul 20, 37, 38
Pavis, Patrice 137, 138
Performance 6, 7, 14, 18, 19, 22, 23, 41, 85, 120, 155, 164, 201, 203, 217n, 220n
Perle, Richard 148–150, 221n
Persian Gulf War (1991)
Persians, The 8, 51, 57–59, 66–69, 217n, 218n
Pinter, Harold 6, 9, 31–34, 59, 68, 97, 122, 195, 196, 207
Powell, Colin 77, 87, 140, 144, 151–154, 176
Portraits of Grief 98, 111, 219n

Question of Impeachment, A 136, 155
Qutb, Sayyid 165

Raffo, Heather 9, 10, 23, 58–62, 72–82, 157, 190, 218n, 219n
Ralph, Philip 136, 142
Ranciere, Jacques 5
Rebeck, Teresa 87, 91, 103
Recent Tragic Events 91, 93
Regime change 10, 47, 90, 105, 131, 133, 148–151

Requiem for Ground Zero 91
Rice, Condoleezza 144, 151, 153, 158
Rumsfeld, Donald 23–26, 58, 77, 90, 97, 140, 144, 150–153, 157, 170, 172, 175, 181, 182

San Francisco Mime Troupe 6, 8, 30, 39–42, 51
Schwarzkopf, Norman 47, 60
Sellars, Peter 6–8, 51, 58–62, 66–73, 85, 217n, 218n
Shawn, Wallace 97
Sheehan, Cindy 14, 24, 80, 88
Shepard, Sam 6, 9, 30, 39–49, 63, 68, 85, 199
Simpson, David 91, 98–101
Simulacral 37, 127, 140
Simulation 5, 20, 35, 124, 127, 171
Slovo, Gillian 9, 26, 120, 136, 155, 173–181
Smith, Anna Deavere 23, 142, 164
Spectacle 4, 7, 8, 15–17, 25, 26, 30, 34, 40–45, 60, 81, 85, 102, 119, 120, 124, 135, 139, 199
State of exception 54, 55, 177, 178
States of Shock 9, 30, 39–48, 84, 216n
Staukhausen, Karl 1–2, 107, 196, 215n
Stephens, Simon 202, 206
Stuff Happens 8, 59, 120, 131–153, 175, 190
Soans, Robin 6, 62, 108, 110, 115–117, 136
Sontag, Susan 1, 2, 23, 90, 91, 94, 184, 215n
Sublime 1, 106–109, 215n
Suicide terrorism 108–116, 129

Taliban 24, 27, 87, 111, 175–181, 199–212
Talking to Terrorists 9, 62, 108, 115–120, 136, 141, 220n
Technowars 17, 30–36, 65, 85, 121, 200
Tectonic Theatre Project 142
Teevan, Colin 206

Thompson, Judith 8, 10, 27, 60, 137, 173, 183–195, 218n
Three Nights in Prague 107–112
Tipton Three 169, 179
Torture 5, 7, 9, 25, 26, 33, 34, 43, 54, 57, 59, 76, 88, 91, 95, 117, 122, 123, 127, 149, 165, 167, 170–178, 182–186, 190–196, 218n
Total television 3, 16, 20, 34–42, 60, 69, 215n
Trauma 9, 13, 25, 26, 47, 48, 79, 80, 83, 87–89, 93, 94, 102, 103, 107, 118, 128, 188, 191, 193–197,
Treatment, The 9, 155, 173, 191
Tribunal plays 8, 135–146, 152
Tricycle Theatre 6, 8, 115, 131, 136, 141–145, 155, 174, 200

Wallace, Naomi 6, 9, 30, 46–56, 65, 85, 186, 193, 217n
War on Terror 9–20, 25–27, 58, 72, 73, 88, 99, 111, 120–122, 127, 135, 143, 155, 156, 172–178, 184, 186, 200, 220n
Weapons of mass destruction (WMD) 87, 126, 132–136, 143–152, 175, 184–189,
Wilkinson, Joy 203, 205
Wolfowitz, Paul 90, 97, 134, 153
Women's rights 72–81
Wood for the Fire 205
Wright, Craig 91, 93
Wright, Lawrence 6, 8, 113, 136–141, 155–157, 162–167, 221n

Verbatim theatre 23, 120, 135–138
Vietnam 29, 30, 37, 40, 43, 46–52, 78, 153, 157, 193, 195, 200, 217n
Vietnam Syndrome 29, 30, 40, 47, 48, 57
Virilio, Paul 3–5, 59, 106

GPSR Compliance

The European Union's (EU) General Product Safety Regulation (GPSR) is a set of rules that requires consumer products to be safe and our obligations to ensure this.

If you have any concerns about our products, you can contact us on

ProductSafety@springernature.com

In case Publisher is established outside the EU, the EU authorized representative is:

Springer Nature Customer Service Center GmbH
Europaplatz 3
69115 Heidelberg, Germany

www.ingramcontent.com/pod-product-compliance
Lightning Source LLC
LaVergne TN
LVHW011813060526
838200LV00053B/3768